The Gender Effect

The publisher and the University of California Press Foundation gratefully acknowledge the generous support of the Barbara S. Isgur Endowment Fund in Public Affairs.

The Gender Effect

CAPITALISM, FEMINISM, AND THE CORPORATE POLITICS OF DEVELOPMENT

Kathryn Moeller

UNIVERSITY OF CALIFORNIA PRESS

University of California Press, one of the most distinguished university presses in the United States, enriches lives around the world by advancing scholarship in the humanities, social sciences, and natural sciences. Its activities are supported by the UC Press Foundation and by philanthropic contributions from individuals and institutions. For more information, visit www.ucpress.edu.

University of California Press
Oakland, California

An earlier version of chapter 4 was previously published as "Searching for Adolescent Girls in Brazil: The Transnational Politics of Poverty in 'The Girl Effect,'" *Feminist Studies* 40, no. 3 (2014): 575–601. An earlier version of chapter 5 was previously published as "Proving 'The Girl Effect': Corporate Knowledge Production and Educational Intervention," *International Journal of Educational Development* 33, no. 6 (2013): 612–21.

Library of Congress Cataloging-in-Publication Data

Names: Moeller, Kathryn, author.
Title: The gender effect : capitalism, feminism, and the corporate politics of development / Kathryn Moeller.
Description: Oakland, California : University of California Press, [2018] | Includes bibliographical references and index. |
Identifiers: LCCN 2017027256 (print) | LCCN 2017033180 (ebook) | ISBN 9780520961623 (ebook) | ISBN 9780520286382 (cloth : alk. paper) | ISBN 9780520286399 (pbk : alk. paper)
Subjects: LCSH: Corporations—Charitable contributions—Case studies. | Girl Effect (Organization) | Nike (Firm) | Corporate image—Management. | Young women—Services for—Developing countries. | Poor girls—Services for—Developing countries.
Classification: LCC HG4028.C6 (ebook) | LCC HG4028.C6 M64 2018 (print) | DDC 362.5/5765082091724—dc23
LC record available at https://lccn.loc.gov/2017027256

Manufactured in the United States of America

27 26 25 24 23 22 21 20 19 18
10 9 8 7 6 5 4 3 2 1

For all the young women in this story and for those I will never know

For Miguel and Sebastián

Contents

Illustrations

FIGURES

TABLE

Preface

A white dot appears and slowly begins flashing. A piano tune and gently ringing bells follow. Words in all caps and bold-faced—*POVERTY, AIDS, HUNGER,* and *WAR*—flash across the screen at a dizzying speed. A question appears, *What if there was an unexpected solution that could turn this sinking ship around? Would you even know it if you saw it?* Thick white lines dramatically cross out *INTERNET, SCIENCE, THE GOVERNMENT,* and *MONEY.* The music pauses. The white dot reappears. Over a series of screen breaks, *It's (dramatic pause) a girl.* The word *flies* circles the bright orange, bold faced, capitalized word *GIRL.* The word *BABY* falls to its feet. The word *HUSBAND* crushes it. The words *HUNGER* and *HIV* rise up and surround it. They begin to fall away as *SCHOOL, UNIFORM, LOAN, COW, and PROFIT* appear. The question, *Are you following what is happening here?*, is followed by *Girl ➔ school ➔ cows ➔ $ ➔ business ➔ clean water ➔ social change ➔ stronger economy ➔ better world. It's called the girl effect. Multiply that by 600 million girls in the developing world.* A black dot appears and multiplies until the page is solid black. *And you've just changed the course of history* scrolls across the screen. A *G* is drawn on the screen. It reads, *Invest in a girl and she will do the rest.* The white dot reappears, flashes, and then disappears. *It's no big deal. Just the future of humanity.*

Description of the Girl Effect video[1]

> Smart businesses appreciate that increased support for girls and women is integral to fostering successful markets for the future. Innovative programs are already producing remarkable results, and far-seeing countries and organizations are finding that reaching out to girls and women deepens confidence, creates opportunity, and raises profits.
>
> 2009 annual meeting, CGI, "Investing in Girls and Women" plenary description[2]

As dusk arrived on International Women's Day, March 8, 2005, I received a press release from Nike, Inc. announcing that it was transforming the Nike Foundation, its philanthropic arm, to focus on adolescent girls in the Global South.[3] The press release lingered in my mind for days. Why would Nike, Inc. dedicate its foundation to the very population that it had been accused of exploiting in its contract factories around the world in the late 1990s and early 2000s? How was the corporation planning to improve girls' lives, well-being, and futures, and what qualified it to do so?

The announcement linked the philanthropic investments in adolescent girls' human capital to the United Nation's Millennium Development Goals (MDGs) on poverty alleviation and gender equality.[4] On such a day, it seemed fitting to think about these interrelated goals. International Women's Day is historically rooted in women's struggles for labor rights, which are, of course, intimately related to ending poverty and achieving gender equity.[5] The day was first instituted in 1909 by the Socialist Party of America to honor female garment workers protesting unfair labor conditions in New York City. The following year it was established as an international day by Socialist International to support women's rights and universal suffrage.[6] While the 2005 press release was deeply connected in this historical genealogy, it did not refer to the radical history of these interrelated struggles. In contrast, it built directly upon a present-day, de-politicized logic that separates ending poverty and achieving gender equality from the ongoing struggles of girls and women for a fair and just global economy. Nevertheless, while labor was not addressed in the press release, it was the silent milieu behind the corporation's announcement.

As I began to research Nike, Inc.'s focus on adolescent girls, I soon discovered that it was part of a broader movement of corporations and corporate foundations that had begun to prioritize poor, mostly Black and Brown girls and women through their corporate social responsibility (CSR), philanthropic, and business policies and practices in the new millennium. At the time, General Electric, Johnson & Johnson, Starbucks, and H&M, among others, all had similar programs. Their focus built on an idea promoted in the early 1990s by economists, such as T. Paul Schultz, Lawrence Summers, and Elizabeth King, that investing in girls' and women's education is the most efficient way to end poverty and promote development. Since then, the world's most powerful development institutions, including the World Bank, United Nations organizations, UK's Department for International Development (DFID), and United States Aid for International Development (USAID), have created programs and policies focused on educating girls and women throughout Asia, Africa, and Latin America.

In 2008, together with financial support from NoVo Foundation and the United Nations Foundation, the Nike Foundation branded this discourse through the Girl Effect, its theory of social and economic change. The Girl Effect is anchored by the idea that the future of humanity depends on poor racialized girls in the Global South. It is promoted as a revolutionary way of looking at girls' latent potential. If granted access to education, girls are imagined to rise from the obstacles that pull them down—poverty, hunger, disease, early marriage, and adolescent pregnancy—to solve the problems that plague our world. They will marry later and delay childbearing, and in doing so, they will generate economic development, limit population growth, educate their children, improve child and maternal health, conserve environmental resources, and control the spread of HIV/AIDS.

If we situate the Girl Effect historically, its power and legitimacy emerge from its correspondence to the authentic needs, desires, and grassroots demands of girls and women for access to quality schooling and training; safe, fair employment; economic security; affordable health care; freedom from violence; as well as legal and human rights. This book puts forward the idea that even as the Girl Effect corresponds to, and fulfills, some aspects of those, it does so not through a transformative logic, but rather using an instrumental gendered, racialized, and classed logic of development. While addressing the problems of poverty, inequality, and uneven development is indeed essential, the logic of the Girl Effect shifts that burden onto poor, racialized girls and women in the Global South by maintaining, and potentially exacerbating, inequitable roles of social reproduction that make them disproportionately responsible for the well-being and futures of others and for resolving the contradictions of development.

The Girl Effect thus transfers the onus of responsibility for change away from the governments, corporations, and global governance institutions whose actions have led to the unequal distribution of resources and opportunities that disproportionately affect the lives and well-being of girls, women, and the poor around the world.

Thus, this book posits that the "gender effect" of corporate investment in girls and women is the potential extension of the corporations' legitimacy, authority, and reach without corporations having to deal with the contradictions in their business practices and in capitalism itself. This has the effect of de-politicizing girls' and women's demands for fair corporate labor practices and a just global economy and disarticulating poverty's persistence from the historical, structural conditions that produce it and for which corporations are often partially responsible.

In this way, this book fundamentally departs from the prominent individuals and institutions who promote this development rationale through their programs and policies.[6] Rather than focus on how to design, implement, and evaluate programs and policies to unleash the purported ripple effect of investing in girls and women, as these actors often do, this book critically examines the logics, practices, and policies of US transnational corporations, such as Nike, Inc.; Goldman Sachs; Walmart; and ExxonMobil, as they seek to empower girls and women.

With access to powerful institutions, including Nike, Inc.; Nike Foundation; the World Bank; and the Clinton Global Initiative, this book focuses on how corporate investment in the Girl Effect is negotiated by diverse, unequally resourced actors with different stakes and meanings attached to the project of development. It uses the case of the Girl Effect to demonstrate the intended and unintended effects corporate programs have on girls, women, and corporations.

The book's ethnographic insights illuminate the "gender effect" at the intersection of corporate capitalism, feminism, and international development as corporations, in partnership with liberal feminists and development experts, seek to free capitalism from the constraints of gender inequality in order to create the conditions for economic growth and corporate profit without necessarily transforming the lives and futures of the girls and women that they claim to serve.

February 28, 2017
Madison, Wisconsin, United States

Acknowledgments

This book has reminded me that we rarely, if ever, accomplish anything on our own. My gratitude to others is profound. Over many years, I have had the privilege to learn from and work alongside brilliant colleagues and mentors who challenged and nurtured me.

This project took root at the University of California, Berkeley, which was an inspiring intellectual space to call home. Patricia Baquedano-López opened her academic world to me at a moment of critical importance. I am immensely grateful for her intellectual support and her faith in me and this project. Paola Bacchetta, Ananya Roy, and Zeus Leonardo provided invaluable theoretical and methodological guidance in this project's development. I am also grateful to Gillian Hart, Roshanak Kheshti, Trinh Minh-ha, Minoo Moallem, Juana Rodríguez, Ingrid Seyer-Ochi, Carol Stack, Stuart Tannock, and Barrie Thorne who inspired different aspects of this project through their courses. My colleagues from graduate school continue to inspire me with their friendship, intellect, and commitments in the world, and they have all read early iterations of this book, including Becky Alexander, Jose Arias, Rick Ayers, Erica Boas, Rachel Branhinsky, Sandy Brown, Emily Gleason, Sera Hernandez, Nirali Jani, Erica Kohl-Arenas, Cecilia Lucas, Alexis Martin, Genevieve Negrón-

Gonzales, Irenka Dominguez Pareto, Poulami Roychowdhury, Nazanin Shahrokni, and Susan Woolley. Becky Tarlau's commitments to theory and activism inspired me while writing this book, and she has lovingly understood when our other writing projects were delayed in the process. Hiba Bou Akar has travelled the entire journey of this book with me. She has provided me with incredible friendship and brilliant advice over many years, and she always saves the day.

My colleagues in the Department of Educational Policy Studies and the School of Education at the University of Wisconsin–Madison have mentored me and provided me with institutional support, including Lesley Bartlett, John Diamond, Jim Escalante, Mary Jo Gessler, Diana Hess, Nancy Kendall, Stacey Lee, Bob Mathieu, Adam Nelson, Bill Reese, Amy Stambach, and Maisha Winn. Bianca Baldridge, Linn Posey-Maddox, and Erica Turner's encouragement, intellect, and humor sustain me. I am also grateful to Kirk Anderson, Dave Douglas, Anna Douglas-Jordan, Sophie Flinchum, Shanshan Jiang, Arashjot Kaur, James LaPierre, Haley Olig, Rachel Silver, Jennifer Tasse, and Miriam Thangaraj for their careful assistance. Selah Agaba adopted this book with care, respect, and contagious enthusiasm—I am very grateful.

Over the years, I've been privileged to receive feedback from countless people who have engaged my ideas and shaped this book: Joan DeJaeghere, Karen Monkman, Jenny Parkes, Ashwini Tambe, Millie Thayer, Elaine Unterhalter, Nelly Stomquist, and Vera Maria Vidal Peroni supported earlier publications from this project. Scholars at the following institutions generously provided me feedback on different portions of this book, including Women and Gender Studies Institute at University of Toronto; the Transnationalizing Justice Workshop of the University of California Multi-Campus Research Group; Núcleo de Identidades de Gênero e Subjetividades at the Universidade Federal de Santa Catarina; Institute for Research on Women and Gender at University of Michigan; The Lemman Center for Educational Innovation and Entrepreneurship at Stanford University; Soka University of America; the Politics of Privatization in Education Non-Conference at New York University; the Department of Geography's Yi-Fu Tuan Lectures at the University of Wisconsin–Madison; and the National Academy of Education/Spencer Foundation. I am also grateful to colleagues at the Global Fund for Women, NoVo Foundation,

Clinton Global Initiative, and Emerging Markets Foundation who invited me to present my research findings.

To all of the people who have guided me and taken chances on me, thank you. Everyone deserves mentors and opportunities like the ones you have provided, including Brian Delaney, Kathleen Hall, Trudy Hall, Marcos Nascimento, Lynn Paine, john powell, Kavita Ramdas, Stephen Silberstein, and Shelia Smith-McCoy.

At the University of California Press, Naomi Schneider supported the idea of this book long before it was written. I am appreciative of her faith in its significance. Thank you to Renee Donovan, Benjy Mailings, and Jessica Moll for their editorial assistance and Lia Tjandra for her cover design. I am grateful for the time, energy, and intellectual generosity of Michael Goldman, Dinah Rajak, and two anonymous reviewers. All errors in the book are my own.

At all of the institutions in the United States and Brazil where I conducted my research, the NGOs in Rio de Janeiro, whose actual names I do not reveal, the Clinton Global Initiative, the Nike Foundation, Nike, Inc., the World Bank, and many other institutions, thank you to all of you who invited me into your offices and classrooms, shared your experiences and perspectives with me, and trusted me to tell this story. I wish I could acknowledge you personally for your generosity and candor. My sincerest gratitude is to all of the young women who welcomed me into their lives and classrooms. I hope I do you justice.

To all of my dear friends who housed, fed, and supported me during my fieldwork and writing, I cannot thank you enough—Juliana Cavilha, Caroline Crown, Felipe Fernandes, Miriam Pillar Grossi, Elizabeth Hauck, Ali Keller, Tiago Losso, Denise Malvehy, Meredith Mazur, Simon Morfit, Carmen Rial, Stacy Sharp, Alberto Struck, Becky Tarlau, Mead Webster, and Katie Wilson. Candida Botafogo's spirit sustained Miguel and me during our many stays in her home in Rio de Janeiro over the years.

My parents, Kitty Moeller and Bill Moeller, have encouraged me to pursue my own path from a very young age. My dad's intellectual curiosity and my mom's unique empathy for others and critical insight on the world have shaped me. Thank you to my brothers, Will Moeller and Carl Moeller, for your love and perspectives on the world, and to Sarah Dolan, Finn Moeller, Reid Moeller, Sra. Jenny Peña, Gabriel Zamora, and Maurito Zamora.

Miguel Zamora's vision of the world inspires my own. He has lovingly accompanied me throughout the life of this book, making many sacrifices along the way so that I could pursue this research. His love and intellect are infused throughout the book. Sebastián was born as I finished this manuscript, teaching me of the beautiful, complex ways our love, care work, and intellectual labor are always deeply intertwined.

. . . . .

Research for this book was generously supported by grants from the National Science Foundation; the Fulbright-Hays Program; the National Academy of Education/Spencer Foundation; the University of California, Berkeley's Graduate School of Education, Department of Gender & Women's Studies, Center for Latin American Studies, and Haas Institute for a Fair and Inclusive Society; and the University of Wisconsin's Department of Educational Policy Studies, Wisconsin Center for Educational Research, Latin Caribbean and Iberian Studies, and Department of Gender and Women's Studies.

Abbreviations

AFD	Alliance for Development
AGI	Adolescent Girl Initiative
AWID	Association of Women in Development
BEMFAM	*Bem-Estar Familiar no Brasil* (The Brazilian Society for Family Welfare)
BP	British Petroleum
BRICS	Brazil, Russia, India, China, South Africa (Five major emerging economies)
CCTs	Conditional cash transfer programs
CGI	Clinton Global Initiative
CPF	Brazilian identification number
CSR	Corporate Social Responsibility
DFID	United Kingdom's Department of International Development
EFA	Education for All
GAD	Gender and Development

GAP	Gender Action Plan
GDP	Gross Domestic Product
GFW	Global Fund for Women
GJO	The Gender Justice Organization
GPF	Global Philanthropy Forum
GRAVAD	Brazilian study on adolescent pregnancy
HIV/AIDS	Human immunodeficiency virus and acquired immune deficiency syndrome
IBRD	International Bank for Reconstruction and Development
ICRW	International Center for Research on Women
IDA	International Development Association
IDB	Inter-American Development Bank
IFC	International Finance Corporation
ILO	International Labour Organization
IMF	International Monetary Fund
INWF	International Network of Women's Funds
IPPF	International Planned Parenthood Federation
IUD	Intrauterine device
LGBTQ	Lesbian, Gay, Bisexual, Transgender, and Queer
M&E	Monitoring and Evaluation
MDGs	Millennium Development Goals
NGO	Nongovernmental organization
OECD	Organisation of Economic Co-operation and Development
PEJM	*Programa pelo empoderamento das jovens mulheres* (Young Women's Empowerment Program)
PSLF	Private Sector Leaders' Forum
RFP	Request for proposals
SAPs	Structural adjustment policies

SEC	Securities and Exchange Commission
STDs	Sexually transmitted diseases
UN	United Nations
UNCSW	United Nations Commission on the Status of Women
UNDP	United Nations Development Programme
UNESCO	United Nations Educational, Scientific, and Cultural Organization
UNFPA	United Nations Fund for Population Activities (now United Nations Population Fund)
UNGEI	United Nations Girls' Education Initiative
UNICEF	United Nations Children's Fund
USAID	United States Agency for International Development
WAD	Women and Development
WBCSD	World Business Council for Sustainable Development
WEF	World Economic Forum
WHO	World Health Organization
WID	Women in Development
WTO	World Trade Organization

Introduction

CORPORATIZED DEVELOPMENT

"It has been called the ultimate emerging market: women," explained Margaret Brennan, a young white reporter for Bloomberg Television's *InBusiness*, while standing in front of the American flag on the floor of the New York Stock Exchange.[1] She continued, "A recent announcement by Booz & Co.," the global strategy consulting firm,[2] "found that about 860 million women are not prepared to take part in the world economy because they lack education, training, access, and finance. Enter the Third Billion." This was February 1, 2012, the day that the Third Billion Campaign was officially launched. I watched the announcement on my laptop from where I was living in San Francisco, California. The campaign was created by "an alliance of corporations, including Coca-Cola, Ernst & Young, Accenture, and Standard Chartered" that was "working with the World Bank and others to invest in these women." A video of women in headscarves walking on a sidewalk played on the screen as the headline "Niche for Global Growth: Women" flashed below.

Brennan then welcomed Beth Brooke, vice chair of Ernst & Young and "one of the world's one hundred most powerful women according to *Forbes* magazine," to the show.

"So tell me, what is this initiative about?" asked Brennan. Brooke, a middle-aged white woman, explained, "The Third Billion Campaign is really focused on just what you mentioned, which is within the next decade, the impact on the global economy of women coming into the workforce, as consumers, as entrepreneurs, as employees, will have an impact as great as China's billion population or India's billion population, which is why we use the term 'the Third Billion.' It's that big of an impact." Brennan sought clarification: "And so, as you have the population growing, it's the participation, and how they participate, that's the issue. Right?"

Brooke responded, "They've got to be prepared to participate, which means be educated, have access to technology, access to capital, access to finance. They've got to be prepared, and they've got to be empowered. There are cultural barriers and things like that, but when prepared and enabled as Booz & Co. reports, there could be the force of one billion additional individuals, who are going to be women, coming into the global economy. And what country and what company right now wouldn't kill for that kind of economic growth?"

Later in the interview, Brennan asked Brooke if there was an existing model that the campaign was using to develop and implement its initiatives. Brooke explained that there was not one clear model. Instead, "Each of us, Ernst & Young in the private sector, countries, nongovernmental organizations (NGOs), everyone can do what they do best. We do a lot around women, for talent, for women entrepreneurs, but we can only do what we do best. Then it takes others who are involved in the Third Billion Campaign. Goldman Sachs, doing what they do. It takes Walmart. Gonna do what they do. Coca-Cola. It takes governments. It takes NGOs. All of us in the Third Billion Campaign are actually coming together to say, if we are aware of each other's efforts, we can collaborate for a collective impact."

I began this introduction with the Third Billion Campaign to provide entrée to the following questions: How and why have these girls' and women's lives and futures become so deeply intertwined with corporations' aspirations in the new millennium? And, more specifically, how has gender equality, particularly in the areas of education, training, and finance, come to be considered a necessary condition for economic growth and, correspondingly, for corporate profit?

This book examines how corporate investment in poor, racialized girls and women in the Global South functions to circumvent a fundamental contradiction inherent in the relationships between US corporations and these girls and women—powerful corporations are often exacerbating inequalities and vulnerabilities for this same population through their business practices even as they claim to be "doing good."

THE THIRD BILLION

As DeAnne Aguirre and Karim Sabbagh of Booz & Co. originally argued, "If China and India each represent one billion emerging participants in the global marketplace, then this 'third billion' is made of women, in both developing and industrialized nations, whose economic lives have previously been stunted, underleveraged, or suppressed."[3] They created the composite figure by using estimates from the International Labour Organization (ILO) of women ages twenty to sixty-five who are considered "not prepared (lacking sufficient education) and not enabled (lacking support from families and communities)" to participate in the global economy.[4] According to their estimated figures, approximately 882 million of these women are located in "emerging" or "developing" nations, while approximately forty-seven million live in North America, Western Europe, and Japan. According to their prediction, as "constraints are alleviated, the Third Billion's movement into the middle class will accelerate."[5] Their potential power in the global economy is considered "akin to stumbling upon a relatively untapped emerging market."[6]

The Third Billion Campaign's coalition was comprised of representatives of powerful institutions, including corporations, NGOs, academic institutions, multilateral and bilateral agencies, and global forums.[7] It originally developed out of an October 2009 gathering at New York University's Villa La Pietra in New York City convened by the university and Vital Voices Global Partnership, with funding from the Paul E. Singer Family Foundation, in honor of the fifteenth anniversary of the United Nation's Fourth World Conference on Women in Beijing, China. The group examined the state of women worldwide, changes made since Beijing, and the present-day "obstacles to women's empowerment and challenges to gender

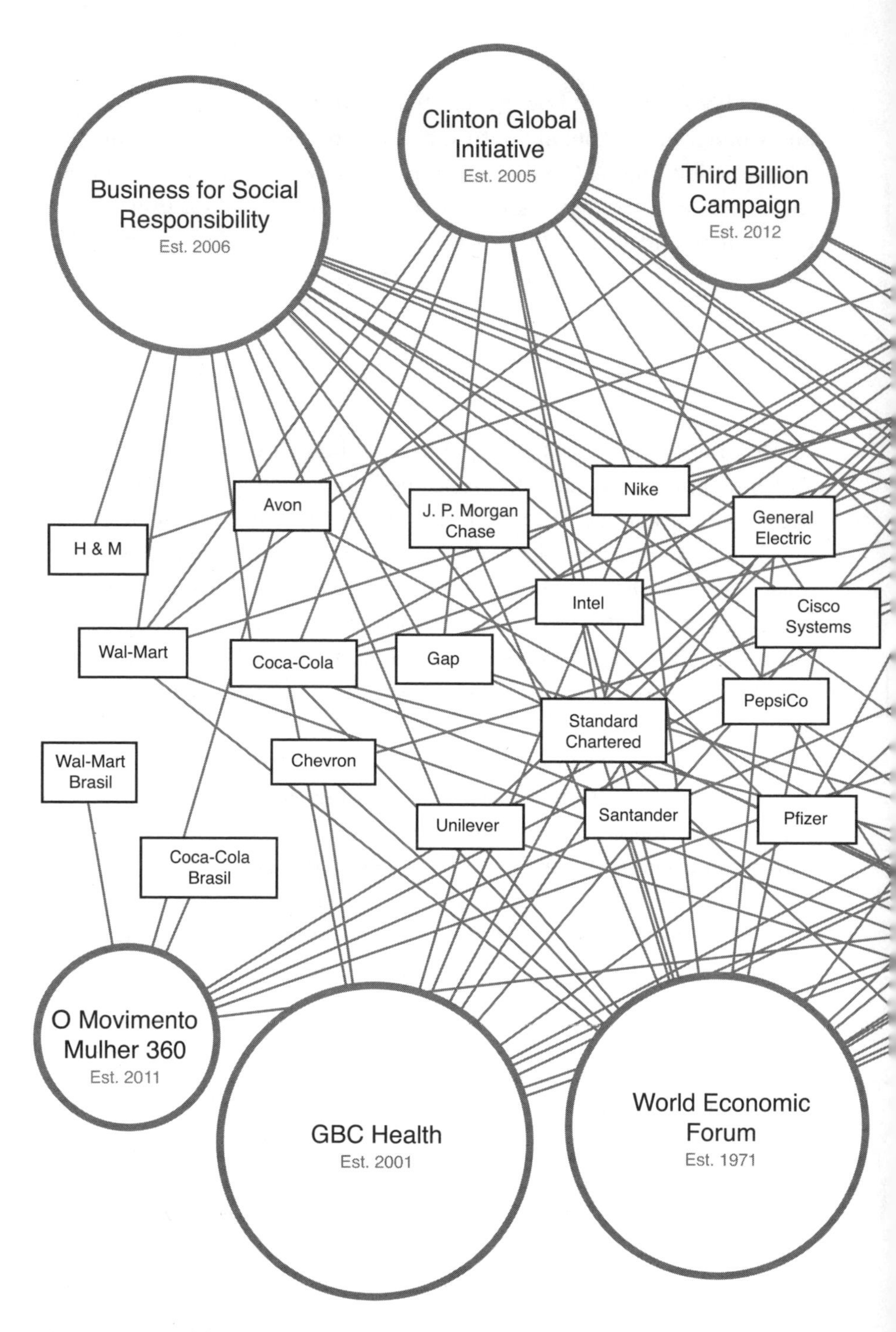

Figure 1. View of the proliferation of transnational networks of corporatized development focused on girls and women.

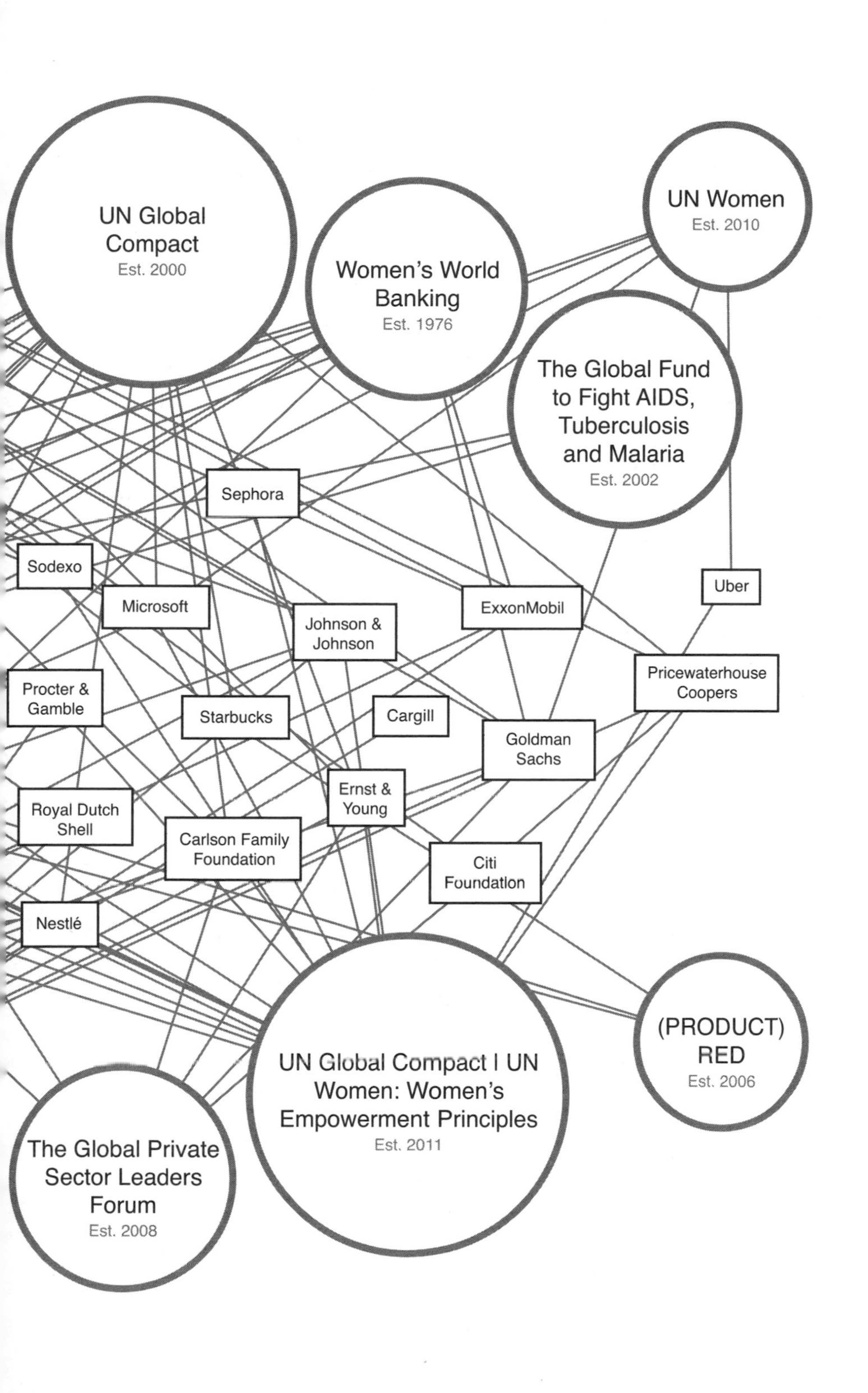

UN Global Compact
Est. 2000
Women's World Banking
Est. 1976
UN Women
Est. 2010
The Global Fund to Fight AIDS, Tuberculosis and Malaria
Est. 2002
Sephora
Sodexo
Microsoft
Johnson & Johnson
ExxonMobil
Uber
Pricewaterhouse Coopers
Procter & Gamble
Starbucks
Cargill
Goldman Sachs
Royal Dutch Shell
Ernst & Young
Carlson Family Foundation
Citi Foundation
Nestlé
(PRODUCT) RED
Est. 2006
UN Global Compact | UN Women: Women's Empowerment Principles
Est. 2011
The Global Private Sector Leaders Forum
Est. 2008

equality." The following year, the group held a second meeting in Florence, Italy, to form the coalition. The coalition's mission is to create an "economic case for women's empowerment and gender equality" by developing messaging and initiatives that "tap women's potential as critical resources, thus leading to stronger economic growth for nations, communities, and businesses around the world."[8] Its agenda focuses on four primary areas, including access to finance, education, and training; entrepreneurship; labor policy and practice; and legal and social status.[9] This agenda forms the basis of the coalition's bottom-billion strategy to invest in girls and women. It has resulted in corporate practices and policies targeting girls and women in order to end poverty and create conditions for economic growth.

Since its launch, the coalition has done relatively little. The campaign itself has fizzled away, and even the website is no longer functional. Yet, the discourse of the Third Billion has become more entrenched than ever as individual corporate members deepen and strengthen their commitment in this area. In many cases, they have continued their participation in other initiatives, such as the World Bank's Global Private Sector Leaders Forum (PSLF), and joined campaigns in different geographies.

Take, for instance, O Movimento Mulher 360, which translates as the Women 360 Movement. Originally launched by Walmart Brasil, the initiative promotes "a 360-degree view of women's economic empowerment" in corporate environments, communities, and supply chains.[10] In September 2015, the initiative became an independent nonprofit association, bringing together Brazilian companies, including Bombril, Grupo Boticário, Duratex, GPA, Itaú, and Natura, with US and other international companies with subsidiaries or offices in Brazil, including Cargill, Coca-Cola, DelRio, Johnson & Johnson, Nestlé, Pepsico, Santander, and Unilever, to reap the purported benefits of investing in girls and women.[11]

THE BUSINESS CASE FOR INVESTING IN GIRLS AND WOMEN

As corporations search for new frontiers of capitalist growth in the context of ongoing economic crises, they have increasingly made a "business case" for investing in poor girls and women in the Global South as an investment with a high rate of return.[12] As Angel Gurria, secretary-general of the Organisation of Economic Co-operation and Development (OECD), explains, this population is the "most underutilized asset in the global economy."[13] By emphasizing how "the potential of women as economic players has been unrealized,"[14] corporations, such as, but not limited to, the members of the Third Billion Campaign, are promoting large-scale investment in particular girls and women to end poverty and promote development and economic growth.

Some of the corporations making themselves known in this area include Becton Dickinson; Booz & Co.; Chevron; Cisco Systems; Coca-Cola; Ernst & Young; ExxonMobil; Gap, Inc.; General Electric; Goldman Sachs; Gucci; Intel Corporation; J.P. Morgan Chase; Johnson & Johnson; Microsoft Corporation; Nike, Inc.; Stella Artois; Standard Chartered Bank; Starbucks Corporation; and Walmart; among others. Their corporate initiatives are typically directed by the corporation itself, often through a corporate social responsibility (CSR) department, or through an established foundation [501(c)(3)] that functions as its philanthropic arm. Philanthropy and CSR are increasingly streamlined within corporations' core business strategies. The initiatives occur through a range of partnerships with development organizations, including international NGOs, bilateral and multilateral agencies, and universities. For instance, Gap, Inc.'s Personal Achievement and Career Enhancement (PACE)[15] program that targets women in its contract factories through local NGOs; Goldman Sachs' 10,000 Women[16] program that partners with local institutions including technical and business schools to offer a variety of training opportunities for women. These programs typically occur through partnerships with traditional development organizations, including international NGOs and bilateral and multilateral agencies, as in the case of Nike, Inc.'s investment in the Girl Effect. As the book's examination of the Girl Effect reveals, corporations are also making new partnerships with venture capitalists, whose access to capital and markets enable previously limited interventions to achieve scale.

Corporate investment in girls and women is predicated on four interrelated discourses: bottom billion capitalism, philanthrocapitalism, gender equality, and Third World difference. The first, "bottom billion capitalism," is the economic theory and practice promoted by those interested in mining the fortunes of what C.K. Prahalad identifies as the "bottom of the pyramid."[17] Prahalad's idea refers to the bottom billion poorest people in the world living in conditions of poverty and marginally positioned vis-à-vis capital markets.[18] Investment in this economic stratum is intended to simultaneously generate economic profit for investors and benefit the poor. As Prahalad and Stuart Hart explain, "Low-income markets represent a prodigious opportunity for the world's wealthiest companies to seek their fortunes and to bring prosperity to the aspiring poor."[19] This rationalization results in what Ananya Roy calls, "the ethicalization of market rule."[20]

As scholars note, bottom of the pyramid ventures driven by the ideology of bottom billion capitalism are often gendered in nature as they seek to harness girls and women as consumers as well as last-mile distribution entrepreneurs or retailers who can supposedly circumvent common barriers to accessing those markets, such as limited infrastructure, consumer dispersal, and product awareness.[21] Girls and women are frequently targeted for gendered products, particularly those that promote the aspirational ideals of class mobility, racialized beauty, and professional status."[22]

For example, Avon Corporation is anchored in a gendered bottom of the pyramid model. Across the world, the company's direct sales model relies on its representatives, the majority of whom are women, to buy the cosmetic products for themselves, and sell and recruit other women to join the network of sellers and buyers. The company boasts to have been the first corporation to empower women by providing flexible out-of-home employment opportunities as early as 1886 when it was founded in the United States. Sales representatives pay an introductory fee, varying by country, to join the sales team, order merchandise, and earn the profit that they make off the merchandise[23] However, as Linda Scott et al. found in their study in South Africa, the women in the Avon network gained some economic and social emancipation from their earnings, but those gains were set against systems of structural violence that continued to threaten their lives and well-being.[24]

Second, the Third Billion concept is also related to the discourse of philanthrocapitalism, the philanthropic practice predicated on the notion of investment.[25] Philanthrocapitalists imagine themselves to be social investors who invest their money to maximize social and economic returns. The returns are defined in social, cultural, political, and economic terms. The corporate focus on poor girls and women is similarly infused with the language of, and the desire for, returns. The high rate of returns—real or imagined—is precisely why corporations target this population. Philanthrocapitalists couple the focus on returns with the employment of market-based strategies and an insistence on measurable, often quantifiable, results.

These proponents claim their approach to philanthropy is new; yet, as Linsey McGoey argues, philanthrocapitalism is historically rooted in liberal political-economic thought, dating back to the eighteenth century, based on the idea that markets are the most efficient mechanism for distributing socioeconomic well-being and, thus, for contributing to the common good.[26] Moreover, it uses the early twentieth century strategies of John D. Rockefeller and Andrew Carnegie, among others, which promote the use of business strategies to solve social problems,[27] and builds upon the practice developed in the mid-nineteenth century of applying rational scientific investigation to human welfare to ensure measured results and accountability.[28]

Beyond the desire to contribute to a particular form of social and economic well-being, philanthrocapitalists are also forthright regarding their own self-interests. There is profit to be made in pursuing the social good. Thus, as a practice, philanthrocapitalism rests comfortably upon a foundation of inequality. Philanthrocapitalists acknowledge capitalism's production of inequalities even as they simultaneously seek to capitalize upon the system's production of wealth to ameliorate the social and economic disparities produced by the system itself, and to produce greater wealth for those who can invest.[29] Their efforts thus obscure the fact that the surplus capital they reinvest in poor, racialized girls and women is often produced on their very backs, thus leaving intact durable, deeply entrenched inequalities across multiple relations of difference.[30]

In this way, the philanthrocapitalism of companies such as Gap, Inc., and Walmart is intimately related to the inequalities their corporate practices create, exacerbate, and/or reproduce in girls' and women's lives. For example, both companies are the ongoing targets of campaigns fighting for safe, non-discriminatory working conditions and a living wage throughout their global supply chains.[31] While both companies target girls and women through their discrete philanthrocapitalist strategies, neither corporation has transformed its core business practices to adequately address the concerns of its majority female labor force and, thus, ensure the long-term health and economic well-being of girls and women.

Third, corporations have taken up the liberal feminist discourse of gender equality[32] through the "business case" for investing in girls and women.[33] They have usurped feminist aspirations of liberating girls and women from the constraints of patriarchy for their goals of market growth and profit maximization.[34] As Isobel Coleman, senior fellow at the Council on Foreign Relations, argued during the days prior to her participation as co-chair of the Empowering Women and Girls track at the 2010 Clinton Global Initiative annual meeting, an event that I participated in for my research: "As companies seek new sources of revenue in developing economies, they will find that gender disparities pose an obstacle. The sooner and harder the private sector works to overcome gender inequality, the better off the world—and companies' own bottom lines—will be."[35]

Feminist scholars of political economy have developed powerful historical and theoretical analyses of how feminist language and desires for liberation have been reframed within market logics. In this way, the market becomes the guarantor of equality as "the dream of women's emancipation is harnessed to the engine of capitalist accumulation."[36] In employing the feminist idea of empowering women to create the developmental conditions necessary for future corporate profit, as Hester Eisenstein argues more broadly, "women replace development"[37] as the most efficient and effective solution to generating economic growth. The World Bank's tagline for its Gender Action Plan (GAP), "Gender equality is smart economics," perfectly sums up this approach. Divorced from its origins in the feminist movement, this economistic discourse on gender equality becomes "an uncanny double that [the feminist movement] can neither simply embrace nor wholly disavow."[38] As documented by Lucy Ferguson and Daniella Morena Alarcón, this creates conflicts for progressive, transnational feminist organizations, such as the Association of Women in International Development (AWID) and women's funds associated with the Prospera-International Network of Women's Funds (INWF) (as well as individuals operating within mainstream development organizations), that have long critiqued corporate capitalism for its violence and marginalization of girls, women, and the poor, yet are in need of funds to support their under-resourced movement toward gender equity.[39]

Underlying this liberal feminist discourse is the assumption that gender oppression is what defines the lives, conditions, and futures of girls and women in the Global South and stands as the barrier to economic growth and corporate profit. This supposition informs the field of "gender and development" as a field of policy and practice that has grown over the past four decades, and its resulting efforts of gender mainstreaming across institutions in the development regime. Yet, even when the term gender is deployed, in practice it is often used as a "descriptive device,"[40] or, more specifically, as a way of targeting girls and women as population categories rather than attending to gender as a relation of power.[41] As João, an NGO staff member in Brazil, remarked to me regarding the Girl Effect's focus: "It's not gender, it's adolescent girls."

To note, all names in the study are pseudonyms to protect the anonymity of the individuals unless the first name and last name are listed. Also, since there were very few people of color employed in the organizations I studied, including the NGOs, Nike Foundation, and the Clinton Global Initiative, I do not note the race, ethnicity, or skin color of individuals in my study as this could potentially make them identifiable. I recognize the limitations this places on the analysis.

Yet, the Third Billion is not actually about girls and women as universalized population categories of gender as the liberal feminist discourse on gender equality imagines. Rather, the concept of the Third Billion is also premised on the discourse around "Third World girls" and "Third World women"[42] that has constructed them as Other within the projects of colonization, global capitalism, and Western feminisms. The term Third World is used here as a sociopolitical concept that does not necessarily map onto geographies of the North and South but rather considers the ways in which centuries of (post)colonial histories and imaginations have shaped understandings of racialized girls and women, as well as places and ways of being that exist within, between, and outside of nation-state boundaries.

Of particular relevance for understanding this is Chandra Talpade Mohanty's critique of how Western feminist texts in international development, in particular, have historically constructed the Third World woman as a singular, monolithic subject.[43] Her work builds on the premise by Western and non-Western feminists of color that gender is necessary though not sufficient for understanding and theorizing the identities, experiences, conditions, and power relations informing lives lived across multiple social, cultural, economic, political, religious, and geographic locations.[44] In relying solely on the concept of "woman" as their central analytical category, and gender as the "single axis" around which difference is understood, hegemonic Western and Anglo-American feminisms often reduce and/or mask how difference operates in relation to and within gender categories.[45] As Trinh Minh-ha argues, "Yearning for universality, the generic 'woman,' like its counterpart, the generic 'man,' tends to efface difference within itself."[46]

While the oppressed woman is generated by an exclusive focus on gender difference, Mohanty's work contributes to understanding how the oppressed Third World woman is imagined to have an additional attribute: "Third World difference."[47] She defines it as "that stable, ahistorical something that apparently oppresses most if not all the women in these countries."[48] Through this homogenizing application of difference, she argues that the texts she analyzes "discursively colonize the material and historical heterogeneities of the lives of women in the Third World."[49]

The Third World difference that defines the subject position of Third World girl in this historical moment constructs her as both oppressed and full of what I identified previously as Third World potential.[50] She occupies a precarious subject position in which she is simultaneously a universalized victim in need of saving and "the answer" to solving the problems of development and growth.[51] Here the act of empowering her to fulfill her potential for development becomes an act of saving her. It is the potential productivity of this contradiction that corporate elites and development experts have embraced, as this book's analysis of Nike, Inc.'s investments in the Girl Effect in Brazil and in partnership with other institutions reveals.

THE GIRL EFFECT

Beginning in the early 1990s, Nike, Inc. emerged as the global target of the anti-sweatshop and anti-globalization movements.[52] Transnational criticism focused on the corporation's well-documented abusive practices against its predominantly young, uneducated, poor, racialized female labor force in the Global South. In its 2005–2006 Corporate Responsibility Report, Nike, Inc. estimated that "80 percent of [their] workers are women aged 18 to 24," and "they are typically poorly educated, living against a precarious backdrop of poverty and insecurity, within emerging economies."[53]

The company which originally began in 1964 as a partnership between Japanese shoe manufacturer Onitsuka and Blue Ribbon Sports to distribute Onitsuka shoes, began manufacturing its own shoes in 1971. It became the Nike brand in 1978. In the years preceding, the company shifted its production from Japan to South Korea as Japanese wages increased, making it less profitable than other locations in Asia with lower wages. In the ongoing race to the bottom that characterizes the global manufacturing industry, the company moved much of its production to Taiwan in the 1980s, and then to Thailand, Indonesia, the Philippines, and Vietnam in the 1990s. Nike, Inc.'s role in pioneering outsourcing led to skyrocketing growth as it secured its place as the largest manufacturer of athletic shoes and apparel in the global economy. Yet, the corporation fell victim to its own success, as the same practices that contributed to its impressive growth rate also led anti-sweatshop campaigns to bring to light the abusive labor conditions in its contract factories.[54]

Responding to tarnishing accusations, including media exposés on child labor, co-founder and then CEO Phil H. Knight publicly stated at the National Press Club in Washington, DC, in May 1998, that "Nike product has become synonymous with slave wages, forced overtime, and arbitrary abuse."[55] Yet, despite Knight's promise in 1998 to transform the corporation's practices, accusations of abusive labor problems have persisted in its contract factories, as reflected in well-publicized worker strikes.[56] Nevertheless, since this moment of crisis, the corporation has focused on remaking itself as socially responsible.

This led to a strategic search for an undiscovered niche in the development market. Knight said he "tapped" Maria Eitel, a white woman, "to create a not-for-profit arm—but had not dictated a mission."[57] A trained communications specialist, Eitel was originally hired by the corporation as its first vice president of corporate responsibility (1998–2004) to

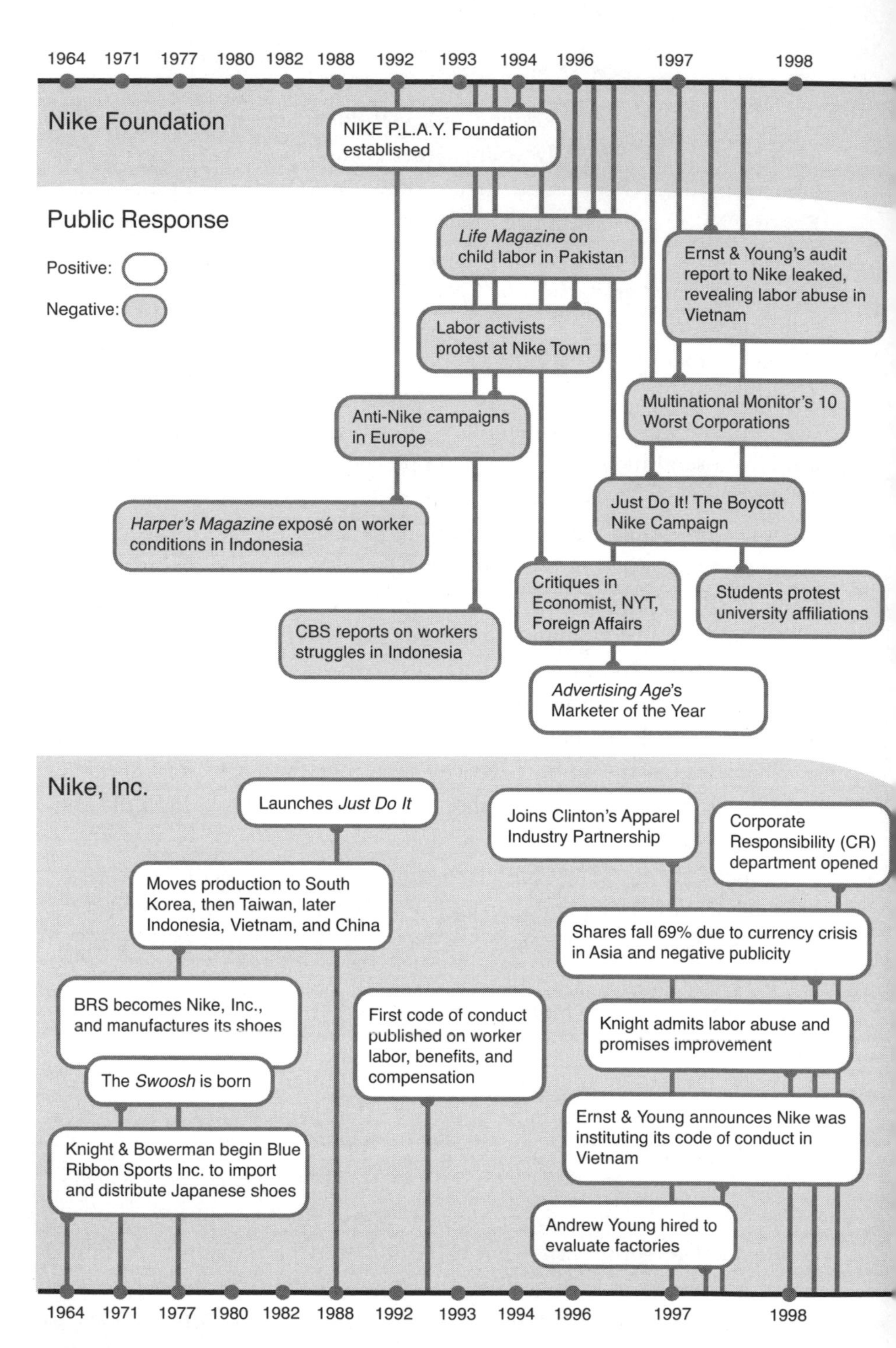

Figure 2. Timeline of Nike, Inc. and Nike Foundation history and public response. For sources to timeline, see p. 210.

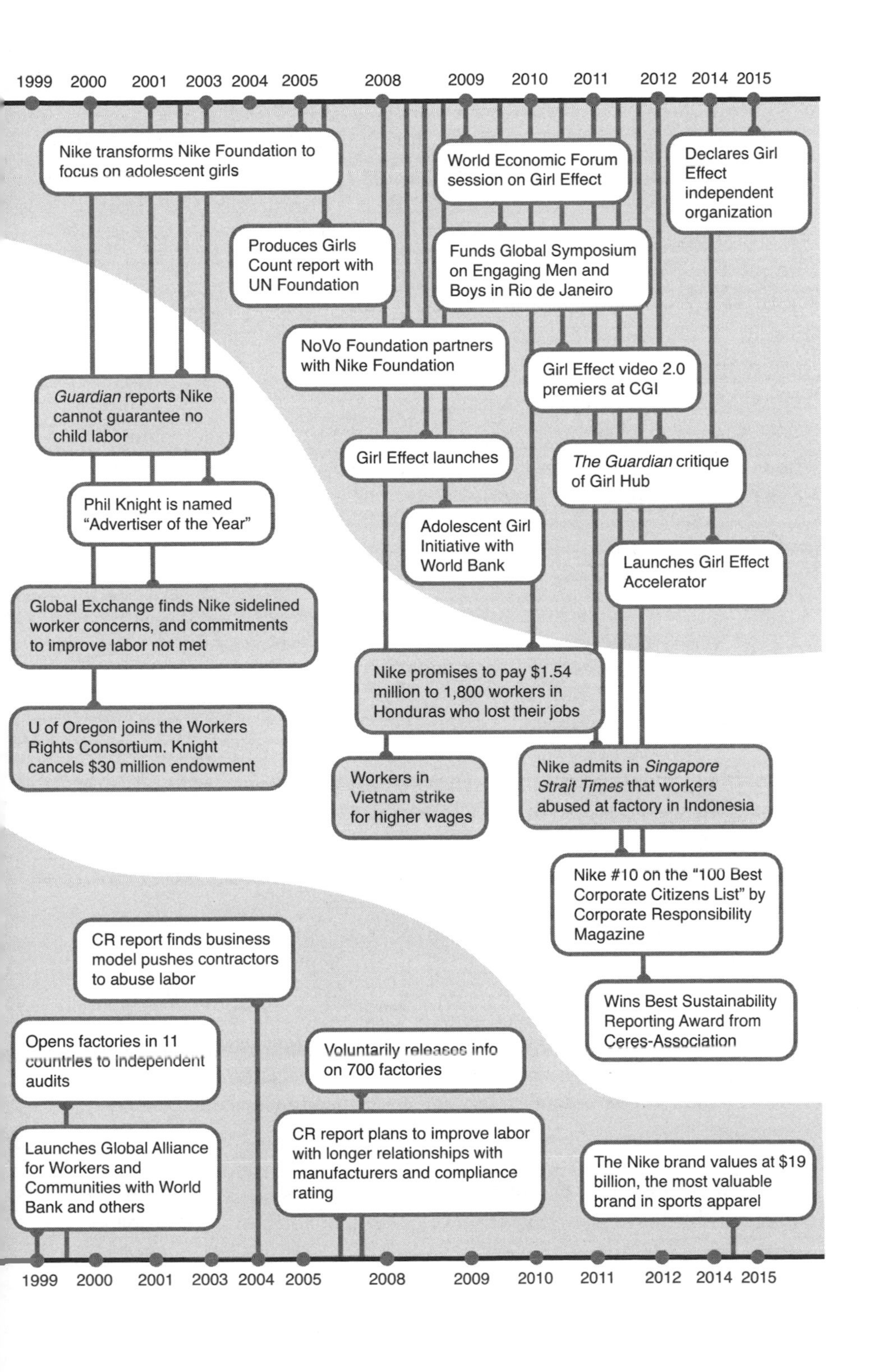

1999
2000
2001
2003
2004
2005
2008
2009
2010
2011
2012
2014
2015
Nike transforms Nike Foundation to focus on adolescent girls
Produces Girls Count report with UN Foundation
NoVo Foundation partners with Nike Foundation
Girl Effect launches
Adolescent Girl Initiative with World Bank
World Economic Forum session on Girl Effect
Funds Global Symposium on Engaging Men and Boys in Rio de Janeiro
Girl Effect video 2.0 premiers at CGI
The Guardian critique of Girl Hub
Declares Girl Effect independent organization
Launches Girl Effect Accelerator
Guardian reports Nike cannot guarantee no child labor
Phil Knight is named "Advertiser of the Year"
Global Exchange finds Nike sidelined worker concerns, and commitments to improve labor not met
U of Oregon joins the Workers Rights Consortium. Knight cancels $30 million endowment
Nike promises to pay $1.54 million to 1,800 workers in Honduras who lost their jobs
Workers in Vietnam strike for higher wages
Nike admits in Singapore Strait Times that workers abused at factory in Indonesia
Nike #10 on the "100 Best Corporate Citizens List" by Corporate Responsibility Magazine
Wins Best Sustainability Reporting Award from Ceres-Association
CR report finds business model pushes contractors to abuse labor
Opens factories in 11 countries to independent audits
Launches Global Alliance for Workers and Communities with World Bank and others
Voluntarily releases info on 700 factories
CR report plans to improve labor with longer relationships with manufacturers and compliance rating
The Nike brand values at $19 billion, the most valuable brand in sports apparel

ameliorate its public relations image during the late 1990s. She was formerly deputy director of media affairs at the White House, then a special assistant to President George H.W. Bush, a manager and director of Microsoft Corporation, and a manager of MCI Communications Corporation. As described in *Fast Company* magazine, "Eitel was in the midst of a yearlong exploration to determine how to make the biggest impact."[58] She consulted with a wide range of development experts, including a number of my interviewees in the areas of formal education, reproductive health, and economic development, as well as "villagers, NGO leaders, and industry titans" before determining that Nike, Inc. should focus on adolescent girls.[59] *Fast Company* recounted Eitel's pitch to the Nike, Inc. board of trustees:

> She remembers the gremlin that whispered in her ear as she nervously waited outside the 2004 meeting where she was to make her case: *Hey, Nike! Let's invest in adolescent girls and poverty! And not in any country where we have factories or businesses! Let's go to places like Ethiopia and northern Nigeria, where no one else dares to go!*" After a perilous few moments of silence, Knight gave her the thumbs-up, the flick that ignited an essential part of a movement.[60]

Beginning in that moment, Nike, Inc. worked to position itself as leading the effort to end poverty in the Global South through the foundation's investments in adolescent girls. As described in the company's press release in 2005:

> "The Nike Foundation is a further step in Nike's evolution as an engaged global corporate citizen," said Philip H. Knight, founder and chairman of NIKE, Inc. "Its philanthropic focus on poverty and gender inequality allows us to further invest in human capital not just where we do business, but where there is the greatest need. We believe the Foundation's investments in human capital will spark a positive cycle of development and complements NIKE, Inc.'s efforts around improvements in our fundamental business practices."[61]

The foundation's focus on adolescent girls was a noncontroversial way to redirect public attention away from ongoing labor strikes and campaigns against the corporation in order to secure its social license to operate and, correspondingly, its financial bottom line.

While the corporation's original intent was not to locate its philanthropic efforts in countries where its business is located, it included Brazil, India, and China in its portfolio from the beginning. These powerful economies, commonly referred to as three of the five BRICS countries, constitute both significant, consistent areas of consumer growth outside of the United States and locations with high numbers of contract factories.[62] They are not, however, countries where the corporation has typically experienced labor unrest. Those countries tend to be geographically situated in Southeast Asia and Central America, including Indonesia, Cambodia, and Honduras,[63] and tend to have the lowest wages and least regulations in the world, as well as governments that suppress labor protests. The Nike Foundation has had relatively few grantees in these regions, with the exception of Bangladesh where it funded Grameen Bank and BRAC, formerly known as the Bangladesh Rural Advancement Committee. The majority of Nike Foundation's grantees have been located in or focused their programs on the African continent throughout all of the phases of the Nike Foundation's development, including countries such as Kenya, Liberia, and Rwanda, where Nike, Inc. neither has contract factories nor significant consumer markets. Nevertheless, the company's interest in the continent has grown over time. As of August 2017, the company has one contract factory in South Africa and three in Egypt.[64]

In 2008, the foundation branded its philanthropic investment strategy by launching the Girl Effect with the United Nations Foundation and the NoVo Foundation, the family foundation of Peter and Jennifer Buffett. Peter is the son of financier Warren Buffett whose investments provided the financial basis for the NoVo Foundation's contribution of $72,700,00 to the Nike Foundation between 2007 and 2013 (see Table 1). During the duration of Nike Foundation's focus on adolescent girls, between 2005 and 2015, Nike, Inc. contributed $94,464,911 to the Nike Foundation, and $6,903,850 in 2004, the year the foundation prepared to launch its new focus (see Table 1). In total, between 2005 and 2015, the Nike Foundation received $191,219,834 in contributions and dispersed $145,594,118 in contributions, gifts, and grants (see Table 1).

The Girl Effect as a branded theory and method of social change was developed through a collaboration between the Nike Foundation's in-house creative team and Nike, Inc.'s long-time Portland-based advertising firm

Table 1 Nike Inc. Revenue and Nike Foundation Asset Value, Contributions, and Disbursements for Charitable Purposes ($US), 2001–2015.

	2001	*2002*	*2003*	*2004*	*2005*	*2006*	*2007*
Nike Inc. annual revenue[1]	9,490,000,000	9,890,000,000	10,700,000,000	12,250,000,000	13,740,000,000	14,955,000,000	16,326,000,0
Nike Foundation fair market value of all assets[2]	1,075,306	799,016	21,556,463	24,369,952	17,971,919	14,506,024	21,932,305
Nike, Inc. contribution	2,785,237	1,173,332	19,204,428	6,903,850	10,875,000	0.00	12,262,000
NoVo Foundation contribution	0.00	0.00	0.00	0.00	0.00	0.00	15,000,000
DFID contribution	0.00	0.00	0.00	0.00	0.00	0.00	0.00
World Bank contribution	0.00	0.00	0.00	0.00	0.00	0.00	0.00
Other contributions	110,443	7,933	5,922	1,783	12,290	7,138	5,227
Total contributions, gifts, and grants received	2,895,680	1,181,265	19,210,350	6,905,633	10,887,290	7,138	27,267,227
Operating and administrative expenses	55,024	95,125	136,873	610,718	946,656	416,443	1,366,328
Charitable disbursements paid	2,336,000	1,372,500	3,838,000	5,218,500	9,543,299	10,040,887	11,939,843
Total expenses and disbursements	2,391,024	1,467,625	3,974,873	5,829,218	10,489,955	10,457,330	13,306,171

1 "Earnings News," Nike, Inc., accessed September 24, 2017, https://news.nike.com/earnings.
2 All financials from the Nike Foundation are from federal tax filings (990s). "Nonprofit Explorer," ProPublica, accessed September 24, 2017, https://projects.propublica.org/nonprofits/.

2008	2009	2010	2011	2012	2013	2014	2015
,627,000,000	18,528,000,000	18,324,000,000	20,117,000,000	23,331,000,000	25,313,000,000	27,799,000,000	30,601,000,000
,174,327	36,033,351	39,761,379	39,698,757	71,495,610	60,378,797	22,893,171	17,549,681
00	8,900,000	7,680,484	6,780,543	5,752,301	7,183,448	18,392,869	16,638,266
,000,000	15,000,000	15,000,000	12,700,000	0.00	0.00	0.00	0.00
00	652,806	3,338,738	4,984,128	0.00	9,736,796	0.00	0.00
00	0.00	0.00	500,000	500,000	0.00	500,000	0.00
600	390,286	1,144,985	1,396,592	523,506	359,263	–32,930	54
,004,600	24,943,092	27,164,207	26,362,725	6,775,807	17,279,507	18,859,939	16,638,302
590,584	1,981,569	6,404,056	13,491,581	16,503,528	20,342,358	17,589,080	825,440
,922,308	16,119,930	17,108,276	13,840,324	10,143,661	6,164,078	9,552,230	21,219,282
,512,892	18,101,499	23,512,332	27,331,905	26,647,189	26,506,436	27,141,310	22,044,722

Figure 3. Photograph of Nike Foundation banner, "The End of Poverty Starts with a Girl," with a reflection of author and a building at Nike, Inc. world headquarters in Beaverton, Oregon. August 2009. Photograph by author.

Weiden + Kennedy.[65] The foundation defined the strategy as "the unique potential of 250 million adolescent girls to end poverty for themselves and the world."[66] It branded particular adolescent girls—poor, racialized, and living in the Global South—with the potential to end poverty in the new millennium.

The potential is predicated on what the foundation calls the "ripple effect" that investing in adolescent girls purportedly has across multiple development indicators, including alleviating poverty, promoting economic growth, reducing fertility rates and population growth, controlling the spread of HIV/AIDS, and conserving environmental resources.

Using this theory of change, between 2005 and 2015 the foundation structured its investments in girls throughout the Global South. The foundation first worked through existing international and national NGOs as it sought to develop a knowledge base on adolescent girls. Once it secured this knowledge, it promoted the brand to bilateral and multilateral agencies, such as the World Bank and the UK's Department for International Development (DFID); powerful private foundations, such as the NoVo Foundation; and global elites in powerful forums, such as CGI in New York City and the World Economic Forum (WEF) in Davos, Switzerland. In its final phase in 2014, it tapped entrepreneurs and venture capitalists in the cradles of innovation in Silicon Valley who were seeking to capitalize on girls' economic potential. Through those partnerships on different scales, the Nike Foundation focused on "driving massive resources to adolescent girls" and "getting girls on the international development agenda."[67] And, most significantly, through Nike Foundation's strategic efforts, the Girl Effect moved into the everyday lives and educations of girls and young women, and their families and communities throughout the Global South.

As the Girl Effect became one of the most prominent corporate philanthropic brands in the world, it reflected a moment of development in which corporations and their foundations were creating philanthropic brands and utilizing their consumer brands to influence how girls and women in the Global South are understood and how development interventions are structured in their name. Yet, as the Girl Effect brand's reach extended far beyond the corporate headquarters in Beaverton, Oregon, it created an unevenly contested political terrain of feminism, development, and corporate capitalism as girls and women in the Global South operated as the site of competing and often contradictory interests.

The legitimacy of the Girl Effect grew from acknowledgments of gendered poverty and inequality in girls' and women's lives. Some of those acknowledgments have been codified in past decades in key international declarations, including the Universal Declaration of Human Rights, Convention to Eliminate All Forms of Discrimination against Women, Education for All Initiative (EFA), the Millennium Development Goals (MDGs), and, most recently, the Sustainable Development Goals. While the Girl Effect builds on these, it nevertheless constructs marginalized girls as a new, efficient resource for poverty alleviation and economic development. As Maria Eitel, then president and CEO of Nike Foundation, explained, "I'll never get tired of saying it: Girls are the world's greatest untapped resource for economic growth and prosperity."[68] In this way, future economic growth resides with girls at the bottom of the pyramid.

Yet, feminist activists and scholars from a range of disciplinary perspectives have increasingly contested the Girl Effect in popular media and scholarly journals as it has traveled.[69] Those include cultural studies analyses of the representations through which the Girl Effect is produced,[70] and ethnographic examinations of how the Girl Effect is taken up in particular geographic locations, often by NGOs, and to what effects for girls.[71] Drawing on ethnographic fieldwork in the United Nations Foundation's Girl Up program, Emily Bent[72] also considers the ways in which the Girl Effect and similar campaigns produce new, relational, and often contradictory, political subjectivities for girls in the Global North. While those are important contributions to understanding the Girl Effect, very little is known about how the Girl Effect is constituted as a global development apparatus or how its logic shapes social relations on multiple spatial scales from an ethnographic perspective.[73] In this way, this book includes, but moves beyond, analyzing the realm of representation or the implementation of Nike Foundation–funded programs in specific locales to consider how the phenomenon is constituted across spatial scales and diverse geographies. It provides in-depth, ethnographic theorizing of how the practice of investing in the Girl Effect is constructed and negotiated by unequally resourced actors—from corporate and foundation executives to NGO educators—in diverse research sites including Rio de Janeiro, Brazil; New York City; Washington, DC; and Beaverton, Oregon.

DEFINING CORPORATIZED DEVELOPMENT

Since the inception of the development regime in the post–World War II era, corporations have been primary beneficiaries of the international development project. The roots of this privileged position originate in the birth of modern capitalism and centuries of colonial empires in which corporations and the state were deeply embedded within one another.[74] Throughout the twentieth century, corporations were one of development's primary customers. Institutions such as the World Bank and the International Monetary Fund (IMF) were designed from their inception, at least in part, to serve the interests of global capital. As a result, corporations were recipients of international development organizations' lucrative contracts to build dams and highways; the inheritors of privatized public-sector services, such as water, sanitation, and energy, as a result of loan conditionalities in structural adjustment programs (SAPs),[75] or, more broadly, the beneficiaries of economic growth strategies favoring corporate interests and global financial integration.[76] Yet, they were minimally involved in the everyday processes of designing, funding, branding, marketing, and executing development programs and policies. As Dinah Rajak explains, today they are both—development's primary beneficiaries *and* some of its principle architects.[77] Since the beginning of the new millennium, US-based transnational corporations and their foundations have become increasingly influential actors in the development regime. They have created new businesses to provide previously public services and forged relationships with traditional development institutions to implement programs and policies focused on a wide array of issues, including the environment, health, infrastructure, formal education, technology, and finance.[78] An increasing number of these corporations have begun focusing on girls and women as a target population for business, CSR, and corporate philanthropic efforts, as the Third Billion Campaign reveals.

Through this study, I identify this phenomenon as an instantiation of *corporatized development*, which I define as the practices, processes, and power relations of corporations and corporate foundations operating in and through the institutionalized regime of power of the post–World War II project of international development as it is embedded within broader historical processes of capitalism. In this way, corporatized development is an articulation of the post-war project of international development and the ongoing, uneven processes of capitalist development as they are historically embedded within (post)colonial relations.[79] On the one hand, corporatized development represents the still emergent, yet disproportionate, weight of corporate actors in funding, advocating, designing, implementing, and branding development practices, programs, and policies in the new millennium.[80] On the other hand, it signifies the use of the logic and strategies of business in solving the problems of development. These include the emphasis on market-based rationales for development interventions, the measurement of rates of return in terms of direct and indirect benefits to business, and the branding and marketing of development populations and projects. While these practices are not confined to corporations alone—the World Bank and the United States Agency for International Development (USAID) have been using these practices for decades—the emergence of corporations in the field has only increased them.

These elements of corporatized development emerge from the interrelated practices of CSR, corporate philanthropy, and social innovation in business. Simply put, these practices are predicated on "doing well by doing good." Consent for doing well is constructed through the other half of the corporate mantra—by doing good. In this particular historical moment, corporatized development sutures them together. As a practice, it enables doing well and doing good to occur in concert rather than in conflict with one another.

Corporations have long engaged in discourses designed to indicate responsibility. From the world's first global trading companies, such as the East India Company and the Hudson Bay Company of the British Crown, to modern day transnational corporations with roots in colonial and US empires, such as the Anglo American Corporation,[81] corporations have participated in trusteeship and improvement practices alongside extractive practices.[82] Yet, in contrast with previous eras, corporations in the new millennium are involved in a performance of making their ethical and unethical practices explicit.[83]

In response to the anti-sweatshop and anti-globalization movements of the late 1990s, corporations were pressured to respond to the demands of transnational networks of critics concerned with their socially, morally, economically, and environmentally deleterious practices. The historical context was defined by mounting social, political, and economic pressures for corporations to remain accountable to "multiple constituencies," including labor, consumers, local communities, governments, and the environment.[84] As Andrew Barry notes, for British Petroleum (BP) and other corporations, the concern with ethics emerged in the midst of public protests and as a way of managing them.[85] In the midst of this crisis of corporate capitalism, ethics became the key "interface between the world of BP and other companies and a global public political realm."[86]

With the support of transnational institutional structures, such as the UN Global Compact, corporations were able to develop a "cluster of techniques" for making the "ethical or unethical conduct of businesses *explicit*,"[87] with techniques such as social auditing and certifications. This "process of ethicalization" has solidified in the new millennium.[88] The movement of corporations and their foundations into the field of development through the discourse of CSR has been critical to this nexus.[89] It has been a powerful mechanism for responding to and recuperating from both external and internal criticism of corporate practices. And, thus, it has been important for revising tarnished images and securing social licenses to operate on different scales and to ensure financial bottom lines. Those development efforts were critical to the restoration of corporate hegemony at the beginning of the new millennium.[90]

As Anke Schwittay argues in her critical ethnography of Hewlett-Packard's CSR programs, corporations are constituted as "ethical actors" and "corporate citizens" through the "actions of others, foremost among them corporate critics" and through the "resulting corporate responses."[91] As her research demonstrates, one observed reaction to corporate criticism is "corporate philanthropy and its technicalization as strategic philanthropy."[92] Nike, Inc.'s investments in adolescent girls through the Girl Effect represents an example of strategic philanthropy, as the corporation restructured its foundation in 2005 to specifically target the very demographic it was accused of exploiting.

For corporate executives as well as CSR proponents, strategic philanthropy is not merely an altruistic endeavor; rather, it contributes to the corporation's financial bottom line by increasing market share, opening new markets, producing new consumers, and securing long-term investments.[93] As Trevor Neilson of GBC Health argues, "The dominant trend in corporate philanthropy is to do giving that reinforces a firm's core strategy"[94] in order to enhance growth and profit. In the context of the global economic crisis and increasing global competition, corporations are increasingly reorganizing their business, CSR, and philanthropic strategies to address the problems that create obstacles for them. For Nike, Inc. and the other corporations involved in the phenomenon of investing in the Third Billion, there is an increasingly explicit focus on removing gender inequality as an obstacle to further growth, in terms of labor, consumers, and general conditions of development.

As demonstrated by Dinah Rajak in her ethnography of CSR focused on the Anglo American Corporation, the "moral economy of CSR" symbolizes "not an opposition to corporate capitalism, nor a limit to it, but the very mechanism through which it is replenished, extended, and endowed with moral authority"[95] regardless of the continuation of a corporation's exploitative practices. This book contributes to debates on if, how, and to what extent corporate beliefs, narratives, rituals, and practices of "doing good" through corporate philanthropy and CSR enable corporations to reconstitute themselves as benevolent institutional actors and extend their moral authority despite the persistence of exploitive profit-seeking business practices.[96]

By the mid-2000s, broad consent for the regime of CSR, as a practice and performance of corporate responsibility, responsiveness, and goodness, made the critiques of sweatshops and globalization from the 1990s appear passé. Its institutionalization through corporatized development enabled corporations to dedicate themselves to ending poverty and promoting social and economic development through a particular set of mechanisms. They signed moral compacts, such as the UN Global Compact,[97] committed to supporting the MDGs, and created and joined organizations, such as the World Business Council for Sustainable Development[98] and GBC Health. Moreover, they participated in an annual circuit of global forums, including CGI,[99] the Global Philanthropy Forum, and the WEF; began initiatives with universities, such as the CSR Initiative at Harvard University's Kennedy School; and channeled their influence through corporate platforms within traditional development institutions, such as the World Bank's Global Private Sector Leaders Forum (PSLF). In short, they rapidly positioned themselves at the forefront of development in the new millennium. And, in doing so, they have become principle "architects" of development.[100]

Yet, in contrast to the first decade of the new millennium, the ground shifted in the beginning of the second. Three decades of neoliberal deregulation and reregulation in favor of corporations in the United States and globally led to corporations becoming disproportionately powerful in fundamental aspects of our lives from finance and housing to health care and education, as global inequality rose to levels not seen since the Great Depression.[101] In response to this, a groundswell of people and communities rose up across the globe through social movements, including the Occupy Movement in response to Wall Street abuses and the Black Lives Matter movement in response to state violence in policing and the prison industrial complex in the United States, and through unprecedented legal cases against transnational corporations, including Walmart, and Chevron,[102] for their abusive labor and environmental practices. Yet, even as public acceptance of excessive corporate power and influence slowly unhinged across the globe and academics and activists revealed the persistent contradictions of "ethical" corporate capitalism, corporations' influence over Third World girls and women through corporate investment has received minimal critique.

On the eve of International Women's Day in 2012, various members of the Third Billion Campaign gathered at an event hosted by the International Center for Research on Women (ICRW).[103] The event was titled, "The Bottom Line: How Big Business Is Empowering Women and Girls." As Third Billion Campaign member Mary Ellen Iskenderian, president and CEO of Women's World Banking, explained on the panel, "There is a way that the business community needs to be interacting with women to unlock that real treasure trove of the market."[104] As Iskenderian's comment reveals, benevolence—doing good—and profit maximization—doing well—have become inextricably tangled around the figures of racialized Third World girls and women. How did these girls and women in the Global South become a means to eliminating poverty and opening new economic frontiers in the imaginary of corporatized development?

"CO-FORMATIONS" OF GLOBAL CAPITALISM

To explore these questions, I begin with the premise that difference matters in structuring the global political economy. From colonialization and slavery through globalization, gendered, sexualized, racialized, and classed differences have been appropriated in the service of global capitalism. These are not arbitrary epiphenomenon that emerge as effects of capitalism, but rather are constitutive of capitalism,[105] albeit in "variable and contingent" ways under different historical and geographic conditions.[106]

Theories regarding the creation of gender and racial categories as a way to justify dispossession beginning with the birth of capitalism provide a way of thinking through this problem. For example, Sylvia Federici analyzes the ways gender and sexual difference was created and expropriated in the service of capital through the witch hunts of the sixteenth and seventeenth centuries in Europe and the Americas. She argues they were as central to the birth of capitalism as colonialism and the enclosures of the public commons. They created a "new sexual division of labor"[107] that reduced women's role to reproducing the labor force. This led to the emergence of a patriarchal system that was predicated on women's subordination and their exclusion from wage labor. She argues further that the "degradation of women" has been one of the necessary conditions of capitalism throughout all phases of globalization, from early capitalism to neoliberal globalization.[108]

During this same moment of the emergence and development of capitalism, scholars from different theoretical lineages within decolonial, race, and feminist theories, such as Aime Cesaire, Anibal Quijano, Cedric Robinson, and Collette Guillaumin, explain how the invention of a new form of difference, the biologic concept of race, emerged as a way of dividing the world's population into a new social hierarchy.[109] Social groups became naturalized during the eighteenth and nineteenth centuries, along with a conceptualization of "multiplicity" or intergroup heterogeneity.[110] This new social categorization allowed colonial empires such as Britain, Portugal, Spain, France, and later the United States to label indigenous populations in Africa, Asia, the Middle East, and the Americas as biologically inferior based on a new ideology of race. This ideology created a fictitious scientific rationalization for the colonialists' system of slavery, and for their territorial and economic expansion as they expropriated labor, land, and raw materials across large territories of the world. Moreover, the burgeoning forms of capitalism depended on this justified inequality between newly designated races. Cedric Robinson's theory of "racial capitalism"[111] is generative for thinking through the ways "the development, organization, and expansion of capitalist society pursued essentially racial directions"[112] from its inception. Robinson and others show how this form of racialization continues as a dominant mode of social organization, one that underpins the global capitalist system and thus strongly influences the ongoing imbalance between labor and capital.[113] As Anibal Quijano explains, while "the racial axis has a colonial origin and character, . . . it has proven to be more durable and stable than the colonialism in whose matrix it was established."[114]

Yet to understand the Third Billion, it is necessary to simultaneously rather than separately attend to the racialized, gendered, sexualized, and classed dimensions of global capitalism. Over the past three decades, Western and non-Western feminists of color have thought through the ways in which gender and racial categories, in particular, work together to generate exclusions.[115] As Denise Ferreira da Silva explains, the majority of those texts examine the "effects of gender on race or race on gender. . . . That is, when coupled with gender, race produces additional gender exclusion, and, when coupled with race, gender produces additional racial exclusion, and so on."[116] Within political economy, this has resulted in scholarship that often privileges one axis of difference (e.g., gender) as a way to think through a particular theoretical, ethnographic, or historical site of global capitalism and as the basis for thinking through or gesturing to the way the other axis (e.g., race) produces the "additional exclusion," to use the language of Ferreira da Silva.[117]

To illustrate, drawing on decolonial and intersectionality theories, Maria Lugones examines how gender operated through the racializing processes of colonialism. She argues that, rather than forcing "precolonial, European gender arrangements on the colonized," colonialism "imposed a new gender system that created very different arrangements for colonized males and females than for white bourgeois colonizers."[118] She considers gender a "colonial concept."[119] The introduction of gender, or multiple genders, as she notes, materially organized the social relations of production, property ownership, ways of understanding, and knowledge production in the colonial world.[120] Building on Quijano's notion of the coloniality of power, in which race is the central analytic, Lugones explains that understanding "the relation of the birth of the colonial/modern gender system to the birth of global colonial capitalism"[121] is critical to understanding the present-day global political economy. Thus, her theoretical project is central to understanding the ways in which racial and gender inequality are inherent in capitalist inequality. Yet, even with Lugones' careful attention to how race and gender work together, the colonial/modern gender system of power and its subjects are still theorized through the modern/colonial world system as a racialized system of power. Ferreira da Silva explains the problem feminist and race theorists get caught in when attempting to explain or elucidate one exclusion in relation to another to understand the racialized and gendered subaltern subject: "What I am suggesting is that precisely this sociohistorical logic of exclusion that makes the racial and gender such a suitable pair also hinders our understanding of how gender and race work together to institute a particular kind of subaltern subject."[122]

The work of Angela Davis on ownership of Black women's bodies during US slavery provides one of the most specific analyses of the ways in which race, gender, sexuality, and class simultaneously came together to attempt to violently control the bodies of Black women to secure the reproduction of the US slave-based economy and its connections to the structures of global capitalism. Rape by white male slave masters was used as "a weapon of domination, a weapon of repression, whose covert goal was to extinguish the slave women's will to resist, and in the process to demoralize their men."[123] But as Davis explains, this attempt was never complete: it was marked by "the accumulated experiences of all those women who toiled under the lash for their masters, worked for and protected their families, fought against slavery, and who were beaten and raped, but never subdued."[124]

To understand how the appropriation of difference functions in today's global economy, I employ Paola Bacchetta's theory of "co-formation."[125] As Bacchetta articulates, critical feminist analytics emerging from postcolonial, transnational, US women of color, and US Third World feminisms have interrogated how difference functions within universalized categories. They have contributed to "rendering visible power, conditions and subjects that were previously unaccounted for."[126] Nevertheless, she argues that, in contrast to feminist theories of intersectionality, it is more productive to "conceptualize powers not as separate axes, vectors or systems, even if intersecting or otherwise combined, but rather always already as multidimensional co-formations."[127] Within this conceptualization, power is always co-constituted, as it operates discursively and materially in different contexts.

Building on her theory of co-formation, I consider how the bodies, lives, and futures of Third World girls are co-formed across axes of difference within the global political economy through the Girl Effect. While the language of the Girl Effect is almost always conceptualized in practice, as well as in critique, as a gender project, its underlying logic of only targeting Black and Brown bodies without naming them as such reflects the ways in which, in the language of Denise Ferreira da Silva, "the racial still constitutes a prolific strategy of power."[128] Yet, the racialized strategy within the Girl Effect continues to be masked by the focus on the universalized category of girl, as the ethnographic focus of this study demonstrates. This project thus takes up the analytic of co-formation to illuminate how corporations such as Nike, Inc. target girls and women through the specificity of their racialized, gendered, sexualized, and classed bodies in particular geographies of interest. While these co-formations cannot be separated, one of the primary empirical and theoretical fields in which the Girl Effect is situated at the intersection of feminism and development is commonly known as gender and development. As both a field of practice and a theoretical field of scholarship, the default way this field is understood is through gender, and at times sexuality, particularly with regard to reproduction rather than identity, but rarely through race. For example, it wouldn't be appropriate within colorblind discourses to call it the Black or Brown Effect rather than the Girl Effect. Scholars of race and development, such as Uma Kothari and Sarah White, have noted this silence on race in the field of development more broadly.[129] As White notes, "Talking about race in development is like breaking a taboo,"[130] particularly when applied to North-South discussions rather than conversations within regions and even when critiquing neocolonialism and Eurocentricism. As Kothari notes, despite the different ways in which racial difference manifests in different geographies and social formations, there are "tenacious strands of racialized forms of knowing and representing in development discourse and practice."[131]

Nevertheless, through my analysis of the empirical and theoretical field of the Girl Effect, I recognize that my default in the study is to often think through how other forms of difference are co-formed with gender or how they play out in relation to girls as a population category even as I put forward a critique of these tendencies. In this way, the discursive boundaries of the fields of theory, policy, and practice we study can generate certain limits or analytic blind spots.

THE FIGURE OF THE THIRD WORLD WOMAN IN THE TRANSNATIONAL DIVISION OF LABOR

To understand how the figure of the Third World woman, and, more recently, the Third World girl, became, in the language of Gayatri Spivak, "the favored agent-as-instrument of transnational capital's globalizing reach,"[132] it is necessary to consider the shift in the transnational division of labor that began in the 1970s. Transnational corporations, including Nike, Inc.; General Electric; and Walmart, adopted new outsourcing and export processing models and moved their production sites to locations in the Global South.[133] The establishment of special economic zones (SEZs) in East Asia and Latin America in the 1980s and 1990s and the initiation of free trade agreements, such as the North American Free Trade Agreement in 1994, assisted this movement of capital.[134]

David Harvey describes this shift as capital's search for a "spatial fix," or, more specifically, the expansionary tendencies of capitalism that lead to the growth of markets within and beyond given geographies.[135] As Jennifer Bair reminds us, "the globalization of production is fundamentally about reorganizing the social geography of industry."[136] This process sparked an ongoing search for the least expensive, most productive laborer whereby shifting the social relations of production in the global economy. The poor Third World woman, at the intersection of multiple interlocking systems of oppression, including patriarchy, racism, and poverty, was imagined to be the paradigmatic worker—docile, dexterous, obedient, and cheap. As Jane Collins explains, "the development of transnational production arrangements was a profoundly gendered process, as the vast majority of new workers in the relocating industries were women."[137] As she and other feminist ethnographers have documented, transnational firms and their contract factories recruited "mostly young, unmarried women without children . . . firing them when they married, gave birth or simply reached a certain age."[138] In factories throughout the global assembly line, documented strategies to control girls' and women's bodies include reproductive control; excessive overtime; verbal, physical, and sexual abuse; and limits on association between workers in the workplace. These illuminate Marx's primary critique of capitalism, as articulated by Harvey, that it "so frequently violates, disfigures, subdues, maims, and destroys the integrity of the laboring body (even in ways that can be dangerous to the further accumulation of capital)."[139]

While the geography of this feminized and racialized labor force continually changes as companies move their production, it is broadly driven by what Melissa Wright describes as the "myth of disposability" of women and girls who work the shop floor. She explains:

> The myth of the disposable third world woman revolves around the trials and tribulations of its central protagonist—a young woman from a third world locale—who, through the passage of time, comes to personify the meaning of human disposability: someone who eventually evolves into a living state of worthlessness.[140]

Even as the discourse on disposability shifts over time and place, Wright claims there is a seemingly "intrinsic quality of disposability" and the "capitalist value" that emerges from the imaginary and materialist networks that constitute global capitalism.[141]

Critical feminists have contributed to understanding how these gendered social relations of production differ across historical moments, geographies, and political-economic formations, whereby contesting homogenizing narratives of paradigmatic Third World woman workers and factories.[142] Leslie Salzinger, for example, challenges understandings of how the hegemonic trope of productive femininity functions in her ethnographic examination of four foreign-owned export-oriented assembly plants in Cuidad Juárez, México. She demonstrates the ways in which gendered practices are (re)constituted through distinct governing practices that operate on interpersonal and structural levels on different shop floors, such that each *maquiladora* produces different femininities and masculinities.[143]

While feminists have challenged processes of capitalist expansion and their repercussions on women,[144] situated local and global feminist responses are not unified.[145] As Manisha Desai explains, they are best characterized as "scattered resistance."[146] Transnational solidarity networks are formed through the coming together of unions, social movements, and feminist activists.[147] These include well-known efforts by organizations in the Global North, such as the Netherlands-based Clean Clothes Campaign, which have waged campaigns against Nike, Inc.,[148] and associations of poor and working class women in the Global South, such as the Self-Employed Women's Association.[149] Yet, diverse groups of actors understand and approach capitalist expansion from different vantage points, leading to seemingly contradictory responses. In Dina Siddiqi's ethnographic research with women factory workers in Bangladesh, she finds disjunctures between local and global feminist concerns about the "sweatshop economy."[150] In such instances, these tensions can undermine the work of local activists while furthering the trope of the Third World women in need of "saving."[151]

INSTRUMENTALIZATION OF GIRLS AND WOMEN

The use of girls' and women's bodies as sites of intervention has deep economic and cultural roots in US and colonial empires. These complex colonial histories created the precedent for using girls' and women's economic production and social and sexual reproduction as instruments to influence development on multiple scales, from individual girls and women to the nation. Take, for example, Lata Mani's discussion of British colonial intervention in the traditional Hindu practice of *sati* or widow self-immolation.[152] This intervention was not always "about women" per se, but rather where the "moral challenge of colonial rule was confronted and negotiated" through the use of colonized women's bodies.[153] In breaking from modernization theory's analyses of *sati,* Mani argues that "Colonial officials sought to justify interference in indigenous tradition, even colonial rule itself, on the basis of women's low position in indigenous tradition as also in contemporary society."[154] She argues, "Women are neither subjects nor objects, but rather the ground of the discourse on *sati.*"[155]

These complex histories in different geographies are, therefore, the ever-present backdrop for interventions targeting poor girls and women in the Global South in the latter portion of the twentieth century and into the new millennium. Just as colonized girls' and women's bodies were a terrain upon which colonization violently occurred, the bodies of racialized girls and women in the Global South are the ground upon which corporatized development is imagined, constructed, and continuously negotiated through competing and often contradictory processes.[156] Girls and women become a means by which corporations enter the development regime through the entangled discourses of bottom-billion capitalism, philanthrocapitalism, gender equality, and Third World difference. Girls and women are imagined to be instruments for achieving a whole set of development outcomes and a new frontier for corporate growth and profit.

The focus on girls and women as a population target in development is related to a debate within economic theory that emerged in the early 1990s, which led to women being positioned as rational, efficient economic actors at the level of the household. As Gillian Hart[157] explains, collective models of the household, such as those created by economists Pierre-André Chiappori, Shelly Lundberg, and Robert A. Pollack, challenged the dominant unitary model of aggregating preferences of household members,[158] as exemplified in the work of economist Gary Becker.[159] These economists "endorse arguments that resources should be channeled to women on grounds not only of equity, but also efficiency."[160] This theoretical move within economics—from conceiving of women as "rotten wives" who are kept in line by an "altruistic male household head" to promoting them as "good mothers"—has undergirded the broader shift toward women's empowerment in development policy and practice.[161]

Over the past two decades, this view of women as the most responsible economic actors at the level of the household has been scaled up through various development programs and policies, particularly as "gender mainstreaming" occurred within traditional development institutions.[162] A product of a historical liaison between liberal development and liberal feminism, one of the results of gender mainstreaming has been particular girls and women becoming key "instruments" for alleviating poverty, reducing population growth, and generating economic growth.[163] Under this logic, investments in them purportedly provide higher rates of return than other development investments, such as technology or infrastructure.

The other side of this discourse is that Third World men irresponsibly spend their money on alcohol, cigarettes, and women rather than prioritizing their families. The relationship between the discourses on Third World women and men has resulted in what Sylvia Chant identifies as the "feminization of responsibility and obligation."[164] This phrase highlights how development programs and policies target girls and women in ways that maintain traditional aspects of social reproduction that undergird capitalism while producing new, heteronormative gender norms based on economic responsibilities and obligations women are imagined to have or should obtain to catalyze future economic growth.[165]

These processes are predicated, in part, on an instrumental logic. Programs and policies with an instrumental logic target girls or women for purposes beyond serving those girls and women.[166] They position them as means rather than ends in and of themselves.[167] While they claim a win-win situation in which girls and women benefit from the educational opportunities, they focus on the return on investment. As such, the content of empowerment programs and policies is structured to reflect the broader goal of achieving a high rate of return. The return is framed not only by the girls and women as human beings with intrinsic value, but in terms of what investing in them will do for poverty, the economy, population growth, health, or the environment. In many cases, instrumentalism may be the result of constrained "political maneuvers by internal advocates" who aim to "highlight the relevance of gender" within institutions that have not traditionally been receptive to it; yet, nevertheless it has had powerful consequences over time as a structuring logic of development.[168]

These consequences can be observed through two streams of development investment. The first is the priority to invest in girls' primary and secondary education in the Global South in the early 1990s.[169] A range of prominent individual and institutional actors heralded girls' primary and secondary education as the development investment with the highest "rate of return." As Frances Vavrus reveals, during this historical moment, girls' education became an "ideal target for development interventions"[170] because it addressed questions of equity without critiquing the broader interventions like SAPs that were disproportionately affecting girls and women.[171] Individual and institutional actors with diverse and, perhaps, contradictory rationales for promoting girls' education coalesced around this issue. Gender equity in education was codified through a series of prominent declarations, including EFA in 1990 and 2000 and the MDGs in 2000.[172]

The second stream of development investment has channeled money to women through a proliferation of microfinance programs,[173] such as Grameen Bank and the BRAC, and government-based conditional cash transfer (CCT) programs, such as Bolsa Família in Brazil and Progresa/Oportunidades in Mexico.[174] Microfinance is the practice of providing banking services, frequently access to credit, to poor individuals or groups, particularly women, who otherwise do not have access to financial services, and CCTs provide cash payments to poor households, mainly through women, who fulfill "behavioral requirements" in the areas of children's health and education.[175]

Both of those development streams aim to strengthen girls' and women's contribution to economic growth and to harness their productivity for poverty reduction in their presumed roles—current or future—as wives and mothers while reducing fertility rates to control population growth.[176] The Nike Foundation's focus united the goals of those two streams. It distinguished its investment focus from the saturated areas of girls' education and women's microcredit and CCTs while remaining focused on their purported benefits—decreased fertility rates and increased economic growth.

ARGUMENT

In the chapters that follow, I examine how corporatized development focused on poor girls and women in the Global South is constituted through the reactionary and expansionary tendencies of corporate capitalism. As I demonstrate, it becomes a means by which US transnational corporations imagine mitigating their short- and medium-term internal and external crises while simultaneously attempting to expand long-term opportunities in new geographic and population frontiers. I show how one company in particular did so by incorporating aspects of the critique waged against it for economic exploitation of female laborers into its response while simultaneously embedding market expansion into it. I argue that consequences of this gendered, racialized, and classed regime are as follows:

First, corporations are investing in girls and women as a means to ending poverty as they seek to create the conditions for development and economic growth. In doing so, they are investing in, rather than transforming, existing inequities across multiple axes of difference—gender, racial, class, religious, and geographic—even as they claim to be ameliorating them.[177]

This occurs through a racialized, gendered, and classed logic that imagines individual Third World girls and women to be responsible for and to possess the agency necessary to solve the structural problems of poverty.

This logic is predicated on inequitable historical and present day sociocultural and political-economic conditions that make poor racialized girls and women of color disproportionately responsible for the well-being and futures of others, such that once they are educated, they are expected to generate a multi-indicator, multi-scalar ripple effect across multiple development indicators from the scale of the family to the world. The theoretical basis of this logic assumes that the combination of their unpaid social reproductive labor, anticipated paid professional or entrepreneurial labor, and increased consumption practices will underpin future capitalist growth and development.

Second, corporatized development positions girls and women as a new frontier for capitalist growth and accumulation. This practice becomes a way for companies embroiled in public relations and/or legal crises, and for those who are seeking a way through ongoing economic crises, to imagine escaping those crises through market expansion. In this way, corporatized development focused on girls and women is part of developing "frontier" markets.[178] Bodies on the geographic and population peripheries of capital accumulation, such as the "Third Billion," are turned into new imagined frontiers for economic growth and development. As Derek Gregory explains, "imaginative geographies" are "constructions that fold distance into difference through a series of spatializations."[179] In this sense, gendered, racialized, and classed difference maps onto a new imagined geography of corporate expansion.[180] Once unemployed women on the edge of ExxonMobil's oil fields or unbanked women on the periphery of Goldman Sach's circuits of financial capital, poor girls and women are imagined to be a new frontier for economic growth as potential future productive, reproductive, and consumptive subjects.

Yet, lastly, as I will show ethnographically, the project of investing in girls and women is fragile and always incomplete. It requires ongoing negotiations on multiple scales as knowledge, money, and other resources move within, across, and between unequal social actors and institutions located in seemingly disparate places around the world, from corporate headquarters and global forums in the United States and Europe to NGO offices in Latin America, Africa, and Asia. As the power of corporations and their foundations grows in international development, diverse actors from across social, cultural, economic, and geographic locations—including educators, NGO practitioners, development experts, feminist activists, and corporate employees—are quietly, carefully, and actively negotiating, albeit on unequal terms, how corporations discursively position girls and women and structure interventions in their name.

OVERVIEW OF CHAPTERS

As I have presented in the introduction, the business case for investing in girls and women has become a powerful prevailing rationality and practice in international development. This book provides insight into the ongoing processes of the feminization and racialization of corporate capitalism, and, in doing so, reveals the uneven consequences of this contradiction for poor, racialized girls and women and for corporations.

I begin in chapter 1 by theorizing the Girl Effect as a global apparatus of power, and reflecting on my role as an ethnographer in and of the apparatus. In chapter 2, I examine corporatized development focused on the Girl Effect as a discursive practice whose history long precedes the historical moment in which it materialized, and I consider how this institutional landscape has developed over the past decade. In chapter 3, drawing on fieldwork at the Clinton Global Initiative, I examine how and why poor girls and women become the means for ameliorating corporate crises and the broader problems of capitalism, and posit that the business of empowering girls and women operates through a gendered, racialized, and classed regime of representation, what I identify as *poverty as spectacle*. In chapter 4, I draw on ethnographic fieldwork at the educational program of one of the Nike Foundation's NGO grantees in Brazil to illuminate how the Girl Effect functions through a gendered, racialized, and classed neoliberal logic predicated on imagined *Third World potential*, and how this influences who embodies this potential. Chapter 5 examines the elaborate, yet continually contested processes of attempting to prove the Girl Effect as a theory of social change. I analyze how knowledge on the purported potential of particular adolescent girls to end poverty is funded, produced, and distributed. In chapter 6, I focus on how diverse social and institutional actors unevenly negotiate consent for corporatized development by examining the material and nonmaterial resources NGOs employ and exploring the boundaries of possibility that result from a curricular, pedagogical, and relational perspective. In the final chapter, I end by tracing the Nike Foundation's movement away from the perceived limitations of traditional development channels and into Silicon Valley's world of fast capital and market-driven enterprise through the Girl Effect Accelerator. The chapter demonstrates the expansionary tendencies of corporatized development as Third World girls are promoted as a potential billion-dollar market and, thus, a valuable new capitalist frontier. The chapter concludes with an analysis of Nike, Inc.'s decision to make the Girl Effect an independent organization and a discussion of the phenomenon of corporatized development in light of emergent trends within transnational feminism.

1 The Girl Effect as Apparatus

To understand the phenomenon of corporate investment in girls and women, I employ the theoretical-methodological conception that the Girl Effect is a global apparatus of power.[1] As articulated by Foucault, a *dispositif* or apparatus is constituted through a set of discursive "power/knowledge" practices[2] that both define and come into being through it.[3] Employing this conceptualization, I move beyond studying discrete institutions, their policies, and their intended effects on social practice, as commonly practiced in research on whether development interventions are successful or not. Rather, I analyze the non-fixed, heterogeneous ensemble of discursive practices, including scientific statements, laws, policies, representations, material products, and institutions, focused on girls as an object of development.[4] In this way, this study is not about girls per se; rather, the Girl Effect is the ethnographic object.

The apparatus that I studied defines adolescent girls as objects of knowledge, or, more specifically, as a population category that is ultimately distinct from girls, women, and youth. But the apparatus is also defined by the category of adolescent girls, without which the formation would not exist. It depends on and is structured by the field of knowledge around the category and thus shapes how the population is understood.

This authoritative knowledge corresponds to and is a result of the creation of a complex set of technologies for producing knowledge that defines and attempts to regulate (although largely unsuccessfully) adolescent girls' bodies, lives, and futures through educational practice. These technologies include, for example, monitoring and evaluation (M&E) programs to assess the success of the programs in unleashing the Girl Effect by gathering data on girls' educational attainment, employment, financial status, consumer habits, and sexual practices, among other indicators. Another set of technologies included counting, tracking, and mapping girls globally through the Nike Foundation's Girls Discovered project with Verisk Maplecroft. The project "aimed to provide development professionals and researchers with a consolidated source for existing, publically available data in a visual format," according to personal communication with Nike Foundation.[5] The maps are among the resources Verisk Maplecroft highlights, along with a Human Rights and Business Dilemmas website it developed, to "help multinational corporations identify and address child labour risks and responsibilities in their operations and supply chains."[6] These resources make apparent how new technologies come together with old forms of social control to regulate bodies and moderate risk for corporations in today's geographies of global capitalism.

As Michael Goldman describes, these forms of power/knowledge practices function in an "exercise of power *through* social bodies rather than merely against them."[7] Power, in this sense, is indeed productive. It operates through the girls who participate in educational, health, and economic programs, the educators and NGO staff members that run them, and the development experts that monitor and evaluate them. Moreover, it functions through the corporate executives and foundation program managers that develop programs in girls' names and the public relations and marketing specialists that brand girls' potential.

While corporate development programs and policies predicated on this logic ultimately fail to end poverty through their investments in adolescent girls, they produce what James Ferguson identifies, building on Michel Foucault, as powerful "instrument effects"[8] of "failed" development projects.[9] In the case of the Girl Effect, the particular effects include distinguishing a population category of development, producing authoritative knowledge on it, and positioning it as an object of intervention and exhibition. The broader effect is the expansion of corporate power and influence within the development regime through these particular bodies.

During my full-time, ethnographic fieldwork (2008–2010), I examined one particular constellation of Nike, Inc. and Nike Foundation's apparatus in and between the United States and Brazil in this particular historical conjuncture.[10] The theoretical conceptualization of the research builds on critical, multisided ethnographic analyses of corporations and corporate foundations,[11] as well as powerful development institutions,[12] from within anthropology, education, sociology, and geography that pursue the complex task of studying up.[13] Drawing on anthropological conceptions of corporations, I conceptualize the corporate form not as a singular or monolithic entity, but rather as complex cultural formations or "social groupings" that are constituted through, and vie for influence over, cultural beliefs, values, narratives, rituals, resources, and practices in the systematic pursuit of profit.[14] How these are controlled, by whom, and for whom, are culturally, legally, economically, and politically contested questions that anthropologists seek to understand. This project understands the corporation as a "temporally, spatially, and socially differentiated"[15] institution comprised of unequally distributed power and multiple competing interests and sources of agency, organized around the dominant goal of profit maximization. It conceives of the corporate foundation to be a distinct, yet financially, politically, and legally associated entity whose beliefs, values, narratives, and practices can align with, support, and/or compete with those of the corporation. The project contributes to debates on where the boundaries of the corporation begin and end, and, correspondingly, to where and whom their responsibilities extend.[16] It does so by examining how girls, educators, feminists, and NGOs become part of the corporate domain, and by considering how ordinary, noncorporate actors in these spaces "enact"—consciously or unconsciously—the socially responsible corporation as they participate in corporatized development programs.[17]

To understand this, the multi-scalar research design focused on Nike, Inc. and Nike Foundation's transnational relationships with four types of development institutions, including two international NGOs in Brazil, the World Bank in Washington, DC, CGI in New York City, and entrepreneurs and venture capitalists in Silicon Valley. I call one NGO, Alliance for Development (AFD). It is the Brazilian affiliate of a Washington, DC–based organization, whose program I call *Programa pelo empoderamento das jovens mulheres* (PEJM), translated as the Program to Empower Young Women, which was funded by the Nike Foundation.[18] The other NGO, which I call the Gender Justice Organization (GJO), is a Brazil-based, international organization. Nike Foundation funded the integration of young women into GJO's work on gender equity with young men. The World Bank is a multilateral development bank whose composition stretches across the world with offices in the majority of countries. Between 2008 and 2015, the Bank partnered with the Nike Foundation on the Adolescent Girl Initiative (AGI) in the first programmatic partnership between the World Bank and a corporate foundation. CGI was founded and led by former US president Bill Clinton. Between 2005 and 2016, it held an annual meeting every September to convene its corporate members with governments, bilateral and multilateral agencies, private foundations, and NGOs around development issues. Former President Clinton and its corporate membership base actively promoted investing in girls and women as a solution for ending poverty and stimulating economic growth. It was critical in constructing a global corporate agenda around girls and women. Nike Foundation played a prominent role in this process. The final set of institutional actors included in the study were entrepreneurs focused on targeting girls in their start-ups in India and on the African continent and venture capitalists from Silicon Valley interested in funding them. Lastly, in addition to this primary constellation of institutional actors, I also engaged with countless other grantees, consultants, and partners of the Nike Foundation during interviews, conferences, and other forums over the years.

Each location functioned as a "fieldwork node,"[19] representing a place within the apparatus of the Girl Effect in which I conducted interviews and/or participant observation.[20] In contrast to traditional conceptions of sites as bounded localities, these nodes were unbounded.[21] They operated as "sites of encounter."[22] They were constituted through interconnected, yet unequal, exchanges and relationships between diverse subjects in disparate locations, many of whom will never have direct contact with one another. Often their only indirect contact with one another came through me as the researcher.

If, as Ananya Roy suggests, "ethnographies are spatialized interventions in fields of power,"[23] this study is an intervention in the multiple fields of power that comprise the Girl Effect. These fields comprise the shifting terrain of feminism, corporate capitalism, and international development as a field of policy and practice. As the fields are global in reach and multi-scalar, my theoretical interventions were developed on multiple scales and across different sites. They were developed through analytical concepts that enable us to read this field of power more closely and understand the relationships between the seemingly disparate sites in the study. In other words, the findings illuminate the global even as they were theorized through my participation in situated social relations in particular ethnographic locations and moments in time.

By carefully examining the articulations of social and economic relations, symbolic meanings, and spatial interconnections in a particular constellation of Nike, Inc.'s investments in the Girl Effect through the Nike Foundation, my analysis elucidates the broader investment logic and the relations and processes that constitute the investments using Gillian Hart's methodology of "relational comparison."[24] I demonstrate how these investments are created, negotiated, and experienced by diverse subjects operating in distinct yet interconnected institutions. These encounters always occur through situated practice—physical or virtual. Encounters in the Girl Effect occur through ongoing, complex interconnections within, across, and between far reaching locales and among unequally resourced social actors who are frequently unfamiliar and, I will posit, ultimately unknowable to one another. Their interconnections occur through uneven exchanges of money, knowledge, representations, stories, expectations, and desires. Yet, in a world perceived as interconnected, practices in the Girl Effect occur as much through disjunctures created through difference as they do through interconnections across difference.

The ethnographic research focused on this particular constellation of institutional actors is not meant to be exhaustive of all of the Nike Foundation's work across multiple countries and with multiple partners over the course of a decade. I also do not expect that the experiences of Nike, Inc., the Nike Foundation, and their institutional partners in any specific geography will be exactly replicated by another set of actors focused on the Girl Effect or by other corporations or corporate foundations investing in girls and women. This book places the ethnographic observations focused on the Girl Effect in specific moments in time and geographies within a larger context of discourse and practice in order to understand the broader world of corporatized development focused on poor girls and women in the Global South.[25] It demonstrates how US transnational corporations and the international institutions supporting them, such as the World Bank and CGI, are developing and implementing policies and practices based on a racialized, gendered, sexualized, and classed instrumental logic of development. It explains how this logic influences the ways poor girls and women in the Global South are understood, how educational interventions are structured in their name, and how this influences their lives and educations. Moreover, it illuminates how these practices extend corporate power and influence over new bodies, institutions, and geographies, and how this occurs without accountability to the girls and women they are supposedly serving and without addressing the contradictions in their corporate business practices, as the case of Nike, Inc.'s ongoing labor problems demonstrate.

RESEARCHER AS SUBJECT IN/OF THE DEVELOPMENT APPARATUS

The question of the researcher as subject in and of the apparatus is relevant to theoretical-methodological conceptions of this research. It relates to Akhil Gupta and James Ferguson's attempt at "decentering 'the field' as the one, privileged site of anthropological knowledge."[26] As they explain, this conceptualization reconstructs the field via Donna Haraway's notion of "situated knowledges."[27] This form of "feminist objectivity" is based on partiality rather than universality.[28] It questions unhistoricized, disembodied claims to authoritative knowledge based on science.[29] These forms of science, including anthropology and Western feminism's claims to truth, have historically and continually created multiple Others. In contrast, feminist objectivity requires a view from the researching body as "always a complex, contradictory, structuring, and structured body."[30]

In this way, I always was, and continue to be, embedded in the power relations that comprise this phenomenon. Following Gayatri Spivak and Sneja Gunew's proposition of "a historical critique of your position as the investigating person,"[31] this book is therefore also a story of my own personal history. I am the granddaughter and daughter of both corporate America and liberal feminism. My grandfather and father were executives of banks and corporations. My grandfather, in fact, worked for General Electric, one of the corporations in this broader phenomenon. I therefore grew up in a corporate family, acquiring the cultural habits it produces, the economic access it affords, and the ways of being it enables. These are inevitably marked on my body and its movements in and through the world. Yet, in contrast to my grandmothers and mother, I was given educational and professional opportunities that they were not granted or encouraged to pursue. Between my generation and theirs, feminism—in its white, liberal expression—enabled me to have other educational and professional options, although it was certainly never explained in that manner.

The peculiar intersection of corporate America and liberal feminism that I study not only runs through figures of racialized girls and women in the Global South, as outsourced laborers or recipients of corporate philanthropy, but through my own body and bodies like mine, albeit in radically different ways. The figure of the white, middle- to upper-class, highly educated American woman—both myself and many participants in my study—is positioned on the other side of the transnational division of labor and corporate philanthropic benevolence; yet, she, too, is positioned at its intersection. Thus, the figure of women like me in my study is the largely unacknowledged beneficiary of corporate America and liberal feminism. As an ethnographer, I was thus intimately part of the discourses that I studied. Disentangling me from the apparatus and my findings is impossible. I was socially, politically, and historically positioned within this field, myself produced in and through it in different ways, and, in turn, producing knowledge in and through my particular location.

As I entered into relationships in the deeply hierarchical institutions in my study, I found myself situated in radically uneven power dynamics within, between, and across the nodes. In particular institutions in the United States, I often shared a highly privileged positionality with my research participants, or as a result of age or professional status, they were in more powerful positions than I was. Nevertheless, it was my own relative positionality vis-à-vis theirs that enabled these relationships to develop. In contrast, at the Brazilian offices and programs of the transnational NGOs where I conducted participant observation for almost a year, the relationships were defined by unevenness. While the NGOs themselves were defined by hierarchical relations of power, particularly as their structures extended far beyond Brazil, I always occupied a privileged position, as my point of entrance into the institutions was through the most senior employees in their Brazilian locations. In each institution, this influenced my positionality throughout the duration of my fieldwork. While the young women in the program were never the objects of my research, the power differentials between us in the NGO classrooms or in their public schools where I conducted observations were certainly the most extreme. From the beginning, however, I sought to make it very clear that they were not the focus of my research and to establish relationships of solidarity with them inside and outside the classroom to the extent that this was ever possible.

In the process of studying this phenomenon I inadvertently found myself becoming an "expert" even as I was interrogating expertise. That occurred because in the context of institutional ethnography, one must make herself useful in order to "sit" in an office setting each day. In particular, I was positioned as a cultural and linguistic translator. As George Marcus explains, the ethnographer's role in multi-sited research as translator of "cultural idiom or language"[32] is more complicated than in traditional, single-sited ethnography.[33] It necessitates careful translation "along unexpected or even in dissonant fractures of social location."[34] Translation is never a neutral act. Thus, these cultural and linguistic forms thoroughly implicated me in the power/knowledge economy of the Girl Effect. Linguistically, I translated between languages (Portuguese and English), serving as the NGOs' translator for visitors from the United States and India, and on conference calls with Nike Foundation. During the time I spent with the NGOs, I also translated baseline data reports, stories written by young women, and program reports, and I wrote case studies in English for the NGOs. These were all sent to the foundation. Moreover, I participated in the ongoing translation of cultural practices, codes, and ways of being that differed between institutions and within institutional hierarchies. My mobility in, between, and across institutional nodes provided me access to powerful forms of social and cultural capital in the apparatus frequently inaccessible to those differentially situated given their gendered, racialized, classed, linguistic, and/or geographic positions.

ON SECURING ACCESS

My access in the different research nodes of the apparatus was always negotiated, tenuous, and never uniform. There were institutional spaces that were very uncomfortable for me, and others that were surprisingly familiar. While I gained acceptance in most of the institutions over time as a "situated, peripheral participant,"[35] there were particular institutions, particularly the Nike Foundation, where I never took for granted the permanance of my access. My choice of data collection methods in any particular node—including interviews, participant observation (physical or virtual), and Internet archival research—emerged from this negotiated access and, thus, was always influenced by it. Methods were therefore specifically tailored to the institutional contexts constituting each node. As George Marcus explains, within multi-sited ethnographies, "not all sites are treated by a uniform set of practices of the same intensity."[36]

And while these data collection methods were structured by access, I sought to be attentive to the relations of power underlying my access and practical choices in these nodes. My ability to choose one method over another in institutional settings with more open access was also an issue of power. For example, at AFD, I was able to sit for hours or full days in the office, hallways, at the kitchen table, and in classrooms. I could freely observe the program participants, educators, and staff members as I participated in the everyday activities, conversations, and movements of the institution. My ability to remain in an institutional setting—to occupy time and space while continually directing my gaze at the Other—was a reflection of power. More explicitly, it was a result of my own privileged position to see, observe, and take notes and to move in and out of spaces, institutions, and physical and cultural geographies with relative ease. This is the position of ethnographer as flâneur or the one who gazes at the Other.[37] My gaze was interrupted at moments, particularly in the act of taking field notes. For example, on the first day I decided to take notes at

AFD, a young woman looked at me and then at the staff member remarking, “She’s taking notes on this?” These were the power-laden encounters, and sometimes awkward engagments, between me and the participants in my study.

In contrast, in powerful institutions, I was constrained in my choice of methods of data collection as there are spatiotemporal limits to fieldwork in such nodes. One often needs high levels of security clearance. This necessitates being vetted through formal channels, where knowing someone or being introduced by someone more powerful is key. Moreover, access often has a time limit. I would walk around with a “one-day pass” sticker stuck to my suit jacket, or my access would be even more limited by particular hours, departments, or even specific elevators and floors.

In these institutions, I would surveil myself in the practice of research as I presumed I was simultaneously being surveilled. For example, rather than freely writing down notes or casually leaving my notebook in the office or classrooms as I often did at the NGOs, in these powerful spaces I would often write the most important information in private. Here, the ethnographer as flâneur is differentially positioned as the object of the gaze or the target of suspicion and surveilance, carefully monitored as she monitors herself.

While I conducted full-time ethnographic fieldwork between September 2008 and September 2010, my observations of Nike Foundation and Nike, Inc. began in 2007 and ended in 2014. In 2004, I began collecting documents on girls’ education from prominent institutions in this field, including the World Bank and UN agencies, and, in 2005, upon receiving Nike, Inc.’s press release, corporations and their foundations also became institutions of interest. I gradually constructed a research archive for compiling, reviewing, and documenting materials on the topic. To do so, I collected historical and current materials located in organizational archives, participated in the listserves of relevant institutions, and created targeted daily Google Alerts to track official, journalistic, popular, and academic accounts of my topic. Gradually over time (2004–present), the information I learned and filed into different folders on my computer became an archive of more than a thousand documents, including articles, press releases, web pages, blogs, photographs, YouTube videos, and event transcripts. This formed the basis of much of my knowledge and methodologically allowed me to develop network mappings of individual and institutional actors. These virtual links formed the basis for my initial conceptualization of the Girl Effect as an apparatus. Over time, some of these transformed into actual individual and institutional relationships. While each institution in this particular constellation is related to and produced in relation to the others in the apparatus, often through shared financing, goals, subjects, and infrastructures, they also operate as individual institutions with their own hierarchies, policies, and regulations on research. Thus, on a practical level, my entrance into each one required a different strategy and time frame. In this way, the process of negotiating this terrain became a rich part of the fieldwork itself.

NEGOTIATING FIELDWORK

I began reaching out to Nike, Inc. and the Nike Foundation in spring 2006. I initially e-mailed the foundation's general address, and later submitted a cover letter to apply for an internship. Both attempts were met with generic responses thanking me for my interest. By spring 2007, I began to carefully plan encounters to meet Nike, Inc. and subsequently Nike Foundation employees and to conduct observations in different settings where they operated. The first such encounter was at the Massachusetts Institute of Technology in Cambridge, Massachusetts, in March 2007 where I met Hannah Jones, Nike, Inc.'s vice president of corporate responsibility. The second encounter was at the World Bank's Global Symposium on Gender, Education, and Development, a small, closed, high-level event at the Bank's headquarters in Washington, DC, in fall 2007, where I was able to meet two Nike Foundation staff, both of whom would become important individuals in my study. Lastly, I attended the Global Youth Enterprise Conference in Washington, DC, in fall 2008 where I met a team of Nike Foundation staff members. The relationships I developed at these three events provided a series of openings over time at Nike, Inc. and the Nike Foundation. Nevertheless, the process of securing initial access to the corporation and its foundation took from spring 2006 to late summer 2009.

Even after three years, my access to the Nike Foundation was never fully secured and could never be taken for granted. Given the high level of anxiety at Nike, Inc. and the Nike Foundation regarding academics and activists, it was a continual process. After months of conversation, my first visit to Nike, Inc. and the Nike Foundation headquarters in Beaverton, Oregon, was scheduled for August 2009. The foundation canceled all of my individual interviews the day prior. The e-mail I received included the following statement:

> Thanks for sending the interview questions in advance. Given the formality of some of the questions, the team would prefer to meet with you as a group as an initial introductory meeting. We are not currently in a position to sign any consent forms nor are we in a position for the meeting to be recorded. I hope you will understand. We realize that this is different from the intent initially set forth, and we apologize for any inconvenience. The group meeting will take place here at the Nike Foundation from 10:30 to 11:30.

Sarah, a Nike Foundation employee, later explained, "Given the company's history of being attacked by radicals," looking down and smiling a little in exasperation, "and even by moderate/middle of the road folks, we need to be extra careful. Any word or phrase could be taken out of context, and we could be attacked for it." Sasha, another senior employee, interjected, "Legally, we even have problems when articles refer to Nike rather than the Nike Foundation." We slowly proceeded with the group questions. The staff took out their recorder for a six-on-one conversation while mine remained in my bag. I took very careful handwritten notes. As a result of being recorded by the foundation, yet having no way of recording myself given their refusal, I carefully monitored how I presented myself, the language I used, and how I discussed my research. Prior to leaving the room, the executive team made it clear that I would not receive further access for individual interviews if I did not share my research with them prior to publication. I was told very directly, "Unless you agree to share your work with us, we really have no incentive to talk with you." They restricted my interviews until I formally agreed to show them my manuscript prior to publication while maintaining the right to my academic independence and integrity. Based on our agreement, this manuscript was reviewed by the Nike Foundation in August 2017. I have noted where I incorporated information provided by the foundation by including quotations and endnotes with the dates of my communication with Nike Foundation.

I visited the Nike Foundation again in the following months to conduct individual, semi-structured interviews with staff members. After this visit, in 2010 and 2012 I continued to interview via Skype a select number of these employees and relevant new employees, as turn-over rates were high at the foundation. For example, I had two extensive interviews with one of the most senior members of the Nike Foundation team, and I interacted with this individual at three multi-day events I observed where Nike Foundation played a prominent role and on conference calls that I participated in through fieldwork with its partnering organizations. Moreover, I conducted interviews with numerous foundation employees, consultants, and other institutional partners between 2007 and 2012. During my fieldwork in Brazil, I also conducted interviews with four employees with a range of responsibilities at Nike do Brasil in São Paulo, the corporation's Brazilian headquarters.

Given the difficulty in securing access to the Nike Foundation, beginning in August 2007 I began reaching out to the Nike Foundation's partnering NGOs in Brazil, the World Bank, and CGI. My relationship with each institution was different, and I tailored my methods of securing access according to the nature of the institution. In the section that follows, I provide in-depth discussion on securing access and conducting fieldwork in each of these institutions.

ON DOING FIELDWORK

The World Bank

My access to the World Bank, which would become Nike, Inc. and the Nike Foundation's partner for the AGI, began with their Global Symposium titled, Education: A Critical Path to Gender Equality and Women's Empowerment in October 2007. After reaching out to the organizers of the symposium, I was given an invitation to participate. Since all of the other attendees were very high-level officials or employees in their respective institutions, from the minister of education in Afghanistan to the president of the Center of Global Development, I was, to say the least, their junior. And yet, since it was a small event of forty to fifty individuals, I had close interaction with them during the events, lunches, and cocktail hours. While this was my first forum, it differed in size, intimacy, and exclusivity from many of the other forums I attended later either as a participant or as a volunteer. The fieldwork relationships I began at this meeting within the Bank and with other institutions were initiated with individuals at a high level, and I did not need to establish my credibility. My other research at the World Bank consisted of two visits, in September 2008 and October 2009, where I conducted interviews with various employees connected to girls' education and AGI. My observations at the Global Symposium were detailed using field notes, and I recorded my interviews using audio recordings.

CLINTON GLOBAL INITIATIVE

Between February 2009 and October 2010, I conducted ongoing participant observation at CGI. My access in CGI initially developed via a relationship I had at the University of California, Berkeley. I participated at CGI as a volunteer consultant and event staff member on its Girls and Women's "Commitment Team" in year-long preparations for and during the annual meetings in New York City in 2009 and 2010. The majority of my participation was virtual, via e-mail and conference calls with staff members and member organizations, including corporations, corporate foundations, and NGOs. I also conducted a total of three weeks of in-person participant observation, often consisting of twelve-to-sixteen-hour days, as an event staff member leading up to and during its annual meetings in September 2009 and 2010. I participated in various capacities, including conducting Internet research, writing and revising documents for circulation to corporate members and NGOs, taking notes at events and on conference calls, writing summaries on events for former President Clinton's daily review during the annual meeting, contributing to talking points for the former president, writing e-mails, participating in choosing individual and institutional participants, and participating in coordinating sessions during the annual meetings. CGI is the one fieldwork node where I never conducted interviews. Given my purpose for observations in this fieldwork node, they were never necessary, as the object of my research was never CGI itself; but rather, I chose it as a node to observe how relationships among its corporate members, NGOs, governments, celebrities, academics, and other individual and institutional actors were constructed through this forum.

I also attended additional global forums including the Global Youth Enterprise Conference (September 2008) in Washington, DC; *Economist* Global Education 20/20 Conference (March 2009) in New York City; *O congresso de grupo de institutos, fundações e empresas (GIFE)* (Congress of the Group of Institutions, Foundations, and Businesses) (April 2010) in Rio de Janeiro, Brazil; Returns to Investing in Girls at the Center for Effective Global Action (CEGA) (April 2011) at the University of California, Berkeley; and AUDACIA: A Global Forum for Girls' Education (September 2011) in New York City, where I presented with Kavita Ramdas, the former president and CEO of the Global Fund for Women.

NONGOVERNMENTAL ORGANIZATIONS

Over the course of four visits to Brazil in August 2007, June 2009, from November 2009 to August 2010, and in July 2011, I conducted participant observation and interviews with AFD and GJO, two NGOs that received Nike Foundation funding. In addition, I also conducted multiple interviews and four weeks of ethnographic observations in June 2009 at the third NGO in Brazil that received Nike Foundation funding. While I was planning to include this site in the research design, my observations at this NGO only lasted for a month because of the NGO's concerns about having a researcher observing their program given the power dynamics between its DC office and the Nike Foundation. I also conducted an interview with a senior staff member of the fourth NGO funded by Nike Foundation in Brazil in August 2007.

Anchoring my research within AFD and GJO enabled me to illuminate how the Nike Foundation localizes its investments in different institutions, and to examine the articulations of social relations and spatial interconnections that constituted these investments and the situated responses to them in different NGOs in Brazil. Given the profoundly unequal relations of power between the Nike Foundation and the NGOs, their staff members, educators, and the young women who participate in their programs, I have been very concerned that my research could negatively affect individuals and institutions in my study in either subtle or profound ways. Consequently, I am revealing only minimal information regarding the NGO staff.

During my observations at the NGO, I participated in daily classroom activities and mentoring, the recruitment events in the community, individual and group selection interviews, staff meetings, e-mail conversations, conference calls with the Nike Foundation, M&E activities, program events, field trips, and everyday socializing in the office, during meals, and at social events during and outside of work. I also translated extensively, including a baseline report by AFD sent to the Nike Foundation, and I was responsible for writing a case study for GJO to send to the Nike Foundation. During these activities, my data collection focused on the goals, structure, curriculum, and pedagogy of the programs; on how the young women were selected, recruited, and supported by the programs; and on the social interactions and the negotiations among the young women, educators, NGO staff, and the Nike Foundation. I also collected an extensive set of documents for analysis, including proposals to the Nike Foundation, curricular and pedagogical materials, M&E questionnaires and reports, and public relations and communications materials.

In each NGO, I conducted interviews with staff members and educators at all levels of the institutional hierarchies and at least five interviews with each of the most senior staff members. These included educators across subject matters, staff members with diverse responsibilities, mentors of the young women, and external individuals with significant relationships to the NGOs.

OTHER CORPORATIONS

I also conducted interviews with individuals at two other prominent transnational corporations in diverse sectors. This enabled me to understand how negotiating access to a corporation and corporate foundation compared across institutions. One interviewee was the president of a corporate foundation, and the other two were the heads of girls' and women's programs in the area of CSR. While these interviewees, as with all of my corporate interviewees, were concerned with anonymity for themselves and the corporations, they were very willing to be interviewed on the first request. The president of the corporate foundation even offered to arrange my visit to their project sites in another country. I also scheduled an interview with a head of the girls' and women's program at another transnational corporation, but for sceduling reasons never conducted the interview. All three corporations were of comparable size, earnings, and brand prominence to Nike, Inc., and had also experienced intense corporate backlash, particularly in the late 1990s, for exploitative practices.

ETHNOGRAPHIC MOVEMENTS

In order to understand a phenomenon like the Girl Effect, the ethnographer must move—virtually, physically, intellectually, and emotionally—between, within, and across institutions and scales in order to experience the power relations, knowledge production, and capital flows that constitute such a phenomeon. This fieldwork required navigating the disjunctures between the world's most marginalized and most powerful people, all of whom constitute the development apparatus I studied, but with very different stakes and meanings attached to the project of development. I transitioned between conversations with poor, racialized young women in NGO classrooms in Rio de Janeiro and a former president of the United States and executives of the world's largest corporations at lavish parties in places like the Metropolitan Museum of Art in New York City. In this way, I moved within this racialized, gendered, and classed regime of power where some have the power to represent and others are represented. While these individuals almost never encountered one another during my fieldwork, except through representation, one such personal encounter illustrates what these disjunctures look like. At a Gender Equity Conference at Petrobras, the Brazilian oil and gas company, with representatives of Brazil's largest public-private companies, Lucia, a young female participant from AFD, the NGO I accompanied, asked Olivia, a staff member from GJO, the other NGO in my study, "Was that data on us?," following Olivia's PowerPoint presentation on poor girls and young women from Rio de Janeiro. In this epistomological encounter, the young woman asked if she was represented in the disembodied data that another represented. In that moment, the young woman became the Third World girl represented by someone else's data. As the book will reveal, the principle challenge of ethnographic research in such spaces is navigating these subtle social relations and the underlying power relations that inform them in which the researcher herself is often deeply enmeshed.

2 The Historical Rise of the Girl Effect

"The Girl Knight," a cartoon figure created by Kenyan artist Eric Muthoga, is a valiant, twenty-first-century heroine who crusades against poverty. Young, Black, and adolescent, wearing a green-and-white school uniform, knee-high white socks, and black Mary Jane shoes, her image was draped on the façade of the World Bank headquarters in Washington, DC, during the World Bank/IMF annual meeting in September 2011. She greeted the central bankers, ministers of finance, and corporate executives who arrived to discuss the global economy in the midst of an escalating financial crisis. In this depiction, she shields her head with a book while slaying the gray beast of poverty with her ballpoint pen. Her education is the means to end poverty. An uppercase "G," the logo of Nike, Inc.'s philanthropic brand, also made an appearance on the corner of the bright orange banner, with the brand's slogan, "The Girl Effect," written below.

This banner, appearing on, arguably, the world's most powerful development institution, brings this particular historical moment of corporatized development into focus. It is a moment when US transnational corporations are talking about committing themselves to ending poverty and promoting economic growth through their CSR, philanthropic, and business interventions focused on poor, racialized girls and women in the Global South.

Figure 4. Photograph of Kenyan artist Eric Muthoga's Girl Knight image, displayed in the courtyard at the World Bank headquarters, Washington, DC, for the annual meeting, September 2011. Photograph by Saul E. González.

Figure 5. View of World Bank building during the week leading up to the 2011 World Bank/IMF annual meeting. The photograph depicts the Nike Foundation's Girl Effect and the World Bank's Think Equal campaign banners, September 2011. Photograph by Simone D. McCourtie/World Bank.

This banner is a public and material representation of the relationship between these two entities—girls and women and US transnational corporations. It signifies their connection in the sphere of traditional development institutions, such as multilateral and bilateral agencies, NGOs, global forums, and national governments. Prior to this moment, this corporate branding of the World Bank was unimaginable. In October 2008, at the launching of the Adolescent Girl Initiative (AGI) (the first formal programmatic partnership between the World Bank and a corporation), the Nike Foundation wanted to hang a banner on the World Bank building. However, according to my interviews with individuals at both institutions, the Bank refused to display a corporate philanthropic brand in that manner. In a span of only three years, the Girl Effect brand was secured and institutionalized in the Bank in 2011.

In this chapter, I analyze the historical conditions that gave rise to corporations investing in girls' education in the first decade of the new millennium, when the interrelated, yet distinct projects of modernization, population control, and liberal feminism converged with a set of US transnational corporations. I argue that this represented the corporatization of "common sense"[1] discourse that investing in girls' education is the most efficient solution for ending poverty and promoting economic growth. These corporations were seeking consent for their business practices through their CSR efforts, as they expanded their economic frontiers through "bottom billion" strategies in the midst of ongoing crises of corporate capitalism following the anti-globalization and anti-sweatshop movements of the late 1990s.

THE GIRL EFFECT AS COMMON SENSE

My analysis builds on Antonio Gramsci's notion of common sense to understand how the practice of investing in girls' education came to function as a natural, seemingly obvious solution to ending poverty and promoting economic growth. As Gramsci describes, common sense is not "false consciousness," as in people not perceiving the "real" nature of their structural realities; rather, it's a contradictory understanding of the world built upon people's "good sense;" in this case, about people's perceptions of the gendered nature of injustice and the very real needs and desires of girls for access to schooling, economic security, and healthy, safe lives.[2] Common sense, in the language of Stuart Hall, is based on "a very contradictory ideological formation,"[3] which is presented as enduring—"the bedrock, universal wisdom of the ages"—even though it is a "product of history."[4] This wisdom, Gramsci would argue, is a statement or belief that is almost patently obvious, so much so that the idea doesn't need justification. It is a popularized way of understanding some aspect of the world.[5]

In the case I am analyzing, the common sense discourse provides an economistic way of understanding the development potential of poor racialized girls in the Global South in relation to poverty and their position in the global economy. This perception obfuscates how the underlying logic of the discourse reproduces unequal structures of power, including gender inequality, by shifting the burden for ending poverty onto girls while absolving corporations and other institutions of their roles in producing and perpetuating it. The social scientific ideas that inform this popular, common sense discourse are human capital theory emerging from economics and fertility reduction and population control from demography. They merged with philosophical ideas of gender equality throughout the latter portion of the twentieth century and into the new millennium to set the stage for the initiatives explored in this book.

To understand the historical construction of this common sense discourse, I employ Gramsci's notion of the "terrain of the conjunctural"[6] as an analytical tool. A conjuncture is a moment defined by the coming together of "different currents and circumstances" that is "over-determined in its principle."[7] In this respect, over-determination is the result of multiple causes, which together determine a particular occurrence that any one cause would not have created. To understand a conjunctural moment necessitates considering how multiple trajectories converge in very specific, yet not inevitable ways, to create a "new political terrain."[8] Considerations include how this over-determination occurs and what its consequences are: How was this common sense created, what is the good sense within it, and what are its effects?

To pull these concepts together, I examine three principal discourses holding sway over time. I demonstrate that the globalized discourse to invest in girls' education developed, first, as the result of transformations in the modernizing, gendered discourse of investing in human capital. Second, it was an outcome of the reframing of population control and coercion as reproductive health and individual choice. Third, it emerged as the fruit of Western, liberal feminism's progressively more strident efforts to ensure equal opportunity for girls and women in education, the labor market, and the development process.

To understand these discourses, I examine relevant documents from within the World Bank Group[9] and the United Nations (UN) agencies. These are the primary institutions shaping the post–World War II development landscape and are critical to understanding the production of dominant history in this broadly defined field. While the World Bank is an independent institution, it is a specialized agency of the United Nations under an agreement from 1947 after the founding of both organizations.[10]

The World Bank, in particular, functions as the "chief arbiter of development," setting the global development agenda in education through its deployment of expertise and finance.[11]

The World Bank documents are sourced from the Documents and Reports Archive (1944–present) of the World Bank's web site,[12] and I situate them in my analysis within the broader historical chronology of the World Bank as documented in the official "World Bank Group Historical Chronology."[13]

Moreover, the UN agencies have been critical to constructing global agendas around girls and women, including the UN Fund for Population Activities (UNFPA), the UN Development Programme (UNDP), UN Educational, Scientific and Cultural Organization (UNESCO), the UN Children's Fund (UNICEF), and the UN Girls' Education Initiative (UNGEI). These organizations' documents and conferences have been integral to how and why girls and women have been prioritized within development since the 1960s.[14] I also included documents from the UN Conferences on Women in 1975, 1980, 1985, 1995, and 2010.

My focus on the historical construction of investing in girls' education as a common sense development strategy is not meant to obscure the multiple, simultaneous, and, perhaps, contradictory aspects of these three principal discourses, the complex practices of resistance to them, or the ongoing struggles for access to education, employment, health care, security, justice, and human rights by girls and women and the organizations that support them. These struggles represent the good sense within this common sense discourse. Moreover, I am weary of instances of glossing over the historical and geographical specificities of these projects. However, given the unprecedented power of this discourse to influence a diverse set of individual and institutional actors and, therefore, to affect policy and practice on local, national, and transnational scales, it is necessary to understand how this universalized logic was constituted during the latter part of the twentieth century. Here I set the groundwork for the analysis in the remaining chapters of the multiple, contradictory practices that constitute Nike, Inc.'s investment in girls. By examining the historical complexity of these present-day processes of modernization, population control, and feminism that influence how poor girls are understood in our contemporary moment, I aim to understand, in the words of Hart, the "terrains of practical action."[15]

MODERNIZATION: INVESTING IN HUMAN CAPITAL

In July 1944, a new global governance structure—the International Bank for Reconstruction and Development (IBRD), commonly known as the World Bank, and the IMF—was established.[16] The following year, fifty countries ratified the UN Charter, and the United Nations was born.

As the era of decolonization unfolded in Africa and Asia, the mission of the World Bank and the United Nations shifted from the project of redeveloping Europe after the war to developing its former colonies in the Global South.[17] The United States emerged as the rising superpower in overseeing this postwar world. As this new institutionalized configuration of power grew, it incorporated institutions in the Global North and the Global South, including multilateral and bilateral agencies, NGOs, global forums, banks, national governments, think tanks, and universities. This new postwar development regime was predicated on the functionalist theory and practice of modernization. Modernization is based on the idea of a linear, evolutionary pattern of progress that all societies supposedly must go through to reach a state of high development within the capitalist political-economic system.[18] It linked the uneven processes of capitalist development to the new postwar project of development. Modernization aroused the "moral commitment, energy, and resources" of the so-called developed North to ensure that developing nations modernized in a fashion appropriate for capitalist development.[19] For W. W. Rostow, one of the key architects of modernization theory, democratic countries of the Global North needed to heavily invest capital, technology, and expertise in developing nations for their economies to "take off" on the path to becoming advanced, industrial societies.[20]

The World Bank institutionalized lending programs and policies linked to modernization. The Bank's wealthiest member nations, such as the United States and Western European nations, viewed these lending activities as part of their broader Cold War strategies to restrain the growth of communism by fueling capitalist economic growth and modernization in the Global South.[21] The majority of its lending focused on large-scale infrastructure projects, such as the construction of highways, electric systems, railroads, and ports.[22]

Although education was not part of the "initial mandate" of the World Bank, the mass expansion of modern schooling was integral to the overall agenda of modernization.[23] Understanding the early influence of human capital theory on the development regime is necessary for understanding why education rose to prominence as a solution for promoting modernization. Human capital theory reframed what had previously been viewed as a form of consumption[24] into a "productive investment."[25] As Theodore Schultz argued, "By investing in themselves, people can enlarge the range of choices available to them. It is one way free men can enhance their welfare."[26] The focus, therefore, shifted attention away from "structural variables onto individuals."[27] The condition of "undeveloped" was constructed as a problem of inadequate human capital with a focus on internal conditions, rather than as a consequence of the racialized political-economic structure of colonial and postcolonial North-South capitalist relations.[28]

The World Bank officially entered the field of educational development in 1962 with the explicit mission of reforming and expanding educational systems to foster economic growth and development. The forms of education promoted were limited to those that increased "manpower" in a country.[29] An October 1963 education memorandum to World Bank president Eugene Black Sr. described the basic elements of the World Bank's education sector policies:[30]

> The Bank and IDA should be prepared to consider financing a part of the capital requirements of priority education projects designed to produce, or to serve as a necessary step in producing, trained manpower of the kinds and in the numbers needed to forward economic development in the member country concerned. In applying this criterion, the Bank and IDA should concentrate their attention, at least at the present state, on projects in the fields of (a) vocational and technical education and training at various levels, and (b) general secondary education. Other kinds of education projects would be considered only in exceptional cases.[31]

The prevailing conception of economic modernization propelled the World Bank's decisions to limit their investments to vocational/technical training and secondary and higher education, because those were understood to drive growth. As described by World Bank president Robert McNamara in May 1969, "It is the IBRD's task to determine, in a given situation, precisely what sort of education contributes most to solid economic growth and to invest accordingly. We have not financed in the past, and we will not finance in the future, any education project that is not directly related to that economic growth."[32]

This Western approach of investing in human capital frequently meshed with the national investment strategies of capitalist-aligned, newly independent countries that were arguing for increased investment in secondary and higher education, in particular, to grow their own professional and intellectual classes.[33]

The development regime, therefore, focused on investing in the "modern man," a figure who was constructed as both the product of, and the necessary condition for, modernization.[34] In contrast, because women's social reproductive labor, both paid and unpaid, was traditionally unrecognized, economists did not categorize it in economic terms or include it in a country's gross domestic product (GDP).[35] This labor was and still is a free resource. It is exploited through its invisibility as it upholds capital accumulation. In modernization theory at this moment, women did not contribute to the projects of national development and modernization. On the contrary, they were viewed as "tradition-bound conservatives and therefore obstacles to modernization."[36] With the exception of UNESCO, their education and skills training were not promoted by the development regime in this historical conjuncture. Moreover, since there was almost no investment in primary education, unlike in socialist countries of the time, there were few opportunities for girls to enter the educational pipeline.[37]

Whereas the World Bank was founded on the framework of political-economic modernization, UNESCO originated as a multilateral institution in 1945 in response to the idea that political economic growth was necessary but insufficient to maintaining enduring peace.[38] UNESCO was centered on the idea that "Peace must be established on the basis of humanity's moral and intellectual solidarity."[39] One of its principle mandates for ensuring peace was promoting education.[40] As Karen Mundy explains, the founding of UNESCO was key to the beginning of a "regime of educational cooperation" as mass systems of education expanded and converged throughout the world in the twentieth century.[41]

From its inception, UNESCO promoted education within a human rights framework in response to the atrocities of World War II. The paradigm of human rights was emerging alongside the growth of the human capital–driven model. The UN General Assembly adopted the Universal Declaration of Human Rights in 1948 and Article 26 was influential in the initial framing of girls' and women's rights to education.[42] One of UNESCO's primary goals was to improve the "status of women" by promoting equality of educational opportunity for girls and women and, more broadly, combating discrimination against them.[43] This emphasis was influenced by the establishment of the UN Commission on the Status of Women (CSW) in 1946, which was "dedicated to ensuring women's equality and to promoting women's rights."[44] In the 1960s, the agency began conducting various studies on girls' and women's access to informal, out-of-school education and elementary education, as well as the teaching profession and education in rural areas.[45] The UNESCO secretariat also convened meetings of ministers of education from Asian and African countries in Cotonou, Dahomey, in 1960, and in Bangkok, Thailand, in 1962, to address "the problem of educational opportunity for women."[46] However, given the institutionalized power of economic modernization and the diminishing relevance of UNESCO, the rights-based focus on girls' and women's education was supplanted in the development regime by the economic focus on female contributions to modernization.

A salient shift occurred in the development regime in the 1970s as the World Bank began to recognize the poor and women as critical to modernization, a shift I will discuss in more detail in the next section. The Bank was an important locus of this shift. Robert McNamara, as president, envisioned a new agenda for the Bank based on his perception of its failure to solve the "problems of poverty and underdevelopment" in the Global South.[47] He shifted the Bank's focus to promote "Redistribution with Growth,"[48] as reflected in an anti-poverty strategy paper. The recalibration of the World Bank included a shift in its investments from "individual loans in specific types of infrastructure to society-wide interventions."[49] In a landscape of increasing school-age populations in the Global South, escalating economic constraints, and growing poverty owing to rising oil prices, McNamara prioritized education as a strategic intervention. The focus was on "how low-cost functional education can enable the poor to participate more effectively in the development process."[50] The World Bank Education Sector working paper describes the motivation behind McNamara's new educational priority:

> An important implication of this expanded development strategy is that mass education will be an economic as well as a social necessity. Education and training systems will need to be designed to enable the masses that have been unaffected by the growth of the modern sector to participate in the development process as more productive workers—by being able to play their roles effectively as citizens, family members, leaders and members of groups involved in cooperative community action, and in many other ways.[51]

To reach this new constituency, the World Bank focused its investment on mass primary schooling instead of secondary and higher education as it had done in the past. This included an explicit goal of targeting women for the first time in the Bank's history. As stated in the World Bank working paper, "Education cannot be restricted to school-age youths. Other target groups such as adults, and especially women, must be included."[52] As described by Michael Goldman, "whereas in the pre-McNamara era, the World Bank loaned no money for primary school education and very little for nonformal education, by the end of his tenure, lending for education increased substantially, almost half of which went to primary and nonformal education to attack the problem of low literacy rates."[53] Figures in the World Bank working paper confirm this assertion:

> So far 72% of the Bank's education financing has been in secondary education. About 23% has gone to universities and post-secondary education and 4% to adult education, while primary education directly (as contrasted to the indirect effect of teacher training) has received little more than 1% of the funds.[54]

The World Bank's increasingly explicit focus on primary schooling and its inclusion of the poor and women in the development process marked a substantive shift in its policy and practices.

During this moment, UNESCO continued to build upon the development regime's focus on the rights of girls and women. In 1970, the "International Education Year,"[55] UNESCO published Jacqueline Chabaud's *The Education and Advancement of Women*. As articulated in the preface, "Equality of access to education for girls and women is a priority subject of concern to Unesco in the field of education" following broader UN efforts "aimed at the advancement of women and the elimination of all forms of discrimination against them."[56] As Chabaud writes, "Such discrimination not only prevents women from achieving complete self-fulfillment as human beings; it also impedes the progress of society."[57] In this conceptualization, the future of girls and women as individuals, their emancipation and self-fulfillment, and the future of nations are at stake. In one of the first statements of gender equality as essential for developmental progress, Chabaud explains, "While the nations of the world increasingly need to make the most of all the possibilities available to them for the purpose of promoting their development, is not the unutilized human potential represented by women a sign of intolerable wastage?"[58]

Beginning in the early 1980s, with a turn toward neoliberal policies, girls and women were increasingly included in development goals, but their education, health, and well-being would suffer. Under neoliberalism, the World Bank and the IMF imposed SAPs in the Global South that broadly called for the decentralization of the state, the opening of economies to global market forces, and the privatization of traditionally public services and sectors (e.g., education, health care, and social security).[59] Within these policies, the state was perceived to be antithetical to economic growth and development. Privatization transferred social and economic welfare responsibilities to NGOs and the citizenry in what is known as "cost-sharing."[60] Women, children, and the poor throughout the Global South disproportionately felt the deleterious effects of this practice.[61]

The primary consequence for women was "the intensification of the trade-off between women's producer and non-producer roles."[62] Women were pushed into informal and low-wage formal sectors around the world, as household incomes decreased due to falling wages and increasing unemployment.[63] Moreover, in addition to paid work in the formal or informal sector, women provided the majority of unpaid, social reproductive work in the world, including child care, elderly care, and household chores.[64] As Eisenstein explains, this continues today as development agencies, corporations, and governments focus on poor women as "a substitute for state-led economic development."[65] In this way, the "crisis of social divestment (under adjustment) is financed from a 'social fund' provided by the superhuman efforts of poor women."[66]

In education, the effect of SAPs included reductions in public spending for education; decreases in available household income for school-related necessities; an increasing dependence on child labor in households; and shrinkage of the civil service sector, and caps on worker salaries, including teachers and other professionals.[67] The economic strain often resulted in families making the difficult decision to suspend their daughters' educations.[68] To compensate for the hardship wrought by austerity policies and to survive a crisis in legitimacy, the World Bank in particular encouraged educating marginalized populations previously excluded from educational systems and formal labor markets as potential sources of human capital and increasing the productivity of the poor's labor. In 1980, nearing the end of his thirteen-year term, McNamara wrote in the introduction to the World Bank's paper, "Poverty and Basic Needs":

> The self-perpetuating plight of the absolute poor has tended to cut them off from the economic progress that has taken place elsewhere in their own societies . . . *The only practical hope, then, of reducing absolute poverty is to assist the poor to become more productive.*[69] (emphasis added)

This statement marks the beginning of a shift in the World Bank's policy from "redistribution with growth" to a neoliberal approach to poverty alleviation that positions individuals as the solution to ending poverty.

Women received growing attention in this shift. The World Bank's promotion of women as a "key priority for the Bank's operation" was integral to its attempt to increase the economic output of the poor.[70] To ease the deleterious effects of SAPs on education, the World Bank intensified its lending. It also focused on "finance-driven education reforms, and increased its emphasis on efficiency over equity issues."[71] Its Women in Development program reflected an attempt to further integrate women into the process of development by "providing support for education and training programs that equip women with skills" and "increasing their access to employment and the market through microcredit".[72] This moment elucidates the initial emergence of what would develop into the common sense discourse on investing in women as an effective tool of modernization and development.[73]

In reaction to the harsh neoliberalization of the 1980s, the 1990s saw a humanizing of the World Bank and the development regime through a new focus on human development. The context of market failure in the 1980s created the conditions for what economic historian Karl Polyani theorizes in his social history of the nineteenth century as a movement to re-embed the economy in society.[74] Within the World Bank and other institutions, this move was visible in efforts to promote human development by once again investing in the health and education of the poor. These programs were racialized and classed, as well as gendered.

The World Bank's focus on investing in women's education, in particular, was first articulated by George Psacharopoulos and Maureen Woodhall in 1985,[75] and later in 1989 by T. Paul Schultz in a World Bank working paper. As Schultz explains:

> The private and social returns are high on investments to improve women's economic productivity—particularly education. Where women receive less education than men, efforts to redress that imbalance deserve priority. Measures to open women's access to information, technology, productive resources, and credit should also be tested far more extensively.[76]

Schultz prioritizes female education because of its instrumental benefits, focusing on gendered disparities in school enrollment rates for support. He claims, "Development agencies have a clear mandate to emphasize this investment gap and encourage countries to raise female schooling rates toward those of males."[77] Following Schultz's paper, World Bank economist Elizabeth King presented initial findings on the financial "rates of return" of women's education on labor force participation. "Although education does not increase the participation of Peruvian women in the labor force (and may in fact decrease it)," she argued, "it alters the occupational distribution of female workers by increasing the proposition of women in paid employment."[78] According to her findings, educated women received higher hourly incomes, and the return was greater for primary education than secondary or post-secondary education. Redressing the gender gap through investment in girls' education moved beyond the World Bank when it was codified in 1990 in the UN Education for All declaration.[79]

However, it was not until the presidency of Lewis Preston, beginning in 1991, that girls' education became a critical priority for the World Bank. The shift is reflected in Larry Summers' announcement as chief economist for the World Bank in 1992 that "the vast majority of World Bank education lending will include specific steps to expand female education."[80] Acknowledging "girls' education might be an odd topic for an economist to address," in a speech at the 1992 annual meetings of the World Bank he explained:

> An extensive body of recent research conducted at the World Bank and elsewhere has convinced me that once its benefits are recognized, investment in girls' education may well be the highest return investment available in the developing world.[81]

He calculated the health and population benefits of these investments. For example, "In India, providing 1,000 girls with an extra year of primary schooling would cost $32,000. It would avert two maternal deaths, forty-three infant deaths, and 300 births."[82] This led him to conclude, "As the social benefits of educating girls are greater than for boys, it is appropriate for females' education to cost less than males' education," a push never actualized by the World Bank.[83] His calculations fit with economistic population discourses that focus on reducing fertility rates and population growth in the Global South to promote economic growth. As Michelle Murphy argues, "Averting births was an investment in future prosperity," and girls' education became a means to do so.[84] It was part of the critical transition from coercion to consent to reduce fertility and population growth in the Global South.

From this moment forward, the World Bank would produce evidence of the purported effects when girls and women are educated. For example, economists King and Hill claim, "Better educated women bear fewer children, who have better chances of surviving infancy, of being healthy, and of attending school. When women are deprived of an education, individuals, families, and children, as well as societies in which they live, suffer. When women are adequately educated, everyone benefits."[85] Theoretical and empirical explanations of the benefits of girls' and women's education for society continued to grow, as regional and country studies provided evidence to support the corporate branding of the idea that girls are the most effective way to end poverty that would come later.[86]

POPULATION CONSTRAINTS ON DEVELOPMENT: FROM REPRODUCTIVE CONTROL TO "REPRODUCTIVE HEGEMONY"

In the postwar era of decolonization, concern grew in the West regarding the constraints increasing world population growth purportedly had on modernization in nominally independent countries in the Global South. Population growth emerged as a salient development issue.[87] For example, in 1962, the United Nations issued a resolution declaring the need to "pay special attention to the interrelationship of population growth and economic and social development, particularly in less developed countries."[88] That discourse linked racialized neo-Malthusian theories of population control to the prospects of modernization in the Global South.[89] Despite the lack of empirical evidence for Malthus' theory of the "law of nature," his arguments regarding overpopulation in relation to agricultural production influenced policy and practice because his views corresponded to dominant sociocultural and political-economic interests[90] of the late-eighteenth and nineteenth centuries when the enclosures in England forced the peasantry off the land, creating a class of landless workers.[91]

When taken up by institutions in the development regime, as described by M. Bahati Kuumba, neo-Malthusian theories have led to attempts to reduce fertility levels and decrease population growth by targeting poor, and racially and ethnically marginalized women.[92] As she describes, these global development policies "simultaneously facilitate racial inequality, class exploitation, and gender subordination,"[93] while serving the interests of global capital. She identifies this as "reproductive imperialism," defined as the "interests served by the foreign domination of Third World wombs in pursuits of profit and power."[94]

Building on the early biological experiments and colonial theories of Raymond Pearl, the dominant discourse of the time promoted the idea that "Population could be engineered toward future economic progress."[95] In doing so, the development regime sought to universalize the particular demographic transition of Europe from feudalism to industrial capitalism.[96] Postcolonial nations became the objects of intervention for demographers, social scientists, and development experts in the Global North and Global South in countries such as Pakistan and Bangladesh.[97] Fertility, in particular, became "a pivotal focus of economization."[98]

The practice of engineering futures brought the energy, resources, and ideology of the "Cold War into the realms of sex."[99] Neo-Malthusian arguments for population control became a US anti-communist strategy. This is reflected in the military and political strategies of US presidents

Eisenhower and Johnson.[100] According to a USAID "Family Planning" timeline, President Johnson's approach was embedded in US foreign policy in 1965 when the US government adopted a "plan to reduce birth rates in developing countries through its War on Hunger and investments in family planning programs."[101] The following year, Congress authorized USAID to create and distribute contraceptives through the Food for Peace Act, and by 1967, USAID was purchasing contraceptives to distribute through its development programs.[102] At the end of the decade, President Nixon declared population growth "one of the most serious challenges to human destiny in the last third of this century."[103]

This was further institutionalized in the development regime through UNFPA, which was authorized to "coordinate the growing international funding and transfer of contraceptive technology to developing-country population programs."[104] It began in 1967 as a trust fund, with operations beginning in 1969 under the UNDP.[105] In 1971, the UN General Assembly targeted population policies as critical to development, and UNFPA sought to "play a leading role within the UN system in promoting population programmes."[106] Institutionalizing this discourse led to the development and funding of notoriously coercive and sometimes violent population programs and policies throughout Latin America, Africa, and Asia to control the reproductive threat to capitalist growth.[107] As described by the World Health Organization (WHO), these programs and policies violated individual rights, particularly of the poor, indigenous people, and ethnic and racial minorities, and often offered incentives or pressures to secure consent, including "offers of food, money, land and housing, or threats, fines or punishments, together with misleading information."[108]

By the 1970s, USAID had risen in global prominence in the field of family planning.[109] The institution used a new supply-side approach, which represented the initial transition from coercion to consent. As Murphy explains, "In other words, offering contraception triggered new desires for it."[110] This represented a strategy for "stimulating consumer desire and choice, not for the sake of profit directly from a sale, but for the sake of altering population and economy."[111]

Although these fertility and population views were highly influential, they were also highly contested. In 1974—the UN "World Population Year"—the UN World Population Conference in Bucharest, Romania, developed the Romania World Population Plan of Action.[112] At the event, US President Ford declared that managing the population crisis is "vital to the future of mankind."[113] Yet, fault lines emerged in conference negotiations along geopolitical lines between the North and the South. The United States, the United Kingdom, and Germany argued, "Rapid population growth was a serious impediment to development."[114] They consequently pushed for policies that combined a focus on economic growth with publicly funded family planning initiatives.[115] In contrast, proponents of the "redistribution position," led by Argentina and Algeria, "believed that the population problem was a consequence and not a cause of underdevelopment and that it could be solved by a new international economic order focusing on the redistribution of resources."[116] From this southern perspective, "Development is the best contraceptive."[117] This division between northern and southern countries fell along highly racialized lines based on colonial histories.

By linking population growth to adverse effects on national development, population discourses began to connect to girls' education. In 1973, UNESCO published "Population Dynamics and Educational Development," which states, "Intensifying and extending education for girls undoubtedly forms an essential contribution to the task of mastering the problems of rapid population growth in Asian countries."[118] In the document, girls' education is understood to be key to postponing marriage age, as well as shaping attitudes toward family planning. This instrumental approach widely influenced the positioning of girls' education as a broader development intervention. Its political benefits included reducing the controversial nature of family planning and contraception, per se, which tends to generate political contestation and anger in some of the target countries for social and religious reasons.

As SAPs emerged in the 1980s, they were accompanied by USAID subsidies for family planning. For USAID and other development agencies, family planning was assumed to reduce the economic burden of bearing children in the wake of rolled back state support for health care and education. In some cases, such as Tanzania and Egypt, combatting overpopulation through fertility control was promoted with other aspects of structural reforms.[119] Beginning in the 1980s, development discourse began to shift away from the explicit population control rhetoric. For example, USAID released a policy paper declaring that family planning programs be "based on fundamental principles of volunteerism and informed choice" as opposed to coercion.[120] This was echoed more broadly at the International Conference on Population and Development in Mexico City in 1984. The conference declaration stated that "all couples and individuals can exercise their basic human right to decide freely, responsibly, and without coercion, the number and spacing of their children, and to have the information, education, and means to do so."[121]

A decade later, the International Conference on Population and Development in Cairo, Egypt, in 1994 and the Fourth World Conference on Women in Beijing, China, in 1995 continued to usher in a shift toward a rights-based approach to sexual, reproductive health, and population policies even as women's fertility was still discussed at these conferences as a barrier to development and a cause of environmental degradation.[122] This shift led to agreement on the "principle of voluntary choice in family planning"[123] in an effort to move from coercive practices toward "full, free, and informed consent."[124] In this way, empowering women to make individual decisions on their reproduction would lead to demographic change. Population education promoted by international institutions under this new model was described by UNFPA and UNESCO as a means to equip women with the capacity to make informed, rational choices and to develop responsible individual behavior.[125] UNESCO director-general Frederico Mayor's address in Cairo marked this shift. He declared, "The regulation of population growth is undoubtedly one of the major and most pressing challenges facing the human community at the present time;"[126] yet, addressing the population issue through the "enhancement of the status of women" must be part of a broader "integrated strategy for sustainable human development." Education was deemed crucial to this strategy:

> Education is essential to slowing down population growth—without which it will be difficult to raise income levels and achieve balanced socio-economic development. Everywhere, in all social and cultural contexts, increased education for girls and women means lower fertility rates, as well as reduced mortality and morbidity levels. This shows that women's reproductive choices depend on a process of empowerment—which can only come from improved educational provision, training for economic self-reliance and the

> enhancement of women's legal and social status. Special efforts need to be made to reach the large section of the female population that has so far proved unreachable—the 29 percent of girls worldwide not enrolled at primary school, the 65 percent of the world's 900 million illiterates who are women. This will call for a whole range of innovative learning and teaching methods, including interactive and distance education, and for learning facilities to be made permanently available to people of all ages, without formal academic requirements.[127]

In his statement, the language of empowerment, education, and reproduction are linked in the argument for moving beyond a coercive model of population control toward one of empowerment, with education playing a key role in the process. At a meeting in New Delhi, India, in December 1993, Mayor further reflected on the institutionalization of this strategy by UNESCO, UNFPA, and UNICEF, as they connected their population focus to the gender equity focus in the EFA initiative. Nine nations considered to have high population growth were a particular focus, including Bangladesh, Brazil, China, Egypt, India, Indonesia, Mexico, Nigeria, and Pakistan.[128] Mayor explains:

> These countries, accounting for over 70% of the world's illiterates and some 50% of its population, adopted an educational plan specifically focused on girls and women. The fact that Prime Minister Narasimha Rao on this occasion announced an increase in India's education budget from 3.6% to 6% of GNP is a source of great hope not only for this huge country but for humanity as a whole. It represents a historic leap forward in efforts to curb population growth.[129]

Population reduction in poor, highly populated countries was still the primary goal. However, the means to achieving that goal shifted from coercion to investing in girls' and women's education. Moreover, Mayor's statement marks an important, early example of the feminization of development. In his vision, women are crucial to achieving the goal of sustainable development through education in their presumed roles as teachers and mothers: "Those who hold the key to this gateway—teachers, parents and particularly mothers—have a crucial responsibility: the world we leave to our children will depend on the children we leave to our world."[130]

I identify this historical moment in the mid-1990s as the beginning of a new regime of "reproductive hegemony." I define the term as the explicit or implicit attempts by the development regime through education, health, and empowerment programs to reduce poor, racialized girls' and women's fertility and population growth through processes of consent, framed in the language of choice, rather than coercion and violence. Here, development interventions focus on creating the conditions for individual girls and women to choose to delay childbearing, reduce the number of pregnancies, and spread them out over longer time spans, particularly through the means of formal and informal education, in order to reduce population growth and increase economic productivity on different spatial scales. The language of choice works through the intersection between neoliberal logic and liberal feminism, linking individual choice to economic efficiency. Reproductive hegemony constitutes one of the primary bases of the Girl Effect's logic. It is, therefore, critical to the story of how and why girls' education emerged as purportedly one of the most effective, yet noncoercive ways, to reduce fertility rates and population growth in the Global South.

Despite the transition to this dominant regime of population management, marginalized individuals and groups, including female prisoners, "people living with HIV, persons with disabilities, indigenous peoples and ethnic minorities, and transgender and intersex persons,"[131] have continued to be coerced into involuntary sterilization long after global governance institutions declared it a human rights violation.[132]

FEMINIST MODERNIZATION: FROM WID TO GAD

With the rise of modernization, liberal, predominantly white, Western feminists operating in the development regime began focusing on women's access to education to secure their role in the labor market and the national development process. Economist Ester Boserup in 1970 laid the critical foundation for the Women in Development (WID) regime in *Women's Role in Economic Development*. She challenged the traditional development regime's view of women as "passive recipients of welfare policies" in the roles of "wives and mothers," bringing them to the forefront of the development process as laborers and equal economic actors.[133] Boserup and others emphasized the rationale that women were contributors to national growth, particularly in women's emerging roles in the new international division of labor, as they attempted to bring women into the economy as equal players. According to Boserup, "As long as girls remain under the twofold handicap of a family education which suppresses their self-confidence and of training facilities in schools and elsewhere which are inferior to those given to boys, they are bound to be inferior workers."[134] Thus, Boserup called "for better-designed education for women to enhance their competitiveness and productivity in the economy."[135]

WID, therefore, remained in the prevailing paradigm of modernization. Frances Vavrus argues:

> The WID view did not challenge the basic tenets of modernization theory, such as its embrace of capitalism, its evolutionary view of social change, and its economic rationale for women's schooling; instead, WID advocacy drew attention to gender stereotypes and prejudices in development policy and practice that prevented women from reaping the fruits of development that modernization is thought to produce.[136]

WID critiqued the international development regime from within the liberal theory of modernization, ensuring its powerful influence in the World Bank, UN agencies, and bilateral development agencies.[137] As development agencies realized the potential of women's roles in national development for increasing economic production, political efficiency, and competition in the global market, they adopted WID's stance on women's education and their broader role in the development process. A productive convergence of modernization and liberal feminism contributed to prioritizing the role and importance of women's education for processes of economic development at that historical conjuncture.

In 1975, declared International Women's Year by the United Nations, the first world conference on the status of women was held in Mexico City.[138] The UN General Assembly declared "the integration and full participation of women in development" was one of the three primary objectives of the conference, along with ending gender discrimination and increasing women's contribution to world peace.[139] To achieve these goals, the World Plan of Action focused on "securing equal access for women to resources such as education, employment opportunities, political participation, health services, housing, nutrition and family planning."[140] The conference set the grounds for the General Assembly's declaration of the UN Decade for Women (1976–1985), and the Convention on the Elimination of All Forms of Discriminations against Women (CEDAW) adopted by the UN General Assembly in 1979.[141] Those events are credited with commencing "a new era in global efforts to promote the advancement of women by opening a worldwide dialogue on gender equality."[142] Rather than "passive recipients of support and assistance," women were now declared "full and equal partners with men" and, therefore, were considered essential to the project of development.[143]

The influence of WID's early focus on girls' and women's economic potential points to ongoing feminist tensions. Some feminists in development prioritize girls and women, first and foremost, as rights-bearing subjects who deserve to be the ends rather than the means of development, as originally prioritized by UNESCO. Others regard girls and women as market actors with the potential to catalyze economic growth and a range of other development outcomes. This tension continues in feminist conversations on how, and to what extent, to engage with corporations investing economically in girls and women.

The WID regime's practices and its incorporation into mainstream development institutions were highly criticized in the 1980s by neo-Marxist feminists attempting to transform the pernicious nature of development.[144] The neo-Marxists, who largely constituted the Women and Development (WAD) regime, rejected WID's approach to investment in education for economic development and their failure to critique the systems of patriarchy and capitalism.[145] Alternatively, WAD proponents argued that schooling reproduced existing structural inequalities and the "status quo."[146] Although WAD activists did not outline a specific agenda for transforming the system of schooling, their traditional approach to women's development focused on a women-only model. Further, they were weary of collaborating with patriarchal development institutions, such as the World Bank and the United Nations. As a result, their perspectives weren't integrated into mainstream institutions, but rather influenced feminist and women's rights organizations as well as other NGOs.[147] Yet, they were critiqued for their focus on women as a class, following their neo-Marxist feminist tradition, and their inattention to the ways difference operates in relation to the category of woman, whereby assuming that women's positions in society will improve if the political economic structures are transformed.[148]

In contrast to the WID and WAD approaches, feminists constituting the Gender and Development (GAD) regime approached questions of development by attempting to understand how political-economic and ideological forces subordinate women.[149] Although the GAD approach was institutionalized in NGOs, such as Development Alternatives with Women for a New Era, it developed more clout in academic development circles than in mainstream development agencies owing to its "language of transformation."[150] GAD advocates, for example, focus on gender as a social construct rather than prioritizing women or girls.[151] Their development approach assesses how gender relations are constituted, particularly through discourse, with schooling as a critical context. Whereas GAD's long-term approach focuses on challenging patriarchal ideologies and institutions, its short-term approaches to development questions frequently mirror WID's regarding its language and target areas, including education and microcredit.[152]

Despite feminist critiques of WID, its integration into the World Bank's agenda of increasing the productivity of the poor throughout the 1980s reflected the material and ideological convergence of white, Western liberal feminism and the international development regime. This coming together reflects the ways in which the liberal feminist desire for gender equality hitched itself to capitalist promises of the market as the guarantor of women's liberation. This intimate, yet contradictory relationship between liberal feminism and capitalism has guaranteed the WID regime ongoing relevance and centrality in the world of international development in a way WAD and GAD could never secure due to their ideological approach and suspicion of traditional institutions.

WID's increasing prioritization of women as key "instruments" of development signaled the initial feminization of development, a harbinger of future policy and practice, thereby securing the roots for a new common sense development strategy as governments increasingly rolled back their services and privatized their assets through neoliberal policies and practices.[153]

THE GLOBALIZED PRIORITY TO INVEST IN GIRLS' EDUCATION

In the early to mid-1990s, the projects of modernization, population reduction, and liberal feminism productively converged to produce a globalized priority in international development to invest in girls' education. This occurred as international development institutions grew increasingly vocal in proclaiming that girls in the Global South were out of school in disproportionate numbers compared with boys. As Frances Vavrus argues, "despite the closing of the gender gap in education in most regions of the world, the 'crisis' in international education has been manufactured primarily in terms of women's lack of access to schooling."[154] Contrary to this popular portrayal of crisis, a mapping of global gender disparities in formal education in the 1990s reveals that although such gaps existed in particular regions in the Global South, the construction of a universal crisis in girls' access to schooling obscured the heterogeneous dynamics operating in regions throughout the global educational landscape. According to the UN Education for All Global Monitoring Report (2003/2004), in 1990 an estimated 108 million children worldwide were not enrolled in school—63 percent girls and 46 percent boys—the majority of whom lived in countries in the Global South.[155] In East Asia and the Pacific, as well as South and West Asia, persistent gender disparities existed in education, with girls constituting 71 percent of out-of-school children in the former region and 75 percent in the latter. In sub-Saharan Africa, a region consistently portrayed at the heart of the "crisis," out-of-school girls accounted for only 54 percent of the total population. The regions of Central Asia, Latin America, and the Caribbean reflected relative gender parity in education.[156] Nevertheless, as the perception of this "crisis" grew, a powerful globalized discourse emerged regarding the benefits of investing in girls' education in the Global South as a development solution in the early 1990s.[157]

I posit that the discourse of investing in girls' education functioned as a handmaiden easing the pain of the World Bank and IMF's devastating SAPs in the Global South during the 1980s and early 1990s. In particular, the World Bank's intensified lending to girls' education during this time was part of their broader strategy to increase the economic productivity of the poor.[158] The power and legitimacy of this discourse grew, leading to efforts designed to increase access to schooling for girls and women in the Global South. It drew on the authentic desires among girls and women for access to education and economic security, and their historical exclusion from schooling and disproportionate burden of the costs of austerity policies.

The convergence of these multiple factors in the early to mid-1990s produced a gendered (neo)liberalism: a fresh, feminized, liberal face on beleaguered neoliberal values. This represented the simultaneous resurgence of liberalism and the furtive, yet dogmatic, persistence of neoliberalism. This gendered (neo)liberalism reorganized institutional priorities and transformed global practices in education, producing a globalized discourse to invest in girls' education as an individualized development solution.

The promotion of the liberal political ideals of equality and human rights for women and girls through this gendered (neo)liberalism was critical to the reconstitution and re-legitimization of the neoliberal agenda after the devastating 1980s. These ideas were codified in the MDGs 2000, which specifically outlined the elimination of gender disparities in education, the promotion of gender equality, and the empowerment of girls and women.[159] However, under these liberal values was a persistent set of neoliberal political-economic conditions promoting the individual subject as an autonomous, rational actor and the market as the guarantor of socioeconomic well-being and individual freedom in the wake of the rollback of the welfare state.

Girls' education was, therefore, prioritized in this historical conjuncture as a necessary investment in human capital to produce empowered, entrepreneurial female subjects with the appropriate knowledge and skills to catalyze economic growth in the Global South.[160] This globalized discourse developed and solidified as a common sense way to address poverty and economic growth in the first decade of the new millennium. A broad set of individual and institutional actors with diverse, and perhaps, contradictory, reasons for investing in girls' education coalesced around it. These included governments and bilateral and multilateral agencies, as well as educational and feminist and women's rights NGOs who were grounded by the good sense of the discourse.

Despite their disparate rationales, these institutions were ideologically connected through their parallel promotion of investing in girls' education, in the broadest sense, in this particular historical moment. Their coming together was accompanied by the concurrent construction of a multi-scalar "apparatus" in the Foucauldian sense—a transnational ensemble of discursive practices, social relations, and symbolic meanings that are constituted in and through relations of power, knowledge, and capital among development institutions operating on multiple scales.[161]

THE CORPORATIZATION OF GIRLS' EDUCATION

Yet, although a plurality of development actors produced this discourse and its corresponding apparatus, US-based transnational corporations and their foundations are increasingly influencing the trajectory of girls' education, health, and economic well-being. Many US transnational corporations entered the field of international development for the first time during that moment. In the beginning of the decade, Starbucks, H&M, Johnson & Johnson, and General Electric, among others, were promoting traditional girls' education through their CSR and philanthropic endeavors. By mid-decade, Nike, Inc., Standard Chartered, Intel, Cisco, ING, and Microsoft moved beyond girls' education to focus on investing in girls, including, most significantly, their economic empowerment. By the beginning of the second decade of the new millennium, another set of corporations were promoting the benefits of investing in girls, including Gucci, Walmart, and Chevron, as they transformed their CSR, philanthropic, and business agendas.

These corporations joined traditional development institutions in investing in girls as the new *homo economicus*. If the object of economic development has always been a gendered subject, it has shifted during the past five decades from the modern, rational man as the homo economicus of the post–World War II era to girls as the future economic woman. Corporations were necessary for this final shift. The movement of corporations into the field of girls' education in the new millennium represents the corporatization of the common sense discourse that investing in girls' education is the most efficient and effective development solution to ending poverty and promoting economic growth based on its high rate of social and economic return. It moved the field from a traditional focus on girls' education to a focus on their economic empowerment.

Yet, corporations and their foundations are not necessarily seeking a direct return. There is nothing profitable, per se, about funding girls' education or economic empowerment, even though CSR efforts certainly improve corporate public relations as well as internal corporate recruitment and retention. Rather, girls' education is conceived as the most efficient way to prepare empowered, entrepreneurial female subjects with the human capital or the appropriate knowledge and skills to reduce poverty and catalyze their economic contribution as a new population of employees, producers, entrepreneurs, and consumers. As Jennifer, a Nike Foundation program manager, and one of the few staff members in the foundation's early years with experience in international development, explained to me in 2007, "What we are really talking about is an economic argument. The carrot on the stick is economic reward."[162] The foundation's strategic move away from the traditional development focus on girls' education toward economic empowerment was described to me by Laura, a Nike Foundation partner, in an interview in 2009 in the following way:

> On the outset, they have very consciously avoided the education sector. Education in a broad sense. They are much more oriented towards economic empowerment. They see the education arena as being overpopulated. . . . Nike didn't see it as their advantage to be working on education per se. Their emphasis is really on economic empowerment. . . . That is the big concept. But how does that get translated into girls' lives? Much more output, explicitly change oriented where as they see education as input training. What can these girls do differently after we are done with them? Because Nike Foundation has such a corporate culture and draws so strongly on the corporate way of doing things, they saw their advantage as economic. How can we connect girls to what we know about—making money, having money in their hands?[163]

In this way, the foundation created a space for its corporatized development efforts through the focus on economic empowerment, away from the overcrowded sector of education where it might not get recognition for its new investment. Moreover, it appears to link its philanthropic focus to its business strategy—if a goal was to ensure girls have money in their hands, it could potentially benefit Nike, Inc.'s bottom line if poor girls were incorporated into its global consumer base in new geographies. Based on my observations, many of the girls in the programs I studied in Brazil were *already* Nike consumers—they wore the company's stylish, yet affordable Converse brand sneakers.

Key to Nike, Inc. making the foundation's work known and marking their presence in the development regime was ensuring their branded logic reached the forefront of global dialogue on the stages of the World Bank, WEF, CGI, and countless other ventures. In late 2007, I attended the World Bank's Global Symposium titled Education: A Critical Path to Gender Equality and Women's Empowerment. The World Bank's relationship with corporations in this field was still in formation.[164] The symposium was part of the Bank's broader program, Gender Equality as Smart Economics: A World Bank Group Action Plan, launched in early 2007 to expand girls and women's economic opportunities in client countries. The Nike Foundation was the only corporate actor included in the small elite gathering. Sarah and Jennifer, the two foundation employees who attended, spent the first day running around with a list of names of those they intended to meet and huddling together in the hall to see who they'd checked off, signaling they were building relationships in the field of girls' education. The following day the Nike Foundation was absent from the afternoon roundtable on multi-sector partners in girls' education in which it was scheduled to participate. As a result, there were no private sector panelists during the two-day symposium.

As a representative of Norwegian Agency for Development Cooperation explained in her remarks that day on global efforts toward gender equity in education:

> So far the private sector has not been a strong voice in these initiatives. Gender as Smart Economics may change this by enrolling the private sector in a dialogue on the Gender Action Plan . . . Reaching the education goals in our partner countries will depend on a national mobilization where all relevant parties are involved, students, parents, teacher associations and NGOs. By linking education to the Gender Action Plan hopefully also the private sector will become a more vocal voice in this national and international dialogue.

By the following year, there was a significant shift in the field of gender and development as corporations became significant partners in the

Figure 6. Photograph of Adolescent Girl Initiative launch at the World Bank headquarters. World Bank President Robert Zoellick (far right) and Nike, Inc. CEO Mark Parker (far back left) shown with young female beneficiaries flown in to perform for the event, October 2008. Photograph by Simone D. McCourtie/World Bank.

World Bank's initiative to achieve gender equality. In April 2008, the World Bank announced two major private sector initiatives: Adolescent Girl Initiative (AGI) and Private Sector Leaders Forum (PSLF). These were two of the six commitments the World Bank made toward achieving gender equality.[165] Catering to private sector companies would define an important aspect of the Bank's new gender program.

AGI launched in October 2008 with the Nike Foundation and the governments of Liberia, Denmark, Norway, Sweden, United Kingdom, and the City of Milan. It sought "to promote the economic empowerment of adolescent girls in poor and post-conflict countries."[166] The Bank's first private sector partnership in a development program, AGI was deemed a "new way for the World Bank to engage with the private sector."[167] Just three years after Nike, Inc. had officially announced its foundation's focus on adolescent girls, it had used its growing influence in development to secure this partnership with the World Bank. Cisco and Standard Chartered Bank shortly followed in Nike's corporate partnership footsteps.

Yet, from interviews with both World Bank and Nike Foundation employees working on AGI, the relationship was strained from the start. Bringing together a fast-moving corporation with a behemoth bureaucratic agency was bound to be challenging for both sides. As Maria Eitel described in her remarks at the CGI 2008 annual meeting just days before AGI's official launch, "It is an unusual collaboration and pretty challenging. But we've made some great progress."[168]

A few months later at the World Economic Forum in Davos, Switzerland, the Private Sector Leaders Forum focused on gender equality was launched over a breakfast sponsored by the World Bank Group, PriceWaterhouseCoopers, and Standard Chartered. As Ngozi Okonjo-Iweala, then managing director of the World Bank, explained at the launch, "So it's not only fair, it's also smart economics."[169] The public-private partnerships between the World Bank Group and leading private sector companies,[170] including Nike, Inc., were developed to support the Bank's gender plan.

By the end of the first decade of the new millennium, corporations and their development partners developed a common sense perspective on the value of girls: Girls are the most efficient way to reduce poverty and promote economic growth in the world.

Nike Foundation represented this idea in graphic form from in partnership with DFID, claiming if adolescent pregnancy goes down 10 percent in Brazil, it will contribute $353 million to the national economy.[171] The statistic in the graph is a powerful reflection of the common sense discourse on the potential of investing in girls, directly linking their fertility reduction to economic gains.[172]

As Stuart Hall explains, "Common sense shapes out ordinary, practical, everyday calculation and appears as natural as the air we breathe. It is simply 'taken for granted' in practice and thought, and forms the starting-point (never examined or questioned) from which every conversation begins."[173] As Sarah, a Nike Foundation employee, told me in 2010, "At the end of the day, you need as many diverse voices saying the same thing as possible for the world to kind of change its view on something, right? For

Figure 7. Family Planning—The Girl Effect Dividend, #fpsummit 2012. Image by UK Department for International Development.

something to be repositioned or to be brought into visible light that has been invisible."

As this chapter demonstrates, this corporatization was not inevitable. In the following chapter, I discuss how a particular set of corporations, including ExxonMobil, Goldman Sachs, and Walmart, all began to say the same thing. Understanding the historical complexity of this phenomenon sets the groundwork for further interrogating present-day corporate practices and their intended and unintended consequences, for girls and women, and for their education.

3 The Spectacle of Empowering Girls and Women

Against a presidential-blue backdrop, leaders from the world's most powerful institutions, including the World Bank, Goldman Sachs, and ExxonMobil, filed onto the ballroom stage for CGI's plenary session, "Investing in Girls and Women," at the Sheraton Hotel in New York City in September 2009. It was the first plenary on girls and women in the organization's five-year history. Bringing together all of development's social actors, from politicians to corporate funders to beneficiaries, CGI, like other global forums, including the World Economic Forum (WEF) and the Global Philanthropy Forum, served as a primary showcase of development between 2005 and 2016.

I stood in the back of the dark ballroom with CGI staff members who were nervously watching the event we had worked for months to organize. Between January 2009 and October 2010 I conducted ongoing participant observation at CGI as an "expert" volunteer and event staff member on the organization's girls and women's team. Meticulous care and endless hours of labor by paid staff, non-paid event staff, such as myself, and an endless stream of young, eager non-paid volunteers were dedicated to creating plenary panels, such as this. Every detail was planned, scripted, and rehearsed. The order of participant appearances was timed, the pronunciation of participant's names perfected, each word was written out in

Figure 8. Photograph of the entrance to the 2009 Clinton Global Initiative annual meeting at the Sheraton Hotel, New York City, for the first annual meeting that featured girls and women as the topic of a plenary session, September 2009. Photograph by author.

"talking points," and every aspect of the event vetted and re-vetted by the former president's team. The fruits of this labor were then displayed upon a perfectly constructed stage, reflected by carefully adjusted lighting, and accompanied by music to trigger one's emotions. Like all CGI events, the plenary was a show, living up to the *Economist*'s name for it—the "philanthropy Oscars."[1] It was a performance of corporate benevolence and this year Third World girls and women were its centerpiece. Goldman Sachs and ExxonMobil were the corporate sponsors of the new "Investing in Girls and Women" track of the annual meeting. Their financial contributions were mutually beneficial for CGI and the corporations. The new track enabled the corporations to showcase their work with girls and women, which was important as these corporations were each deeply embroiled in ongoing public relations crises for their business practices. It was equally relevant for CGI to have two of the world's most powerful corporations in distinct sectors—finance and oil and gas—supporting its program. It symbolically assured CGI ongoing relevance within the corporate world, and, thus, provided material reassurance to a membership organization dependent on the annual financial support of its corporate base, particularly in the midst of the global financial crisis. Consequently, CGI took special steps to ensure its corporate sponsors were satisfied. Their work with girls and women was visually highlighted throughout the meeting on wallpapered images and television screens showing repeating footage of the Black and Brown female beneficiaries of their programs.[2] Their CEOs, Lloyd Blankfein of Goldman Sachs and Rex Tillerson of ExxonMobil, both white American men, were given high profile speaking positions on the plenary panel.[3]

This chapter tells the story of how and why transnational corporations embroiled in public relations crises, such as ExxonMobil, Goldman Sachs, and Walmart, have been known to publically commit to investing their philanthropic, CSR, or business resources in the lives, educations, and economic futures of poor racialized girls and women in the Global South in this context. It shows how forums, such as CGI and the WEF, facilitate these corporatized development practices and to what effects.

As corporations seek to ameliorate their short- and medium-term internal and external crises while expanding long-term opportunities for economic growth and corporate profit in new geographic and population frontiers, forums like CGI create private, highly securitized spaces where corporatized development is enacted, affirmed, and amplified without much fear of dissent. In particular, these forums create the conditions for corporations to reimagine themselves and rewrite their narrative in a space where few will question their intentions or protest their business practices. The forums allow them to perform this new version of corporate self to other global elite—the upper echelons of the corporate, political, philanthropic, and celebrity worlds. Because there are multiple forums like CGI each year—along with countless other venues of less prestige, and mechanisms for amplifying their message to move diverse publics, such as press releases, videos, blogs, Twitter, and Facebook—each time a corporation performs this new narrative and asserts its authority on girls and women, it becomes more true.

In this way, the corporate version is amplified over countervailing voices and forms of knowledge which are subjugated in these spaces and through the transnational networks where these elite subjects circulate.

To demonstrate, this chapter had its beginning with a panel I helped construct during my participant observation at CGI in 2009. It illustrates how two corporations embroiled in controversy reimagined themselves as benevolent, yet strategic, development actors committed to poor girls and women. I use the example of how these corporations operate within the space of CGI to develop a new way of thinking about the potential productivity of gendered, racialized, and classed regimes of representations of Third World poverty and corporate benevolence.

"INVESTING IN GIRLS AND WOMEN" PANEL

In his introduction to the panel, former President Clinton told the audience, "I think empowering women is central to what the world has to do in the 21st century." As he continued discussing girls' and women's empowerment, I thought back to my participation in developing his speech. During the prior week, I was introduced to his speechwriter by Julia, a senior CGI staff member: "K is our in-house girls' expert." She recommended the speechwriter connect with me about statistics on girls and women that were to be included in Clinton's introduction to the plenary. The next morning the speechwriter requested I write a set of talking points based on statistics on girls' and women's health, economic empowerment, and education, in order "to drive home the importance of the issue." I wrote the talking points, but I changed the broader framing of each area to more accurately describe the conditions they reflected.

For example, the following statistic was located under the heading "economic empowerment": "If you invest in a girl or woman, she puts 90% of her income back into her family whereas a boy or man only puts 30%." This statistic is often used to represent the purportedly high rate of return generated by investing in girls and women. Yet, contrary to the understanding of those who employ this statistic, it reifies racialized gender inequality rather than empowerment. Thus, the purported social and economic return reflected by this statistic, as heralded by those who cite it, is generated by gender disparity at the level of the household. It reflects profound inequity or, more specifically, the disproportionate burden some girls and women bear for the lives and well-being of others.[4] As such, I changed the framing I wrote from "economic empowerment" to "economic inequality" to accurately represent the gender relation the statistic describes.

As I stood in the back of the room that day, listening to Clinton's speech, I was interested to discover that "economic inequality," my suggested term, had been replaced by "economic empowerment," the term defining the dominant development rationale for focusing on Third World girls and women. For CGI's purposes, it simply wasn't on-message to point out that the foremost statistic used to promote the high rates of return supposedly generated by investing in girls and women is predicated on inequality rather than empowerment. Moreover, after searching for the statistic's origin, I realized that its inability to be traced to any particulars endows it with universalizing power in the development imaginary. As the people, conditions, and context from which the statistic is derived are erased, they are replaced by the image of a Third World woman, who is always responsible for more than herself, and a Third World male, who irresponsibly spends his money on alcohol, cigarettes, and women.

After Clinton concluded his speech, the moderator, Diane Sawyer, reflected on the significance of the increasing global attention given to girls and women in that particular historical moment. "Don't we all feel that there are times when we can mark the year, mark the millennium in which there is a great convergence? In which that giant river of what is right meets the river of what is needed and suddenly propels history forward at an unexpected pace. And I think it has begun. And we can all feel it. These are some of the power hitters riding that river," she asserted while gesturing to the panelists.

In addition to Rex Tillerson and Lloyd Blankfein, the panel also included Edna Adan, a Black Somali woman, a nurse, midwife, founder of a maternity hospital, former UN diplomat, and former foreign minister and first lady of Somaliland; Melanne Verveer, a white woman, US ambassador-at-large for global women's issues; Robert Zoellick, a white man, president of the World Bank; Zanib Salbi, an Iraqi American woman, the founder and president of Women for Women International; and television journalist Diane Sawyer, a white woman, as the moderator.

Sawyer first turned to Lloyd Blankfein, seated beside her, to ask him about 10,000 Women, Goldman Sachs Foundation's initiative launched in

2008 to provide business and management education to female entrepreneurs in emerging markets. More specifically, she asked, "Why women? Why not women and men equally?"

"I think in this group I don't have to defend the point, but the best place to invest is women. There is research that shows it. When you invest in women, you invest in families. And it is really, frankly, the highest leverage, partly because they are starting from such a low position, but largely because of the way they go back and invest in their families and communities," Blankfein explained, highlighting the purported multi-scalar ripple effect generated from investing in girls and women.

Sawyer followed up, "I've heard you say that maybe these aren't the women you will be hiring immediately at Goldman Sachs, but their children will be," revealing the corporation's interest in the investment's intergenerational potential. Pausing, Blankfein responded, "That's right." He then went on to describe the 10,000 Women initiative in more detail.

Sawyer then turned to Ambassador Melanne Verveer, asking, "Is it necessary?" to invest in girls and women. Ambassador Verveer responded, "No country can prosper if it leaves half its people behind. And investing in women, the potential of women, and the realization of that potential is one of the most powerful forces for good that our world can unleash. And, regrettably, much of it is yet still untapped."

Turning to US defense strategy, Sawyer followed up by asking, "We have heard the Joint Chiefs say that the single biggest force or one of the biggest forces in combatting extremism is empowering women. . . . What's the strongest argument you can make that educating women will combat extremism in the world, that it will change the world politically?"

Verveer responded, "Well, the most dangerous places in the world, frankly, are those places where women are put down in the greatest way. It's where societies implode and where states fail. And women are on the frontlines of moderation. And to the extent that women are invested in and educated, it makes a great deal of difference in terms of the future of those countries and the forces that succeed or don't succeed."

Sawyer then turned to World Bank president Robert Zoellick. She remarked, "Adolescent girls. We heard the president talk about it earlier. Why concentrate on adolescent girls? You have the 2007 Gender Action Plan you've launched."

Zoellick responded, in part, by discussing the World Bank's Adolescent Girls Initiative with the Nike Foundation and Denmark. He described how their pilot in Liberia under the presidency of Ellen Johnson-Sirleaf would focus on three thousand girls over the next three years. He explained, "And what it does is it takes them between age 16 and 24, keeps them in school, makes sure their education is connected to a job, gives them some mentoring. And what you can see is the benefits in terms of not only their lives but their children's lives." Echoing Blankfein, Zoellick highlighted the intergenerational aspects of the development intervention.

Later in the panel, Sawyer stated, "We are looking at two corporations here which have earned the wonder of the world." Pointing at Tillerson, she said, "The second largest corporation in the world" in reference to ExxonMobil. "Give me the philosophy. What is the responsibility of businesses that make billions and billions of dollars? Is it a 10 percent tithe toward these countries you're in? What's the right amount, and what is the way to get everybody on board?"

Tillerson explained, "Well, philosophically, we are committed to this space because it is critical to our own sustainability in the countries in which we operate. A large part of our activities today and in the future are going to be in lesser developed parts of the world, so our longer term success is built around the ability to have a productive workforce, have communities that are stable, and growing and participating in the economic benefit."

Sawyer returned to the issue of corporate funding, in particular. She explained, "I want to button this issue of money, and the role of corporate America in supplying this money . . . Lloyd, will you ask Rex the toughest question you can ask him. The two of you ask each other the toughest questions about the role of corporate America and its profits in funding developmental issues."

Blankfein began, "So now, let me ask Rex a question that we ask ourselves. Are we at capacity for our investment? In other words, having said what I said, are we at the point there where an incremental dollar wouldn't help? And, secondly, how about countries where the needs are higher but maybe the advantage, maybe you're not located there because there are not [oil] reserves and you're not operating in those countries. So do you start with the point of view of where you are and look for the neediest or do you go to the neediest and a happy coincidence but not a necessary coincidence if you happen to be there for your commercial interest?"

Tillerson responded without actually addressing Blankfein's question regarding how they determine where they focus their investments in girls and women. After two more questions to Tillerson from Sawyer and Blankfein, it was clear Tillerson did not plan to directly answer questions regarding Exxon's resource allocation strategy. Moving beyond him, on the same topic, Sawyer turned to Zoellick, "Bob, creating the infrastructure, isn't that about money too?"

He replied, "Yes, it is, but this conversation has come to, at least in my mind, an interesting point. There are a lot of people with good will. There are good intentions. There is a charitable spirit. But what we are talking about is kind of moving to a different level. We've done a lot of research at the World Bank on the theme of gender economics is smart economics. You won't find that people in countries will act solely out of charitable impulses. You gotta do it in their self-interest. Let me give you an example. The Mexican Opportunidades program, which Mayor Bloomberg has talked about, which has money going to the poorest families, consciously makes the payments to women. They have to send the kids to school to get the payments. They have to get health checks, so it has probably done more for women's health than anything in history. But we know that by giving the money to women, you get a better result. So I could give you a whole series of examples like that where you draw women into the system."

As the panel concluded, Sawyer asked Blankfein a question from one of the audience members, "What do your shareholders think of these programs?"

He responded, "I think at the end of the day, we are people and reputation. And we have to do whatever it takes to attract and retain the best people. And, oddly enough, this is a recruiting tool for our firm. And by the way, it is a retention tool for the firm . . . And when I talk to shareholders, I make that point and, frankly, they see that too . . . So when you are doing these activities that make people feel more complete and engaged, that's very, very, very good for our franchise."

He later concluded the panel, saying "At the risk of sounding too much like a finance guy, which I am. This is really the highest return on risk space you can have, really for two reasons. One, the need is so great. And the people, on the other hand, the people with whom you operate are so capable and passionate that you can actually have a terrific effect. I'm not sure there aren't places with more needs and there are people more capable, but the combination of the two here allows us . . . we are in the business of trying to find these things to work on, and maybe again I am saying it a bit differently, slightly differently than Rex said it along the same lines. This is where you get an enormous return, if other people aren't going to be in the space. I regret that in a lot of ways, but I tell you, in that there is an opportunity for us because I don't think we have to be, to squeeze ourselves into spaces between two other people here. There is a wide-open area for us to go. We'll let the next generation of people who want to make the investment worry that there is nothing left to do. There is plenty for us left to do here."

WHY DO CORPORATIONS INTERVENE?

Through Blankfein's and Tillerson's promotion of their corporate philanthropic and social responsibility programs, they starkly revealed the "business case" behind investing in girls and women. While neither of them publically referred to their public relations and legal crises, or their strategy of investing in girls and women as a strategic means of turning the public's attention away from those, that was the broader context in which they were speaking.

Instead, the executives focused on how the strategy was critical to securing consent internally in addition to ensuring long-term corporate growth. As Blankfein articulated, 10,000 Women was an internal employee recruitment and retention strategy. It worked to promote employee satisfaction, regenerate employee fulfillment in their finance jobs, and ensure they continued working for the company. With levels of public approval at all-time lows, the financial firm needed to build up the image of the company in order to recruit top candidates and retain successful employees, particularly women, as much as it needed to secure its external image.

Both men revealed how the strategy was key to developing long-term investment conditions. As Tillerson explained, investing in girls and women was part of securing conditions for global economic growth in these "lesser developed parts of the world" by ensuring the locations have trained, productive workforces and stable, economically viable communities. As he explained, this was directly linked to the corporation's "own sustainability in the countries in which [they] operate" and to their "longer term success" in these geographies. In this respect, both CEOs sought an intergenerational effect. As Blankfein alluded, although Goldman currently does not recruit from or have offices in many of these countries, it was potentially training the next generation of employees as the firm moved into new geographies throughout the world.

In contrast to the CEOs, the government and multilateral representatives moved back and forth between the economic imperatives of investing in girls and women in the context of the global economic crisis and the political needs in the midst of the US War on Terror. Zoellick's comments promoted a political-economic strategy while Ambassador Verveer spoke about the practice as a political-military strategy for battling terrorism. In this way, educating girls and women is a handmaiden to military strategy, as seen in Iraq, Afghanistan, and Pakistan. And, lastly, as anticipated by the CGI staff during the organizing of the event, the civil society representatives—the only people of color, the only women of color, and the only individuals from the Global South—talked about the social, cultural, political, and economic needs and benefits in equal proportion, while also emphasizing women's sheer determination for survival and for securing better lives for themselves and their children. Edna Adan highlighted the realities of maternal mortality and the benefits of educating girls and women on social, cultural, and political practices, whereas Zanib Salbi raised questions regarding accountability, women's participation in decision making, and creating viable economic alternatives to traditional cultural practices for families and communities.

Salbi challenged Tillerson's remarks on funding, in particular. Turning toward him, she explained, "Women and girls get a very small, miniscule amount of funding for any development dollar. According to research funded by the Nike Foundation and NoVo Foundation, one cent out of every development dollar, less than one cent, goes to girls." She continued to press him later, asking, "Are we including women in decision making? Are we accountable for the impacts of our projects? Are we measuring the decisions on not only how much money is going in and who is making the decision, but also, what's the impact of the decisions?"

Underlying all of the panelists' contributions and contradictions was a prioritization of the gendered human capital discourse of investing in girls and women, and, with the exceptions of Adan and Salbi, an explicit focus on the economic returns of those investments.

Besides Salbi's gentle jabs at Tillerson, the "Investing in Girls and Women" panel was representative of the entire 2009 annual meeting. The concerted effort by CGI to highlight the corporate initiatives in the field, particularly, but not limited to Goldman Sachs and ExxonMobil, was met by praise despite broader public critique of those corporations' business practices. To explore the question of how girls and women became a new frontier in the context of ongoing capitalist crisis, I turn to the crises in which ExxonMobil and Goldman Sachs were then embroiled, and how they directed their resources toward poor girls and women as an indirect way of mitigating those external and internal public relations disasters.

EXXONMOBIL

ExxonMobil,[5] one of the world's largest energy companies, is based in Irving, Texas. Exxon's roots are in John D. Rockefeller's Standard Oil Company. In 1999, Mobil Oil merged with Exxon to become ExxonMobil.[6] For decades it has been subject to ongoing public relations crises related to its environmental, labor, and human rights practices in communities where it operates both in the United States and globally.[7] Michael Watts theorizes the violence associated with oil extraction as "petro-violence." He identifies this violence as "*ecological* violence perpetrated upon the biophysical world"[8] and "*social* violence," seen in the "criminality and degeneracy associated with the genesis of petro-wealth."[9] Petro-violence is linked to unprecedented wealth creation and corporate growth in the oil industry; and yet Exxon has never been found criminally liable. In 2016, *Fortune 500* ranked it the second most profitable company in the world, falling to fourth in 2017.[10] Thus, the violence of its petro-wealth creation and its benevolent philanthropic and CSR practices operate as two sides of the same coin.

The most infamous incident of ecological violence for the company was the 1989 Exxon *Valdez* oil spill in Alaska's Prince William Sound. Eleven million gallons of crude oil spilled into the sea, creating the largest oil spill in US history at the time. More than one thousand miles of coastline were damaged, and hundreds of thousands of animals died.[11] Seared into the public's conscious, helped by the ubiquitous media images of suffering animals covered in oil, the disaster became difficult for the corporation to escape. Yet, the *Valdez* spill wasn't the end of ExxonMobil's destructive footprint. Ongoing incidents reveal the toxic nature of the company's relationship with local communities in which it operates.[12]

In addition to its direct effects on the environment, the company has been accused of actively influencing international and government policies on greenhouse gas emissions and climate change, funding organizations that argue against global warming science, and seeking to curb government interventions to reduce fossil fuel emissions.[13] Those efforts occured despite the company's early internal knowledge that burning fossil fuels increases carbon dioxide in the atmosphere.[14] In November 2015, the New York attorney general opened an investigation into whether ExxonMobil deceived the public on climate change or lied to its investors on the potential risks to its business.[15]

On the question of human rights, the major transnational oil companies, including Royal Dutch Shell, Chevron, and ExxonMobil, have long been accused of working alongside foreign governments and paramilitary groups. In the Nigerian context, the Economic Community of West African States ruled in 2012 that the government of Nigeria and oil companies, including the transnational conglomerates ExxonMobil, Royal Dutch Shell, and Chevron, have violated human rights, including the "right to a general satisfactory environment and the right to natural wealth and resources, as guaranteed under the African Charter on Human and Peoples' Rights ratified by Nigeria in 1983."[16] In Indonesia, eleven villagers filed a 2001 lawsuit, *Doe I v. ExxonMobil*, against the corporation in a US federal court, claiming that the company was complicit in human rights abuses committed by Indonesian security forces in the Aceh province who were paid by the company to patrol its oil fields. In 2014, a federal court ruled that the villagers can proceed with their claims against the company, followed by a 2015 ruling that the plaintiff's claims sufficiently "touch and concern" the United States.[17]

Educating Girls and Women

In the context of ongoing crisis management, in July 2005 ExxonMobil began its Educating Women and Girls Initiative. According to the company, the program focused on "providing and improving educational and training opportunities for women and girls in the developing countries where we live and work."[18] In developing its investment rationale, Tillerson cites the World Bank's influential discourse on the ripple effect: "The research is clear that improvements in education and increased opportunities for women and girls serve as a foundation for economic growth, development and societal progress. We believe this initiative will support international development goals and have a profound and lasting impact on individuals, their families and the communities where we operate around the world."[19]

The program began in 2005 with $1.6 million in grants focused on countries including Chad, Indonesia, Kazakhstan, Qatar, Equatorial Guinea, and two global partnerships.[20] The initiative strategically linked its philanthropic practices to regions that are important to ExxonMobil's business geography.[21] By 2007, its grant giving cumulated in more than $11 million on the African continent and in other important oil-producing regions where the company works, such as Asia, the Middle East, and the Caspian region. These programs sought to give the girls and women leadership, business, teacher, and vocational training as well as to construct and renovate schools and provide support for girls' education. In 2009, the company shifted away from formal education toward economic empowerment as it launched its new Women's Economic Opportunity Initiative to replace its education initiative. The rhetoric and logic of the ripple effect accompanied that shift. As Jackson explains:

> And my observations from working with women all over the world is that, when given access to training and resources, they take whatever is given and take it to the limit. They are so resourceful in making the most out of every opportunity. So the research findings that you often hear talked about in terms of women using 80–90% of their income and putting it back into

> their families and communities—I've seen that at work. I've seen them generate enormous amounts of resources relative to the opportunity, and then do incredible things to make their families and communities better off. And it's our personal observations along with the research that makes us so comfortable that we've picked the right investment area.[22]

That updated initiative had a dual focus in promoting women's economic opportunities, citing the same statistic I had sought to be removed from former President Clinton's talking points. The first focus was investment in technology under the umbrella program called Technologies to Improve Women's Economic Livelihoods, which the former president announced at CGI in 2009, the year ExxonMobil co-sponsored the "Investing in Girls and Women" track with Goldman Sachs. As Tillerson explained in a press release of the initiative, "As a global technology company, ExxonMobil can make a lasting contribution by helping to identify and deploy new technologies to improve and strengthen the economic livelihoods of women . . . This focus area is consistent with our own belief and experience that technology and innovation are critical to addressing many of the world's major challenges."[23]

The second focus was on investing in women in management. This continues ExxonMobil's work with CEDPA's Global Women in Management program, a grantee carried over into the company's new focus on economic opportunity. One of the first efforts in this area was a partnership between ExxonMobil and Cameroon Oil Transportation Company (COTCO) designed to prepare "high potential African women leaders to assume increased responsibilities and accountability in their personal, institutional and community lives by bolstering skills in program and financial management, leadership, fundraising and proposal development, strategic communication, supervision, and advocacy."[24] The program clearly linked the corporation's philanthropic focus with its geography of oil extraction, and emphasized the common sense discourse on the feminization of responsibility and accountability.

GOLDMAN SACHS

As the global financial crisis took the world's markets by storm, public trust in the global banking industry was deeply shaken. Goldman Sachs was one of the institutions at the center of this intense mistrust. In the first decade of the new millennium, its revenue rose dramatically. Prior to the global recession, it experienced an unprecedented revenue boom—between 2005 and 2007, its revenue almost doubled as it fed off of the housing market bubble through mortgage-backed securities and collateralized debt obligations—from more than $24 billion to more than $45 billion. While the corporation's revenue fell at the beginning of the global financial crisis in 2008, losing more than $23 billion, it returned to its pre-crisis revenue of more than $45 billion by 2009.[25] In 2010, the Securities and Exchange Commission accused the firm of securities fraud in a civil lawsuit that claimed "the bank created and sold a mortgage investment that was secretly intended to fail."[26]

As revealed in the US Senate subcommittee investigations on the financial crisis in 2011, this was not a single incident. As subcommittee chairman Senator Carl Levin (Democrat-Michigan) explained, "The 2009 Goldman Sachs annual report stated that the firm 'did not generate enormous net revenues by betting against residential related products.'" Levin said, "These emails show that, in fact, Goldman made a lot of money by betting against the mortgage market."[27] In the series of e-mails presented by the subcommittee, chairman and CEO Lloyd Blankfein, who participated in the CGI plenary discussed at the beginning of the chapter, wrote to his top colleagues: "Of course we didn't dodge the mortgage mess. We lost money, then made more than we lost because of shorts."[28] As Senator Levin states, "There it is, in their own words: Goldman Sachs taking 'the big short' against the mortgage market." He further explains:

> Investment banks such as Goldman Sachs were not simply market-makers, they were self-interested promoters of risky and complicated financial schemes that helped trigger the crisis. They bundled toxic mortgages into complex financial instruments, got the credit rating agencies to label them as AAA securities, and sold them to investors, magnifying and spreading risk throughout the financial system, and all too often betting against the instruments they sold and profiting at the expense of their clients.[29]

The firm's aggressive speculation during the housing bubble was only one instance in its history of profiting off of speculative bubbles.[30]

In the wake of the world financial crisis, the firm weathered fierce internal and external critiques.[31] The firm's reputation was ranked "very poor" immediately following the crisis, later rising to "poor" in 2015, placing it in a category with other financial services providers, such as Bank of America Corporation, Citigroup, Inc., and J. P. Morgan Chase, according to the Harris Poll, which measures the reputations of the most visible US corporations.[32] Nevertheless, in 2015, the company ranked very last on the list of the one hundred most visible US companies, as ranked by the general public.[33] In comparison, Nike, Inc. ranked twenty-five, ExxonMobil ranked eighty-two, and Walmart ranked eighty-four.

10,000 Women

The firm took various steps to address its public relations problems. One of those is its work in women's business education. In the midst of the crisis, in March 2008, Goldman Sachs announced it was donating "$100 million to give at least 10,000 women a business education and, more broadly, to develop and enhance business education programs at universities in Africa, the Middle East and other developing regions."[34]

As explained in its progress report, "The founding objective was to spur economic growth and build stronger communities by opening doors for women whose financial and practical circumstances would otherwise prevent them from receiving a traditional business education."[35] Between 2008 and 2013, it enrolled ten thousand women in its program, according to Goldman's reporting.

The corporation based its initiative on two research reports commissioned by the company—"Womenomics" and "Women Hold up Half the Sky." The underlying argument in those reports echoes the discourse of the multi-scalar ripple effect—investment in girls and women's education has a high return on investment. On the micro level of the girl or woman, Goldman reports it affects wages, fertility, maternal and child mortality, and health, among other indicators. On the macro scale, one report states:

> Female education is a key source of support for long-term economic growth. It has been linked to higher productivity; higher returns to investment;

> higher agricultural yields; and a more favourable demographic structure. The economic growth that results from higher education feeds a virtuous cycle, supporting continued investments in education and extending the gains to human capital and productivity.[36]

The report delves into the specificities of these potential returns in the BRICS as well as the N-11 countries, a term also coined by Goldman Sachs' Jim O'Neil for Mexico, Indonesia, South Korea, Turkey, Bangladesh, Egypt, Nigeria, Pakistan, the Philippines, and Vietnam. The report explains, "Greater investments in female education could yield a 'growth premium' that raises trend GDP growth by about 0.2% per year."[37] Moreover, "Narrowing the gender gap in employment—which is one potential consequence of expanded female education—could push income per capita as much as 14% higher than our baseline projections by 2020, and as much as 20% higher by 2030."[38]

While internal and external criticism for Goldman Sachs' business practices reached unprecedented levels in 2009 following the crisis, 10,000 Women is still cited throughout the development world as a paradigmatic example of a corporation investing in women.[39] As reported in *deveximpact,* an initiative of USAID, "In the world of corporate philanthropy, few programs are as recognizable as Goldman Sach's 10,000 Women initiative," which has garnered praise from governments and nonprofits, and has developed a brand for itself as a leader in corporate social responsibility for women."[40] The program continues to remain relatively untouched by the public criticism.

MANAGING CORPORATE CRISIS

Within a historical context of mounting social and political pressure for corporations to remain accountable to multiple constituencies, including labor, consumers, local communities, and activists, corporations such as Goldman Sachs and ExxonMobil have been forced to respond to, and recuperate from, criticism of their business activities in the United States and globally that harm the environment, labor, and communities.[41] In an effort to secure their social licenses to operate and, correspondingly, their financial bottom lines, companies have adopted an array of "corporate social technologies"[42] to reconstitute themselves as benevolent institutional actors and extend their moral authority despite the persistence of exploitive profit-seeking business practices, leaving their constituencies without recourse.[43] As Stuart Kirsch explains in his ethnography of the mining industry, central to this is the co-optation of their critics' discourse by "promoting themselves as responsible, sustainable, and transparent."[44]

One channel for doing this is their efforts to empower girls and women. While feminist and women's rights organizations have long critiqued corporations for their deleterious effects on the lives of girls, women, and other marginalized communities, companies have effectively depoliticized women's rights and feminists' demands for a fair and just global economy while also incorporating their language through their instrumental prioritization of girls and women. As one executive director of a women's organization explained on a conference call I participated in through CGI in 2009: "Great that corporations and governments are using our rhetoric but at the same time a lot of their work is what we're up against. ExxonMobil has put women at risk. And we are willing to fight."

As Kirsch explains, this "ability to neutralize criticism often leaves the public resigned to the harms they produce."[45] This process occurs through CSR or philanthropic activities, which enable companies to "continue externalizing the costs of production onto society and the environment, despite making widely publicized claims about the social benefits of their activities, their commitment to abide by existing laws and regulations, their willingness to cooperate with the state, and their responsibility as corporate citizens."[46]

This is the move from antagonism to hegemony. It is about securing consent for current and future production and consumption by incorporating poor girls and women as well as corporate critics into their domain, a tactic similar to that used to disarm the environmental movement.[47] In order to survive, corporations need to ensure consent with their diverse constituents in the uneven geographies where they operate. The practice of "doing good" to girls and women becomes one way to construct consent for "doing well."

In doing so, corporations have integrated gender equity into their common sense. These are the kernels of "good sense"[48] in this discourse, to employ the language of Gramsci. This is the result of decades of efforts by feminist and women's organizations to get "gender equity" on the table through gender mainstreaming and more progressive efforts; yet, what is disarticulated from these corporate practices are the explicit or implicit critiques of how corporations marginalize girls and women. Since corporations have become the dominant institutions structuring this agenda, these critiques are also marginalized.

As Michael Goldman explains, the moment of hegemony is when the dominant historical bloc "poses the questions around which the struggle rages."[49] The questions being asked are not whether corporations are harming girls and women through their business practices, whether in their retail stores, sites of oil extraction, financial practices, or contract factories, or whether corporations can be pressured to transform their business practices; rather, the questions focus on how corporations are doing good to girls and women, and how they can scale-up these efforts.

As this occurs, the contradictions of capitalist production, particularly as they influence poor girls and women, are not resolved. Rather, as Kirsch states, "They can only be negotiated in new forms" by institutional actors, including states, corporations, NGOs, and multilateral organizations such as the World Bank.[50] The case of corporatized development focused on girls and women thus represents a negotiated form of corporate capitalism where corporations are responding to critiques of their practices, yet they are doing so in ways that do not attempt to address the root of those business problems. Rather, they are employing practices of strategic philanthropy that align with their business model, but may or may not correspond to the lives, needs, and desires of the girls and women they target. But this is not the point. It is the perception of those actions in the public sphere that matters, not necessarily by their fiercest critics, but by the general public who might otherwise (or still) be swayed by stories of sweatshops and child labor, or human rights abuses and financial exploitation. Spaces like CGI and the World Economic Forum create opportunities for corporations to build those messages while forging strategic relationships with NGOs, state actors, and development institutions. For corporations to guarantee their hegemony, a moment when the relations of force are in balance, consent must be secured in each of these arenas despite their failure to shift their business practices.

CIRCULATING COMMON SENSE, KNOWLEDGE MANAGEMENT, AND TRANSNATIONAL NETWORKS

In order to survive, despite continual threats to their hegemony, corporations need to expand, generating and internalizing new frontiers. Through these processes, market expansion enables "capital's expanded reproduction" as corporations overcome crisis, at least temporarily in particular geographies.[51] As Bob Jessop describes in his analysis of David Harvey's work on spatial fixes, "crisis-tendencies can be overcome in the short- to medium-term through investments that absorb *current* surplus capital and increase its *future* productivity and profitability. This involves both senses of 'fix'. For not only are these typically long-term investments, they also provide a potential escape from crisis via market expansion."[52] For Harvey, as Jessop explains, this aspect of the "internal spatial fix as temporal displacement" includes "long-lived physical and social infrastructures," including education, "that take many years to return their value to circulation through the productive activity they support."[53] The investments of transnational corporations participating in this phenomenon include both—possible short- or medium-term escape from crises of legitimacy, as Goldman Sachs, ExxonMobil, and Nike, Inc. have all experienced, which often contribute to, or are feared for their potential to, spur market contraction—*and* long term investment in geographical and population expansion, as Blankfein and Tillerson described on the CGI panel.

Global forums, such as CGI, and their networks are critical in constructing and sustaining this imagined frontier. They are essential to understanding how particular types of authoritative knowledge and expertise on girls and women travel, are translated, and are taken up by corporations. Over the past decade—together with CGI—WEF, PSLF, and La Pietra Coalition's Third Billion Campaign, among others, have structured the global development agenda around girls and women as a corporate agenda. Since its inception in 2005, former President Clinton and CGI's corporate membership base actively promoted "investing" in this population as a solution for ending poverty and stimulating economic growth. Along with those other institutions, it decided what knowledge of girls and women counts, what circulates, and who has authority over it. It enabled transnational corporations to reimagine, reconstruct, and publicize their relationship to poor girls and women in the Global South. It did so, in part, by subjugating the knowledge of feminist and corporate critics as well as subaltern girls and women whose bodies have become the ground upon which corporatized development is enacted.[54]

CGI's facilitation of Walmart's re-imagination of its relationship to girls and women presents an interesting case. In 2001, six female Walmart retail workers filed a lawsuit, *Dukes v. Wal-mart Stores, Inc.*, against the company for gender discrimination in pay and promotion policies and practices; and, in 2003, they amended the lawsuit to include 1.5 million present and former female workers, making it the largest class action lawsuit for workplace bias in US history. However, in 2011, the Supreme Court ruled in favor of Walmart, citing that the plaintiffs did not constitute a class.[55] While the ruling did not decide if the company was liable for discrimination, it was a clear victory for the corporation over its female employees. Nevertheless, the lawsuit itself clearly indicated that the company had a gender problem, which could generate problems with constituents across its geographies, including its female workers, consumers, and shareholders. After the Supreme Court ruling, the original plaintiffs filed another class complaint, "alleging Walmart managers in the retailer's California regions systematically discriminated against female employees."[56] In July 2016, the plaintiffs reached private settlements with Walmart.

In the wake of the Supreme Court's decision, Walmart launched the Global Women's Economic Empowerment Initiative at the CGI annual meeting in September 2011 to "help empower women across its supply chain."[57] As explained by Sarah F. Thorn, senior director of federal government relations, the initiative "aims to harness our company's unique size and scale to help empower women across our supply chain. Through the initiative, we are helping to provide training, market access and economic opportunities to nearly one million women—ultimately allowing them access to the economic opportunity they deserve."[58] In its press release, Leslie Dach, Walmart's executive vice president of corporate affairs explained:

> We do not believe that a company has to choose between being a successful business and a responsible one. We have a model for making a difference

> that works. When we combine the Walmart model with women's empowerment, we have an incredible opportunity to make a difference on the big challenges facing our world.[59]

Here the company sidesteps its gender discrimination problem by placing its concern for women in its supply chain on display at CGI, even while gender discrimination in its retail stores continued to be an issue at the time.[60]

As Penny Abeywardena, former director of girls and women integration at CGI, explained in a 2014 Clinton Foundation blog that showcases Walmart's gender empowerment efforts, the company "leveraged the CGI platform to empower girls and women over the past several years—including in 2013, when the company rolled out a dedicated space on Walmart.com that gives shoppers the opportunity to buy unique products while supporting small women-owned businesses around the world."[61] As she wrote, CGI provides a platform for corporate leaders to "discuss their views on the opportunities, and the imperative, for business executives to reimagine their approach to gender inclusion."[62] Yet, what does gender inclusion mean for a company like Walmart if gender discrimination allegedly continued in its workplaces as evidenced by continuing lawsuits against the corporation? As Walmart claims to empower women across its supply chain, women in its retail stores continue to claim gender discrimination.

In this way, influential platforms like CGI for knowledge sharing and resource mobilization by powerful elite individuals and institutions facilitate what Jamie Peck identifies as a "fast policy regime" that circulates dominant policy ideas on girls and women without holding corporations accountable for changing exploitative practices of capital accumulation.[63] Sarah, a Nike Foundation senior staff member, shared this insight with me in an interview in August 2010:

> If there were champions of girls that were in those circles, we would work with them to help them sharpen their language and messaging so we are all sort of sending a similar message and an inviting tone so we could encourage others to kind of come in. And in the end, those forums are critically important to public opinion because they are all thought leaders who end up having a voice in the community, in their respective

> communities so the more voices that are there that understand and believe in the message we have been sending and can carry on that messaging, the better.

Corporate and foundation employees recognize the significance of these spaces for crafting and spreading their messages. As Stephen Ball writes, these forums enable corporations to come together with powerful foundations, NGOs, and governments in "new networks and sites of policy outside of the framework of the nation state,"[64] creating minimal conditions for public accountability and transparency. Spaces such as CGI and WEF are highly securitized spaces that operate within what CGI staff members called the "secret service bubble." The security apparatus, along with the vetting process, ensure that there are no disturbances or rogue attendees to question the content or power dynamics of the event.

As a consequence, during two years of participant observation during the annual meetings and in the months of preparation leading up to them, I only observed one publicly vocalized critique of corporations' contradictory roles in funding and advocating programs and policies focused on poor, racialized girls and women. During a closed, invitation-only session at the 2009 annual meeting, a prominent feminist stood up, declaring the contradiction of ExxonMobil's sponsorship of the girls and women's track at the annual meeting when grassroots women's and feminist organizations in Nigeria are dealing with the consequences of its environmental degradation and human rights abuses. The remarks were met by silence. The moderator thanked her for the comment. Lorie Jackson, director of ExxonMobil's Women's Economic Empowerment Initiative, entered the room a few minutes after the remark, but no further conversation ensued in her presence.

The only other critiques I heard were whispered to me. The executive director of a transnational NGO that receives corporate funding from two prominent corporations said, "I'm so tired of this. They are robbing girls." She was critiquing the lack of corporate accountability and transparency over money spent on marketing and public relations campaigns. Yet, in her public role, she spoke diplomatically about the general need for transparency and accountability in the field rather than directly critiquing the corporations. Even those modest calls were met by relative silence. Urging one another to be transparent and accountable seemed anything but a priority for the institutions in attendance.

POVERTY AS SPECTACLE

The knowledge and expertise on poor girls and women in the Global South that circulates in these forums is deeply reductionist.[65] It circulates through representations of gendered, racialized poverty and predominantly white corporate benevolence. The "Investing in Girls and Women" plenary I analyze in this chapter is an example of that gendered, racialized, and classed regime of representation.[66] The powerful, mostly white participants represent the poverty and potential of Third World girls and women as a site for consumption and investment. Those representations also circulate in their promotional materials, including posters, videos, infographics, Tweets, and Facebook posts, that amplify those forms of knowledge.

Those representations are not about poverty experienced by poor gendered and racialized subjects as a material condition of deprivation or systematic exploitation in capitalism. Nor are they representations of poor, racialized girls and women as human beings or agential subjects. Rather, I identify those representations as constitutive of what I call *poverty as spectacle*.[67] Poverty as spectacle is not merely a set of images of poverty and the poor.[68] It is an uneven social relation between people mediated by racialized, gendered, and geographically imagined representations of the poor, the condition of poverty, and, correspondingly, of those who imagine and work toward poverty's end and the interventions they create.[69]

To develop the concept, I build on Stuart Hall's theorization of the "spectacle of the 'Other,'" as constituted through a racialized, gendered, classed, and geographically marked regime of visual representation.[70] On one side, the regime is based on "racialized knowledge of the Other;"[71] on the other, is what Tiffany Willoughby-Herard identifies as a "global regime of whiteness," which is sustained, in part, through the practices of corporations and philanthropy.[72] Together they are, in Edward Said's language, "deeply implicated in the operations of power."[73]

The social relations of this regime of representation are informed by present day and historical power/knowledge practices that reproduce the underlying, uneven social relations perpetuating gendered and racialized poverty even as the producers, distributors, and consumers of the spectacle claim to work toward poverty's end. While poverty as spectacle circulates far beyond CGI and the site of corporatized development, in these spaces it is dominated by representations of Third World girls and women created by mostly white corporate employers, philanthropists, and development experts. And while not all of the subjects in my study at institutions like CGI were white, there were only a few non-white staff members at the primary institutions, including the Nike Foundation, CGI, and the NGOs in Rio de Janeiro; yet, more significantly, this regime of power operates through a logic of whiteness and practices that uphold centuries of social-cultural and political-economic relations predicated on white racial superiority from colonization through globalization.

This spectacle can be seen in the CGI plenary on Empowering Girls and Women, but it is also evident in the Girl Effect video, the Girl Knight banner, the data on girls presented at Petrobras, and on the billboard of the Sheraton Hotel for the CGI annual meeting, just to name a few moments depicted in this book.

In the realm of the spectacle, poverty is detached from its material conditions of deprivation. The "freeing" of poverty from its materiality results in poverty's alienation from the actual lives of the poor. Poverty as spectacle—in an ironic twist—denies the material conditions in which the poor live and often die. On one hand, those material conditions are produced through long histories of systematic exploitation, and thus are conditions of struggle as individuals, communities, and nations fight for freedom from poverty and the oppressive sociocultural and political-economic relations that produce it. At the same time, while those are not conditions to be romanticized, they are the material conditions in which human beings relate to others as human and through which agency is born. And while the spectacle does not actually free the poor as human beings from those conditions, it negates their humanity and frees itself (and those who produce, distribute, and consume it) from the material conditions of poverty. As Guy Debord reveals, the spectacle is "a visible negation of life—a negation that has taken on a visible form."[74] Poverty as spectacle is also a "negation" of poverty and the poor in a very visible, yet deceiving form. It is through this negation, as Hall explains, that "representation and reality" become blurred.[75]

Thus, within poverty as spectacle, poverty and the poor exist only through representation. In the case of corporatized development, it occurs through corporate representations of gendered and racialized poverty and the poor Black and Brown female beneficiaries of their projects. Yet, the spectacle is not just a set of images; rather, poverty re-materializes through poverty as spectacle. It has become the objective way poverty is understood in spaces such as CGI. Poverty as spectacle thus becomes real—it comes into being through the material life of ending poverty. Through this material life—including the videos, posters, and performances that animate development—the poor, poverty, poverty's imagined end, and those who work to end poverty exist in the spectacle. This re-materialization through the spectacle both reflects and has very real material effects on social relations in our historic moment. Thus, poverty as spectacle's alienation from poverty as a material condition and poor subjects is indeed productive.

In contrast to historical representations of racialized girls and women in the Global South that depicted them as objects on display or passive subjects in need of saving, as Stuart Hall, Anne McClintock, Chandra Mohanty, and many others analyze,[76] these corporate representations of poverty also represent racialized girls and women as empowered, efficient, and educated subjects with Third World potential to end the structural problems of poverty and to promote economic growth through corporate interventions.

Through the spectacle, there is a reversal of the presumed relationship between these Third World beneficiaries and their First World benefactors, as corporations and their employees, such as those represented in the plenary, become the primary beneficiaries of those performances. The spectacle reflects their benevolence toward those marginalized subjects despite their ongoing labor, environmental, and militarized practices across the world that often exacerbate conditions of vulnerability for girls and women and against which women's and feminist organizations and corporate critics have organized for decades.

In this way, the poverty spectacle works to obscure the exploitative practices of corporations, such as those depicted in this chapter, while promoting new representations of themselves in the image of poor Black and Brown girls and women in the Global South. They ultimately distract those consuming these forms of knowledge from understanding the ways in which corporate business practices are gendered, racialized, and classed in often exploitative ways, as the cases of these corporations reveal.

Institutional efforts in spaces such as CGI are critical to assuaging public critique of the corporations' exploitative practices and to maintaining corporate hegemony in the context of ongoing corporate crises. In the language of James Ferguson, they function as "anti-politics machines," depoliticizing, undermining, and often silencing claims for redress and fair treatment in the presence of violent and exploitative practices of many of these companies. By influencing corporations to channel their focus on girls and women and rewarding them with publicity for these efforts, CGI provided them with a legitimized platform for their philanthropic, CSR, and business efforts. As such, CGI facilitated the extension of corporations' legitimacy, authority, and reach, without necessitating that they deal with contradictions in their business practices or their forms of self-representation.

After my first year participating on CGI's Girls and Women team, I spoke candidly with Julia, a senior staff member, about the representations of poverty as spectacle. She agreed with my analysis. Yet, in a member-based organization, that perspective didn't matter. She explained, "Kathryn, what you hate is what our members love most." Despite the critique both CGI staff and I presented, those representations of poverty as spectacle continued.

To conclude, the business of empowering girls and women is constructed on the terrain of poverty as spectacle. It produces it and functions through it. This gendered, racialized, and classed regime of representation thrives in forums, like CGI, that provide a legitimizing space for companies like ExxonMobil, Goldman Sachs, Walmart, and Nike, Inc. to secure their hegemony by incorporating and neutralizing critiques of their business practices in order to continue generating unprecedented wealth creation, in part, through the representations of their benevolence toward, and on the backs of, Third World girls and women. In this way, these poverty spectacles reflect and reproduce the dominant power/knowledge relations between corporate wealth and gendered, racialized poverty in this moment of global capitalism.

In the chapters that follow, I show how one corporation and its foundation constructed their branded spectacle, the Girl Effect, as they generated and affirmed a new narrative of corporate self on the world stage.

4 Searching for Third World Potential

The Girl Effect, *n.*
The unique potential of 250 million adolescent girls to end poverty for themselves and the world.[1]

Beyond Barra de Tijuca, a wealthy, coastal neighborhood in the Zona Oeste (West Zone) of Rio de Janeiro, high-end shopping malls and corporate parks give way to large open swaths of flat land. An intricate maze of lagoons forms a natural boundary between the geographies. As I looked out the window of the bus to the west on my first day of fieldwork, new construction emerged on the horizon. A sea of high-rise condos and construction cranes populated the stretched-out landscape. They were densely clustered in the midst of the desolate buildings from the 2007 Pan American Games. The entrances to those buildings were closed. Grass grew in the cracks of the concrete parking lots. It was November 2009. The city had just won the bid for the 2016 Olympic Games. Brightly colored Rio 2016 banners hung on the buildings, draped as the promise of things hoped for. The bus headed west away from the lagoons toward a seemingly out of the way community. The paved road met unpaved side roads. As preparations for the Olympics began, the community where I was beginning my fieldwork was on the periphery of a soon to be central geography of the city. The space would become the new Barra Olympic Park, where the largest concentration of sporting events would be hosted, and the construction of the TransOlímpica Highway would soon traverse the community, rapidly linking it to more centralized spaces in the city. For now, the community waited in anticipation of forced removals as the main roads were widened and the highway construction began.

After the bus arrived at my stop, I walked up a concrete path, beyond a maze of white institutionalized-looking structures; a small, isolated building sat on an incline with a forested area behind it. There were no signs, just a closed door. Inside was the Alliance for Development (AFD), an NGO whose program, *Programa pelo jovens mulheres* (PEJM) (Program for young women), I was coming to observe. The program's large white poster featuring an orange soccer ball filled with a yellow flower greeted me as I opened the door. It read, "*A vitória começa com elas*," (Victory begins with them) (using the feminine form of *them*).[2] The faces of three very young, poor Brown girls in tattered T-shirts and long expressions appeared in the bottom corner of the poster while an older, wealthier white girl chasing a soccer ball in athletic clothes, cleats, and shin guards was positioned along the poster's edge. I would come to learn that neither the poorer-looking young Brown girls nor the wealthier-looking, older white girl represented the young women in the program. As Susanna, a senior staff member, would later tell me when looking at the poster, "Those aren't our girls."

The program's two sponsors, Nike Foundation and Nike Foundation and a regional funder,[3] were also listed on the poster, along with the government institution from which for the time being AFD rented its office and program space.

In this chapter, I examine how AFD conceptualized and then searched for adolescent girls with the "unique potential" to end poverty to join a session of its Nike Foundation–funded educational program.[4] This search, with the goal of recruiting one hundred adolescent girls, provides a lived and embodied way of understanding how the category of adolescent girl is constructed through the logic of the Girl Effect, and its consequences on the ground. It enables us to consider how the discourse of the Girl Effect managed to create a population category of "potential," and sought to fill it with actual people.

I argue that AFD's search was predicated on finding adolescent girls with an imagined Third World potential to end poverty. The Girl Effect branded particular adolescent girls—those racialized, classed, and situated geographically as Third World girls—with the potential to end poverty for themselves and their families, communities, nations, and the world. In my analysis, I elucidate how the Nike Foundation understood this potential, who embodied it, and who was intentionally or unintentionally excluded from it. I examine how the program sought out a population with potential; yet, if that potential was perceived as foreclosed or nonexistent, as in the case of the pregnant girls, older women, and young men, they were not recruited. This occurred despite the desperate need of the NGO to populate its program and the very real diversity of educational needs and desires in the community where the program operated.

SHE'S AN ECONOMIC POWERHOUSE

AFD's program was part of the Nike Foundation's joint philanthropic portfolio with the NoVo Foundation, called "She's an Economic Powerhouse: Economic Empowerment Models for Girls." The foundation launched the portfolio in October 2007[5] and gave one round of three-year funding to the NGO grantees in the portfolio. As articulated in the request for proposals (RFP), the portfolio was based on the following conceptualization of adolescent girls:

> We see girls as economic powerhouses. She's powerful today as the backbone of her family's economic and social health. She could be even more powerful tomorrow, if her role as an economic actor is shifted. The potential impact of this approach will complement ideals of gender equity and basic human rights. That's what this set of RFPs is all about.[6]

The portfolio sought to increase girls' power—as adolescents and future women—to end poverty:[7] "We want to see this power increase. But that growth relies on an unspoken truth: unless more of the 500 million adolescent girls living in the developing world today make safe passage to productive womanhood tomorrow, this means of ending poverty will plateau."[8] The portfolio included NGO grantees operating in diverse sociocultural and political-economic contexts, including Brazil, Paraguay, the Dominican Republic, Kenya, Burundi, Uganda, and Mongolia.[9]

According to AFD's grant contract with the Nike Foundation, this Brazilian-affiliate of a Washington, DC–based international NGO was required to provide informal "economic empowerment" education and training to 1,400 adolescent girls between 2008 and 2011. AFD was working with two subgrantees in Rio de Janeiro that were also implementing the program, and it had plans to expand the program beyond the city in future years. While I visited one of the subgrantees on a few occasions and observed both of them at the graduation ceremony, my observations were primarily limited to AFD. The primary courses "Technical Administration" and "Entrepreneurship" focused on developing skills useful for becoming an administrative assistant or an entrepreneur. Additional courses for each participant included training in basic computer and mathematics skills; writing and reading; and legal, gender, and human rights education.

Prior to its relationship with the foundation, AFD had worked with both young women and men. Nevertheless, since adolescent girls were the Nike's Foundation's target population, AFD developed a proposal that focused exclusively on adolescent girls rather than young men and young women. AFD was not alone in this approach. Beginning in 2005, the Nike Foundation's money targeting adolescent girls represented a new funding stream in development. The globalized focus on adolescent girls as a category of development distinct from girls, women, and youth emerged, in part, through the Nike Foundation's focus on the Girl Effect. Consequently, organizations working across the world—from small NGOs to large bilateral and multilateral organizations—shifted their focus to adolescent girls, even without organizational experience working with this population or substantive feminist training. The result for AFD and other NGOs in Brazil and beyond was a reworking of organizational programming without the experience or background to do so. Yet, rather than use the term adolescent girls, AFD, like the other two NGO programs in Brazil funded by the Nike Foundation, used the term *jovens mulheres*, translated as young women, when referring to the actual participants in their programs, who were approximately ages sixteen to twenty-four.

THE SEARCH

AFD's activities to recruit one hundred young women for the second session of its program spanned the months between the end of November

2009 and the beginning of March 2010. The terrain I traversed with the program staff covered an expansive, sprawling area on Rio de Janeiro's periphery. On some days, Susana, a senior staff member, and I spent our time in the surrounding community, walking through the quiet, dusty streets.[10] We hung program posters in the windows of beauty parlors and Internet cafés. We left flyers on desks and tacked posters to the bulletin boards of other local NGOs.

In February, during the week before *Carnaval*,[11] we visited a nearby neighborhood association in the late afternoon. The poster I described earlier hung on the closed door of the president's office. As we entered, the president, a middle-aged Afro-Brazilian woman, greeted us. When we sat down, we were joined by an older Afro-Brazilian woman from the neighborhood. After a brief conversation, Susana explained that the program was beginning a new session. She asked the president if she knew of any young women from their neighborhood who might be interested or eligible. The president asked which age groups we were recruiting. Susana responded, "Between sixteen- and twenty-four-years-old." The president explained in a matter-of-fact tone, "I know lots of young women, but they are all *buchinho*," using popular slang in Portuguese for describing a pregnant woman. Directing her question to both women, Susana asked, "Are there a lot of pregnant young women?" The president and the older woman nodded their heads in apparent disappointment. The president discussed how pregnancy ruins these young women's lives. It eliminates opportunities, she said, explaining that no one will hire them while pregnant. I anticipated that Susana would include the pregnant young women in the recruitment, because several young mothers were in the first session of the program. However, she did not.

Before we left, the older woman asked with a sarcastic laugh, "Do you have a program for adults?" Susanna responded, "No, just young women." The woman continued, "I am unemployed." Susanna asked, "What type of work do you do?" Looking down, the woman replied, "Cook." She paused for a moment, stating with more confidence, "I am a cook." Noticing the woman's discomfort, Susanna explained, "I ask because I might know of an opening." As the conversation ended, Susanna handed the president a new poster and a set of small informational flyers. She asked if she could take down the old poster on the door. After realizing it was stuck, almost glued to the glass, the president said that she would place the new one over it.

On other days, we traveled to more distant communities. On the first of March, the rains had already begun. Summer was ending. We hoped it would be the last day of recruitment. Despite the low numbers of recruits, the program was scheduled to begin in early March. As rain inundated the streets early in the morning, four of us from the program arrived at a public high school in a community approximately thirty minutes away by bus from AFD's office. Our group included Susana; Gabriella, a new employee; Vanessa, a fifteen-year-old intern and former program participant; and me. For six hours, we climbed up and down the school's stairways, entering more than sixteen classrooms. We interrupted academic lessons and provided teachers with unanticipated coffee breaks. In each classroom, we stood in a line before rows of young women and men seated at their desks in narrow yet deep rooms. Susana and Gabriella introduced the program as Vanessa and I walked around the classrooms passing out small flyers to interested young women. "SPORT – QUALIFICATION – WORK" was written in Portuguese on the flyers in bold, letters. A description of the desired participant was printed below in bold letters: "Female sex, 16–24 years old, and interested in entering the labor market or becoming an entrepreneur." In each classroom, Susana would introduce the program to the young people. During one introduction, she explained, "The course objective is preparation for the labor market. . . . We work to develop abilities that the labor market looks for, like teamwork, discipline, respect." She described the commitment, explaining to them, "The program has two main courses: technical administration and entrepreneurship. It is a five-month-long, intensive course, Monday through Friday, from eight to noon or one to five." In Rio de Janeiro, students attend public school either in the morning, afternoon, or evening, which enabled them to also attend the program while school was in session. The young people's eyes grew wide when they learned of the course's intensity. She further explained to them:

> Our program is completely free. Many times you see a program that says it's free, but then when you arrive there, you have to pay for the materials. We don't charge you even one *Real* because our funder, the Nike Foundation, already paid for you to participate. The Nike Foundation supports us for this program. You will receive a program T-shirt, the materials, and a very

> simple, small snack. But the program requires a lot of you—a lot of dedication and discipline. It may not pay off in the short or medium term, but in the long term, it will pay off. Right, teacher?

She leaned over to seek the teacher's reassurance. The teacher responded, "Yes." As I handed out flyers in the back of one of the classrooms, a young Afro-Brazilian man shyly asked me if a program also existed for men. I explained the program was currently only for young women. I asked him, "Do you want to participate?" He responded, "Yes." I handed him a flyer and told him to call the program the next year when it may serve young men as well. Addressing that dilemma, Susana told the young men in the room not to be disappointed. "The organization will have another program for young men and women in the future. But right now, it is only offering a course for women." Taking advantage of the young men's attention, she told them, "If you have a sister, a girlfriend, or a neighbor who fits the profile, you should take a flyer for her."

By the end of the long day, we had distributed all of the materials we brought with us, including a small strip of paper with information for the group interview the following day. The next day, we waited anxiously at the office for the dozens of young women we had invited to interview. Only two came. Who was the adolescent girl we were looking for? Did she exist? Where was she, and why was she so difficult to find?

CATEGORICAL COMPLICATIONS IN THE GIRL EFFECT

The search process reminded me of Gayatri Chakravorty Spivak's reflection on her search to reconstruct the Rani of Sirmur[12] in the colonial archives of British India. She writes:

> As I approached her house after a long series of detective maneuvers, I was miming the route of an unknowing, a progressive *différance*, an "experience" of how I could not know her. . . . There were no papers, the ostensible reason for my visit, and of course, no trace of the Rani. Again, a reaching and an un-grasping.[13]

The search for adolescent girls in Brazil was also "a reaching and an ungrasping." After months of searching, "adolescent girls" eluded us even as we anxiously pursued them. One hundred adolescent girls were neither found nor educated during the session I observed. This session officially began with a celebration of International Women's Day on March 8, 2010, with seventy participants. Moreover, after the first day, young women began to leave the program for various reasons, including needing to work, inability to pay for transportation, and health problems. By March 20, the program was down to sixty-four participants. The leaders of AFD explained to me that future sessions would compensate for the insufficient numbers in this one.

In spite of AFD's anxiety regarding recruitment, the length and location of the search were not factors in the insufficient number of recruits: There were adolescent girls nearby and the search had lasted three months. The problem instead was that the search for adolescent girls was part of a linear trajectory with an imagined beginning—the category of adolescent girl—and a fictitious end—the unleashing of the Girl Effect.

To understand how the category of adolescent girl is constructed within the Girl Effect, I draw on David Valentine's methodological approach to understanding the origins, meanings, and institutionalization of population categories. As Valentine notes, categories and the values attached to them are never neutral. Language is constitutive of the power relations operating in the discursive production of categories.[14] By considering what he identifies as "categorical complications" or, more specifically, who was included in and excluded from our search for adolescent girls, I elucidate the development discourse of the Girl Effect brand as the Nike Foundation and its partners sought to intervene in particular young women's lives, molding them into desirable developmental subjects.

The categorical complications I identify occurred as the knowledge, money, and other resources shaping this program moved within, across, between, and among unequal social actors and institutions in seemingly disparate places such as Beaverton, Oregon, and Rio de Janeiro. Many of these actors were unfamiliar and often ultimately unknowable to one another. Many of them will never be aware that they are imagined within, excluded from, or participating in the production of this category. These complications were created by profound relations of difference, yet they were ultimately constitutive of the category.

The official profile of the adolescent girls we were looking for was written in Portuguese on the program's flyers and posters: "Female sex, 16–24 years old, and interested in entering the labor market or becoming an entrepreneur."

Those generic characteristics reflected the Nike Foundation's mobilization of the universalized category. Yet, while AFD was officially looking for girls who fit this profile, as I will show, a range of nonofficial characteristics influenced recruitment. Those were less tangible and more conditional, and they emerged from AFD's idea of who constituted the target population in terms of class position, race, education level, employment status, and fertility. Those unofficial characteristics were, in part, a result of pressure—real or perceived—to achieve successful program outcomes. That pressure imbued the everyday of the program and created an ongoing aura of anxiety, particularly around recruitment. Consciously or unconsciously, the pressure influenced which participants the program selected even though the Nike Foundation has reiterated in communications that it was "inclusive of all adolescent girls, regardless of status, race, or any seen or unseen characteristics." Based on communication with the Nike Foundation "Nike Foundation grantees developed their own recruitment and retention strategies for their programs. These profiles and strategies varied widely within the grant portfolio (of several hundred grants totaling millions of dollars made by Nike Foundation) and included programming that was inclusive of a diversity of identity profiles."[15]

In relation to class, because the broader goal of the Girl Effect is to end poverty, the young women were poor, but not too poor. On two occasions, Susana told me about the daughter of a street recycler who left the first session of the program after only a few weeks. Susana surmised that the young woman's low class status meant she had little in common with the other participants. On the other hand, if a young woman's family earned even a small amount over the federal minimum monthly wage, she was considered to have too many resources at her disposal. In another example, the employer of a young woman's father paid for her private school tuition. Susana was concerned that she wasn't "needy" enough, as her access to the additional resource of a private school education gave her a significant advantage over the other young women.

Despite the official color-blind nature of the Nike Foundation's broader deployment of the category "adolescent girl," the search for recruits was also a racialized process. On one level, the search mapped onto the "racial formation"[16] of this Brazilian city, where the deeply uneven spatial distribution of opportunity occurs along race and class lines. The search for adolescent girls took place mostly in or on the edge of *favelas*, poor areas of the city where the majority of residents are Afro-Brazilian, mixed race, and/or darker skinned.[17] With a few exceptions, the young women in the first two sessions of the program identified as Black (*Negra*) or Brown (*Morena*) on the baseline survey the young women filled out. They differed from the young women in the nearby whiter, middle- and upper-class neighborhoods where residents have better access to opportunities, particularly high-quality, private primary and secondary education.

On a discursive level, the official, color-blind characteristics of the search and the broader mobilization of the race-neutral adolescent girl corresponded to US and Brazilian color-blind discourses in which AFD and Nike Foundation were enmeshed where race talk and racial differences are muted despite everyday racial discrimination and broader structural racialization.[18] As Susana once explained to me, "We focus on gender, not race." Although gender was the official focus of the program, as developed through the collaboration between AFD's Washington, DC, office and the Nike Foundation, in reality, the race of the young women could not be separated from their class positioning, the condition of poverty in which they lived, and their geographic location in neighboring favelas. Therefore, in practice, AFD was neither race-neutral in the search nor cognizant of the racialized dynamics through which it functioned. In this way, AFD mirrored Nike Foundation's broader practices which, despite being entirely focused on poor adolescent girls, included a majority of participants who were Black or Brown in countries across the Global South with different racial formations.

From an educational perspective, the young women needed to be in, willing to return to, or graduated from high school. If they were pursuing an education or training degree beyond high school, they were considered overqualified. An unemployed, twenty-four-year-old with a nursing degree, for example, was turned away from the program, as was her friend who was already enrolled in a professional program in oil and gas, a burgeoning field in Brazil. Since age was less of a sticking point and numbers were low, young women ages fourteen and fifteen were admitted, despite their limited employability in accordance with Brazilian labor law. Because the program focused on employability, the young women the program sought were also expected to be unemployed unless the employment was informal, very low-skilled, or within their family.

Based on my observations, the program also did not recruit pregnant young women, even though staff knew otherwise-qualified young women were in the surrounding communities and mothers had successfully completed the first session of the program. According to the Girl Effect logic, pregnant girls would no longer hold the potential to end poverty or, in other terms, they would be too reproductive to still be considered productive. The rationale for excluding older female adults is similar. They are imagined to no longer hold the potential to end poverty. As described in "Girls Count: A Global Investment and Action Agenda," funded by the Nike Foundation, older female adults have already moved into their "adult roles as wife, mother, worker, and citizen" and, thus, the moment for intervention has passed.[19]

The program also did not recruit young men even though numerous young men or their parents approached me to express interest in the program either during recruitment or at the program site. For example, a mother came to the program staff to ask if they would accept her stepson and, on another occasion, a young man and I discussed his interest in the program as he waited for his female friend during her interview. At the time, none of these young men had an equivalent educational opportunity in the community.

When asked during a group selection interview why the program only recruited adolescent girls, Carolina, a staff member, explained that they had decided to focus only on girls because when you invest in girls and women, everyone wins. To illustrate, she asked the girls, "If you go to the beach for the day, and the others do not have money, who pays?" The girls all responded, "the woman," nodding their heads. One of the girls stated, "The woman pays for transportation and lunch." Carolina asked, "And who wins? The woman and everyone around her," she explained.

In the logic of the Girl Effect, adolescent girls hold this unique potential given their presumed responsibility for the education, health, safety, and economic well-being of their children and communities. In communication with Nike Foundation, the organization has stated, "belief in the human potential of adolescent girls is not a statement about the potential of boys or the human potential of any other individuals and communities."[20] Yet, as the search revealed, this program and the other in Nike Foundation's Economic Empowerment Portfolio in Brazil accepted only adolescent girls, even though each of the NGOs had previously worked with young men and women and would later return to working with both after their grant funding ended.

The categorical complications illuminated through the search are based on the class position, race, education level, employment status, and fertility of the adolescent girls for whom AFD was searching. The complications reflect how a supposedly universal adolescent girl masked a very particular girl that the program actually targeted. In spite of the ostensible neutrality of her official profile in AFD's promotional materials, a Third World girl with the purported potential to end poverty was recruited. If girls lacked this potential, then they were not recruited—despite AFD's desperate need to find enough participants and the genuine diversity of educational and economic needs and desires in the community.

ADOLESCENT GIRLS AS A POPULATION CATEGORY IN THE GIRL EFFECT

> Adolescent girls aren't just "future women." They are girls.
> They deserve their own category.
>
> They need to be a distinct group when we talk about aid, education, sports, civic participation, health, and economics.
> Yes, they are future mothers.
> But they actually live in the present.[21]

Through the Girl Effect, the Nike Foundation insisted on an adolescent girl who is distinct from either girl or woman. At a small, invitation-only gathering I observed of elite philanthropists, corporate executives, and NGO directors at the CGI annual meeting in New York City in 2010, a senior

Nike Foundation staff member stated, "The category needs to be called out." Yet, distinguishing adolescent girls from girls and women creates contention and exclusions in the field. Later in the same meeting, a well-known and powerful philanthropist responded to this statement. She said, "It's incumbent upon us to make sure we don't allow the divide and conquer between women and girls. We need to stay strong about the issues that affect all females, and all need to be paid attention to." Despite contestations in its deployment or the difficulty in finding subjects, the category continued to be "called out," as the Nike Foundation senior staff member declared. In considering the category of girl, it is necessary to examine its roots in authoritative modern, Western conceptions of the child and the corresponding developmental stage of childhood. Both are socially constructed, varying across society and historical period. Yet, despite this variance, there is a conception of the "essential nature of childhood" that brings together psychology and sociology.[22] Wyness argues that the "legitimating power" of this "dominant framing" functions "to render childhood as a universal fact of life" regardless of context.[23] Within this framing, children are conceived of as dependent, malleable, and impressionable.[24] They occupy a stage preceding adult rationale, agency, and voice. Childhood as it intersects with gender produces the powerful binary of boyhood and girlhood.[25] The boundaries of this gendered dichotomy are carefully delineated and constantly monitored by the institutions of the family, the state, education, and religion.[26] Thus, if a child does not "naturally" fall within the binary, s/he is manipulated discursively and/or physically via technology to fit within the accepted gender categories.

Within this dichotomy, girlhood is conceived of as a sacred stage. It represents a period of sexual innocence and ethical purity for the female body prior to womanhood. Thus, a girl who is sexually active, pregnant, or a mother is barely legible as a child. Moreover, girlhood is understood as a moment of dependence. This relationship of dependence is conceived in physical, financial, and emotional terms. Thus, a girl who is perceived as independent—as a laborer, a street child, a mother—is outside the boundaries of girlhood and, thus, understood as a child in crisis and in need of saving.[27] Efforts to ensure girls as well as boys experience childhood, as conceived within a Western framing, are the frequent aim of campaigns targeting them throughout the Global South.

Through the Girl Effect and similar discourses, the girl is separated from womanhood through corporeal, sexual, temporal, sociocultural, ethical, economic, political, and other distinctions. Adolescence is the moment when the distinctions between girl and woman are concretized in the female body. Yet, as Catherine Driscoll argues, "Despite how obviously puberty seems to define a boundary between girlhood and womanhood and a field for female adolescence, adolescence is not a clear denotation of any age, body, behavior, or identity, because it has always meant the process of developing a self."[28] This self is understood to come to fruition during womanhood, the development stage at which a female purportedly takes on gendered roles as "wife, mother, worker, and citizen."[29] As Driscoll explains, "Feminine adolescence is always retrospectively defined, always definitively prior to the Woman it is used to explain."[30] In this respect, adolescence in the Girl Effect is defined as the moment prior to the development of the woman who will either reproduce or end poverty through appropriate, limited reproduction. It is a moment that is full of potential, and those girls who are still not reproductive are deemed to have the "unique potential" the foundation is seeking. It represents a temporal shifting of the developmental logic that has largely targeted women up until this point.

Through the Girl Effect discourse, adolescence becomes universalized as a moment of human development for all females without regard to cultural context and the constraints or demands of the conditions in which they live. Despite the dominant perception of adolescence as a transcultural, transhistorical concept, the adolescent girl is a late-modern Western concept.[31] In Driscoll's words, adolescence is critical to the construction of modern subjectivity:

> The concept of adolescence is central to the development of the modern subject, and the difficult negotiations and performances of feminine adolescence are crucial data for modern theories of subjectivity, where they most often figure as a definitive failure of subjectification (of coming to be a coherent self-aware subject).[32]

In this conceptualization, the discursive and material move from girl to woman is predetermined. It is the very anticipation of this transition that creates the impetus of the Girl Effect program to shape her through

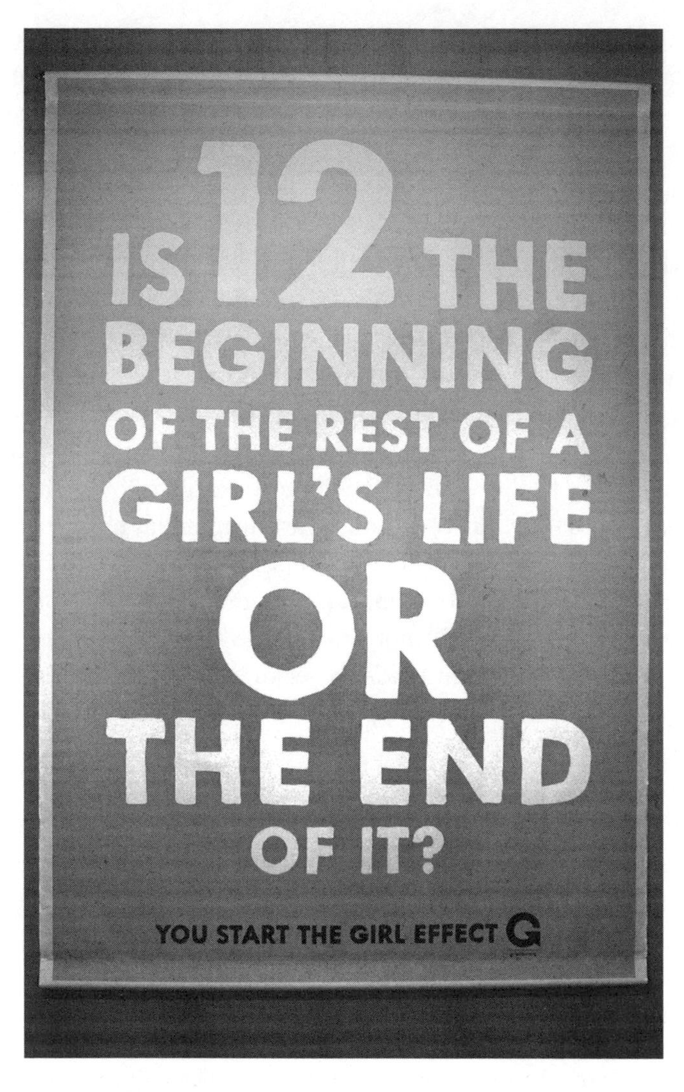

Figure 9. Photograph of Nike Foundation's poster, "Is 12 the beginning of the rest of a girl's life or the end of it?," displayed at "The Revolution Will Be Led by a 12-Year-Old Girl: The Girl Effect Exhibit," Mercy Corps Action Center Gallery, Portland, Oregon, January 2011. Photograph by author.

adolescence. As a moment, it is understood as central to the success or failure of girls becoming desirable subjects of development. Defining this perspective is a question posed at the entrance to the Girl Effect Exhibit. The rotating exhibit, paid for by Nike, Inc., was set up from November 2010 through January 2011 at the headquarters of Mercy Corps, a Nike Foundation grantee, located in Portland, Oregon, near the corporation's world headquarters. When I visited in January 2011, there was a large orange poster hanging on the wall with the following question: "Is 12 the beginning of the rest of a girl's life or the end of it?"

This question fundamentally concerned the potential success or failure of a girl to become a valued subject of development. To ensure her success, the intervention to mold her into this imagined woman must occur during the moment of adolescence, as Nike Foundation president and CEO Maria Eitel urges, "before it's too late for them—and for us."[33] Through its investment strategy, the Nike Foundation aims toward "smoothing her path from girlhood to womanhood."[34]

The pathway, it claims, is "riddled with trapdoors," such as pregnancy, child marriage, and HIV/AIDS.[35] The Nike Foundation consequently seeks to "close the highest leverage trapdoors" so that adolescent girls remain on the desired path.[36] Eitel describes her understanding of these pathways in an interview in the *Huffington Post*:

> Even though not nearly enough was being done, there were a few innovative programs out there showing that with the right opportunities, she could finish school, marry and have children when she's ready, stay healthy and pass all of that to her future children. That's one path a girl can take.
>
> The other more common path is where she turns 12 and all of her opportunities are shut down. She gets pulled out of school to face early marriage, pregnancy, risk of HIV infection. When that happens, things are pretty much set for her and for the next generation.
>
> We realized to solve poverty, we'd have to get to her before she arrived at that intersection; we had to figure out how to get her on the first path. And if we could do that, it wouldn't just be an investment in her, but an investment in everyone around her.[37]

In this theoretical conceptualization, the path an adolescent girl takes determines whether she is a recognizable subject of development. If she survives the trapdoors, she is valuable as a developmental subject. The preconditions for her potential to be unleashed are secured. If she falls through a trapdoor, she continues the "intergenerational cycle of poverty." As Eitel describes later in the interview, "This is urgent and everyone is losing. To change her life and her possibilities, she then transforms every child who will be born into poverty. She has the opportunity to break that intergenerational cycle and that's very unique to an adolescent girl. What happens to her at that transitional moment will determine whether her family is on an upward spiral or a downward spiral."[38]

These pathways echo the "culture of poverty"[39] discourse and the millennial discourse of the "end of poverty."[40] The Nike Foundation focuses its intervention during adolescence in an effort to simultaneously safeguard and manage the female body in the formative interstitial moment between girlhood and womanhood when it is imagined that she can be molded as the conduit for ending poverty rather than the vehicle for the intergenerational continuation of it.[41] Her presumed (hetero)sexuality triggers anxiety regarding the literal reproduction of poverty. Thus, if she has the potential to become the vehicle for the intergenerational cycle of poverty, she is also positioned as the potential conduit for the millennial notion of the "end of poverty" if she could be caught in time, as echoed by Ngozi Okonjo-Iweala, then-managing director of the World Bank, at the "Girl Effect on Development" session at the 2009 World Economic Forum.[42] As Okonjo-Iweala explained, elaborating in her remarks on the World Bank's catchphrase, "Gender equality as smart economics," from its 2007 GAP,[43] "Investing in women is smart economics, and investing in girls, catching them upstream, is even smarter economics. If you invest in girls, if you educate girls, if you get girls into jobs, you solve so many problems."[44] Her statements were attributed to the power of the Girl Effect. They are unimaginable outside of its logic. Within it, girls theoretically represent the potential future rather than the present fate of a family, a community, a nation, and even the world.[45]

Although those two imagined paths informed who was included and excluded from the population category during AFD's search for adolescent girls, an adolescent girl neither holds poverty inside her nor determines its future. To conceive of such a possibility is to create a reductionist view of girls and women. Moreover, this conception creates an individualized, girl-centered solution to ending poverty. It positions Black and Brown girls as disproportionately responsible for solving the structural conditions and problems of poverty created by histories of exploitation in capitalist development.

DIFFERENCE AND THE ADOLESCENT GIRL

When the Nike Foundation launched its website, it featured the quote, "Adolescent girls are adolescent girls, whether they are living in a rural village in Africa or the center of Paris or in New Jersey. If you know more than one teenage girl, this you know."[46] This quote reflects the universalizing aspiration of the Girl Effect. It flattens difference across geography. Despite their shared gender and age, adolescent girls in suburban towns in New Jersey, the city of Paris, and villages in the African continent do not have equal or even similar subject positions. This statement masks critical differences among race, class, sexuality, religion, language, nation, and geography that radically structure and differentiate girls' and young women's lived experiences, educational possibilities, and employment opportunities throughout the Global North and South. Adolescent girls do not constitute a unitary category, and all subjects in it are not equal. To understand how the category of adolescent operates within the Girl Effect, I examine the multiple, hierarchically differentiated, yet invisible subject positions operating within it. I do not conceive of them as fixed or essential subject positions; rather, I employ them as heuristics for examining how they are constructed and deployed in the Girl Effect.

The first subject position I identify is the privileged, unmarked female subject of the Global North. "Co-formations" of difference across history and geography produce varying racialized, classed, sexualized, religious, linguistic, and national landscapes of privilege.[47] This unmarked subject—perhaps a middle-class, white girl from New Jersey in the United States—occupies legally, politically, and socially protected spaces of the nation-state and is able to move across borders. She is presumed (hetero)sexual, and she is responsible with her sexual choices. She is the "empowered" girl, defined by her level of education, future employability, consumer status, and desirable reproductive potential. She is revered in late-modern Western conceptions of girlhood, occupying the space from which the always already disempowered Third World girl is compared.

The second subject position is the privileged, unmarked female subject of the Global South. During the search, the racial and class positioning, education, and potential employability of this white or lighter-skinned, mixed-race, middle- or upper-class subject made her invisible in the recruitment, even though a representation of her was featured in the recruitment poster I described in the beginning. It was as if she did not exist in the zone of the city where the program operated, even though the program desired that all of the young women they recruited attain her levels of class, education, and future employment. Following David Valentine, I flag this historically unmarked subject to make visible the circulating power relations within the Girl Effect.

In contrast, a poor girl of color in the Global North is neither the Girl Effect's Third World object of intervention nor is she one of the privileged unmarked subjects of the Global North and South with which she is implicitly compared. By occupying a marginalized subject position within a geopolitical location of privilege, she represents the face of the periphery within the core, the Third World within the First World. Her subject position corresponds to centuries of colonial exploitation and forced migrations, as well as ongoing transnational migration and labor, causing the rigid construction of First World/Third World binary to be blurred. Despite her location in First World cities where the institutions that produce the Girl Effect are situated, she is invisible in the Girl Effect. In an equation of imagined value creation, her potential returns are low and, therefore, her needs, desires, and demands are obscured.

TOWARD A CRITIQUE OF THIRD WORLD POTENTIAL

The search for adolescent girls in Brazil has served as an ethnographic entrée into understanding the category's constitutive nature within the Girl Effect. It reveals which adolescent girls were sought out and why, which returns me to the premise of this chapter. Based on my observations, the subjects who were recruited for the program were imagined to hold the Third World girl potential imagined, branded, and promoted by the Girl Effect.

Yet, what did the program look like for the young women included? The young women who entered this program came with high hopes for their futures. As an educator, I was excited on the first day of the program when the young women went around the room telling us their professional goals despite the multiple constraints on their lives—one wanted to be an architect, another a veterinarian, a doctor, and so on. Yet, by the end of the six-month program, the same group of young women went around the same room telling a former Nike Foundation staff member who was visiting that their professional aspiration was to become administrative assistants. It was striking. The visitor actually turned to me, quite startled, and asked in English, "Why do they all want to be administrative assistants?"

The professional desires of the young women had been shaped by the program's curriculum. Despite the focus on training administrative assistants and entrepreneurs, the program was largely unsuccessful in finding the participants jobs either before or after graduation or helping them to launch new businesses; when successful, the program channeled the participants into insecure, often temporary, low-wage employment in businesses such as telecommunications centers, supermarkets, and bus companies. There were few exceptions. In reflecting on this problem with João, a researcher from Gender Justice Organization (GJO) (the other NGO where I conducted fieldwork in Rio de Janeiro that was contracted to conduct the monitoring and evaluation [M&E] for AFD), he explained: "To what point is the program going to qualify them? Qualification is structural." He emphasizes, "80% of the young women are Black. Racism is a structural problem. You can tell them the laws, inform them of their rights, but with such low levels of education, what are you going to do?" As João reflected, because the Nike Foundation was interested in proving their economic empowerment model, the program focused on quick results rather than the more difficult, yet necessary task of addressing core educational, social, and economic inequities in their lives—those inequities due to co-formations of racism, classism, patriarchy, and poverty that result in low quality schooling, challenges in completing secondary education, difficulties pursing higher education, and intense discrimination in the labor market.

If the program had been focused on actually transforming their futures, it potentially could have worked with the participants to pass the *vestibular*, the rigorous, highly competitive national exam to enter the high quality, free public university system in Brazil. That would have enabled the participants to pursue the stable professional jobs they expressed a desire for and that their white, middle-class, wealthy counterparts will have access to. But passing the exam requires a solid educational foundation and extensive tutoring, and the classes, which are mostly private, were well beyond their means. While the work of scholars such as Martin Carnoy and David Plank[48] has demonstrated the persistence of these structural educational challenges in Brazil, the program could have tailored its resources to address those educational barriers in the Brazilian context. During the time of the study, many of the state and federal universities had adopted affirmative action quotas from which the program participants could have potentially benefited. By 2012 it would become law for federal universities to reserve 50 percent of spaces at the university for students "coming from public schools, low-income families, and who are of African or indigenous descent."[49] Yet, from my observations, entering the university was not a primary goal of the Girl Effect.

The limits of Third World potential were revealed during various moments in my fieldwork. One of those moments was a conference call I participated in between representatives of AFD, its DC office, GFO, and the Nike Foundation. I was translating the call for João. During the call, Jim, the senior staff member overseeing the program from AFD's DC office, stated, "I am surprised by the numbers who want to go to the university. The program helps them to do that, but there are other things before." Drawing on the numbers from the M&E questionnaire, he asked the Nike Foundation staff, Jennifer and Erica, "What can we do to better position them to make that dream possible?" Erica commented, "Young people often don't know what to aspire to. University is the one thing they are familiar with. The reality of whether they would be able to take advantage of it." She further explained, "Asking about aspirations is one thing. But it is a limited response." Marcela, AFD's executive director, referred to a "decrease in those who aspire to the university," revealed between the baseline and the end line results. Jim said, "It could be attributed to a different understanding of what else there is." Erica further explained, "The university is not an end line aspiration. Now they may realize that there are other ways to reach their aspirations, such as through an apprenticeship, start their own business. There are other ways to reach those goals." Erica's response reminded me of a conversation João and I had recently had when I returned to GJO after an interview with Tiago, a senior white male executive at a European transnational corporation in Rio de Janeiro who was one of the most active mentors in AFD's professional mentoring program for the young women. As I had recounted to João, Tiago told me in our discussion about AFD's training program, "We need to have more workshops for the young women with examples of those who are *pedreiras*, female bricklayers." In response, I asked, "But in Brazil, attending the public university is free if you can qualify. Shouldn't the program be preparing the young women for the *vestibular* or helping them to find free preparation courses for the exam?" He responded to me, "They don't need to go to the university. It is not a requirement. If later down the road they want to, then that's fine." As I finished telling João, he had a look of disgust on his face, "He would never say that for his daughter."

In this way, the Girl Effect is about "Other people's children,"[50] to borrow the phrase from educator Lisa Delpit. As Erica and Tiago revealed, it is not what a white corporate or foundation employee from either the United States or Brazil would aspire to for his or her own child. They would want their daughter to pursue higher education. The Girl Effect is about adolescent girls and young women from Other races, ethnicities, classes, religions, or languages and from Other communities, nations, or regions of the world. It is about adolescent girls and young women from places that most of the corporate participants in my study will never visit and about girls and young women they will never physically meet.

As I observed the power and influence of the Girl Effect grow over time, I also witnessed a range of people quietly yet actively contest, albeit on unequal terms, the underlying logic of the Girl Effect and its understanding of girls and young women.

Toward the end of my fieldwork in Brazil Marcela shared this idea during a staff meeting, "[The young women] are not all going to be leaders or change the reality in their communities." She asked us, "What do you ask of your child?" Another staff member remarked, "To be someone in life." Marcela continued, "The girls first need to take care of their own lives. We need to stop with this idea," pausing, "that they are going to take care of the streets." During a personal conversation, she furthered her critique: "Sometimes I think we are asking too much of [these young women]. So, they will do what their mothers and grandmothers did." Her comments point to the possibility of reproducing gendered patterns of social reproductive labor rather than transforming them through the logic of the Girl Effect.

The Girl Effect asks these girls and young women to be responsible for the lives, well-being, and futures of those far beyond themselves, including their families, their communities, their nations, and the world, without seeking to provide them with the same opportunities its corporate creators would imagine for their own child. It is based on the assumption that these girls and young women are already responsible for more than themselves and that investments in their education and training are enabling them to unleash this potential on multiple scales. If these girls and women are more responsible for the daily survival and well-being of their families and communities, their responsibility is based on a particular set of historically produced, sociocultural and political-economic conditions. They are not naturally more responsible or selfless than other girls, women, or men. Nor are they inherently "excellent resource managers" or "proactive investors," as my Nike Foundation interviewees' market-based language imagined them. If they are these things, it is because they are structurally positioned to be so.

However, given the monetary power of corporations and corporate foundations, as well as the dependency of NGOs—such as the one I studied—on funding institutions, AFD's staff were wary of potential backlash from current and future corporate funders and, thus, carefully considered the character, depth, and public nature of their critiques. As Marcela explained to me, "I don't want to be developing a machine that I don't believe in." Yet, as she further explained, "If we conclude that the best investment is not in young women, will we take the risk to tell Nike that? No, we cannot. If we were independent, I would, but we are not independent of our funder." To my knowledge, Marcela never told the foundation that she questioned the focus on adolescent girls. AFD's focus on adolescent girls' Third World potential did not persist beyond its grant contract with the Nike Foundation, which ended in 2012. Adolescent girls disappeared as the target of its programming. It had strategically employed the category to secure funding; yet, when it did not receive renewed funding, the organization returned to its prior focus on young women and young men. This demonstrated that the category itself was ephemeral.

AFD's strategic, temporary employment of the adolescent girl simultaneously reveals the influential nature of corporate and other development funding on NGO programs and the contingent, rather than persistent, power that corporations have on NGO practices and, correspondingly, the lives, educations, and futures of girls and women. The fact that the category was eclipsed demonstrates how these corporate efforts are deeply tied to financial resources and accompanying forms of authoritative knowledge. This consequently reveals both the power and the fragility of corporate efforts aimed at particular girls and women.

By ethnographically documenting the rise and fall of this particular category, this chapter provides evidence of how powerful yet transitory population categories are in development. In doing so, it offers a framework for conceiving of the construction and operation of development categories, whether they are adolescent girls, small farmers, street children, or any of the ever-shifting population categories targeted in development. This enables the examination of how such categories obscure the broader structural forces that influence them and how their employment through development interventions can reproduce, rather than transform, existing relations of power.

5 Proving the Girl Effect

She should be a statistic.[1]

Early one afternoon in late November 2009, I sat down alongside six young women who were being interviewed to participate in the second session of AFD's economic empowerment program. Two other young women, Luciana, age sixteen, and Luiza, age fifteen, were standing with Susana, the senior staff member, at the front of the classroom. Susana explained to the interviewees that she had invited Luciana and Luiza, who were completing the first session of the program, to share their experiences because, as she said, "Who better to talk about the program than them?"

Luciana spoke with certainty and confidence. She described the long selection process she and her colleagues completed before they entered the program. At the end of this description, she was emphatic about one point. When talking about the baseline questionnaire they had to complete before beginning the program, she said, "They ask you about *everything. Everything.*"

Everything refers to the data the Nike Foundation collected through a questionnaire in its monitoring and evaluation (M&E) strategy to prove the Girl Effect as a theory of social change. From my interviews with employees to conversations I participated in at global forums, the foundation repeatedly made strong claims that the development world did not have sufficient

Figure 10. Photograph of the primary classroom at AFD in Rio de Janeiro, July 2010. Photograph by author.

knowledge about adolescent girls. At a small, invitation-only gathering I observed of elite philanthropists, corporate executives, and NGO directors at the CGI annual meeting in New York City in 2009, a Nike Foundation senior staff member explained to the group, "Girls are *missing* and *invisible* from the statistics. For accountability, we need to *count* and *track* her." The questionnaire asking adolescent girls about "everything," as Luciana suggested, contributed to this effort. As quoted above, it enabled the foundation to create a compilation of statistics it could use to promote its programs, justify its budget, employ as evidence to advocate for resources, and convince more important development institutions, such as the World Bank or DFID, to focus on girls. In its interactions with AFD, Nike Foundation staff members made contradictory statements regarding why this information was necessary. In a conference call among staff from AFD, its Washington, DC office, and GJO, Erica, Nike Foundation's staff member, explained, "Data collection is only to help the program," as they discussed the problems with data collection, particularly around low participation in the baseline and endline questionnaires. Yet, earlier in the call, Jennifer, another Nike Foundation staff member, repeatedly asked for translated tables from Portuguese to English with data from the baseline, explaining, "For us at the Nike Foundation, when we want to pick this up and use the data for presentations, it will be difficult."

The Nike Foundation's quest for data did not go uncontested, however. In a conversation following the Nike Foundation senior staff member's assertions of missing and invisible girls at the CGI annual meeting, an executive director of a transnational NGO, a grantee of the Nike Foundation, told me in an angry whisper, "We don't agree with that. There is a lot of data on girls." Regardless of whether this was true or not, by saying there wasn't sufficient data on girls, the foundation created a niche for itself, a purpose for collecting and controlling its own data.

As Sarah, a Nike Foundation senior staff member explained to me in an interview, the foundation was developing a "knowledge base" on adolescent girls through its M&E strategy. This knowledge base was predicated on historical familiarity with the trope of Third World girl, learned through centuries of colonial interventions targeting colonized, racialized girls and women. These interventions informed how she was understood by the Nike Foundation in the present and made her knowable regardless of where she was geographically, politically, or culturally located. Thus, even prior to knowing actual girls, the Nike Foundation built on universalized knowledge of the trope of Third World girl. However, as Anna Tsing[2] reminds us, aspirations to the universal are "an always unfinished achievement."[3] In this sense, the project of producing knowledge about this universalized subject was always incomplete. It required the ongoing labor of knowledge production across profound relations of difference. This occurred in part, through an elaborate and well-coordinated, yet regularly contested, process of attempting to prove the Girl Effect through the creation and use of M&E technologies.

It was a recursive process of knowledge production and educational intervention predicated on a particular epistemological understanding of, or way of knowing, Third World girls. On one level, this knowledge informed, and was informed by, the educational interventions funded by the foundation. On another level, the knowledge created about adolescent girls through its programs was disseminated to multiple audiences to advocate on girls' purported potential to end poverty. These diverse audiences included the corporation's and foundation's own employees, their current and potential partners from small, cash-strapped NGOs, and ministries of finance in the Global South, as well as other corporations, bilateral and multilateral organizations, and public audiences in the Global North. The foundation educated these different publics on what they should know about adolescent girls, why it matters, and how they should act upon it. While the foundation's messaging changed depending on the audience—from soft messaging, such as a viral Girl Effect video that tugs on the public's heart strings, to hard economic figures on returns on investment and effects on GDP for ministries of finance and World Bank officials—the foundation universalized the data it collected on diverse girls around the world to shape its messages on their value for development.

Within this model, based on my experiences, the foundation measured the "success" of its programs in two ways. The first was whether or not it was effective in unleashing the Girl Effect, and thus whether its theory of change was true. The second was whether it was successful in influencing more powerful institutions in the global economy, such as the World Bank, WEF, and DFID, to transform their programs and policies to focus on girls. Consequently, the actual young women and their education were not the end goal. Rather, as the foundation extended its power over new bodies, institutions, and geographies by asserting itself as an expert on girls, the girls became a means for creating broader development change and for establishing relationships between the corporation, foundation, and these "bigger players," as one interviewee described them. The success of such an educational program should be measured based on the program's ability to serve the educational needs, aspirations, and rights of young people. Their education should be promoted because they matter in and of themselves rather than because of their potential value as instruments of development change.

THE NIKE FOUNDATION'S MONITORING AND EVALUATION PROGRAM

Over time, the Nike Foundation developed an extensive M&E program to prove its theory of change is true and to disseminate its findings to influence other institutions. As explained in the RFP for its Economic Empowerment portfolio, the "goal in issuing this RFP is twofold: (i) to test, validate and further refine our Economic Empowerment model as a comprehensive economic empowerment model for girls, and (ii) to develop and/or test other comprehensive programmatic and investment models that deliver economic empowerment for girls."[4] The ultimate goal of the RFP was to prove that the theory of change was correct and the model of economic empowerment was successful.

Laura, a Nike Foundation partner, explained to me how this worked in an interview in June 2009:

> They have this M&E framework into which the grantees' work is supposed to feed. The reason we are supporting you is because we want to say this after we fund you. It is really particular and really easy for them to be disappointed. . . . They have big plans for the messaging around the M&E, which is why they are trying to set up the M&E so carefully. It is almost pre-messaged. Let's see. Its engagement with grantees is set up in such a way that their findings are already anticipated. Can we say this, can we say that?

Laura told me how she felt uncomfortable with this approach:

> "I am very committed to advocacy and very earnest. But I feel as though they play a little fast and loose from what they can actually say from the data. You cannot say that for every $5 dollars a girl makes that it delays marriage for five months. That has been an ongoing tension. They want to grab it and run with it. But then they want the legitimacy of the research. They want the fireworks."

The Nike Foundation originally contracted with International Center for Research on Women (ICRW) to develop its strategy and implement its program. ICRW provided the foundation with extensive expertise and leadership when they entered the field of gender and development. The Nike Foundation brought the program in-house after tensions arose between the organizations, and it decided that it wanted to keep the knowledge and money internally. Sarah explained this shift:

> It is so integral to the heartbeat of how you make decisions that we ended up pulling it in and investing internally. It is to make sure that the knowledge

> actually stays internal to help make decisions on future investments and so that we actually also keep money that is spent on M&E kind of tightly focused, if you like.

This decision also signaled that the foundation no longer needed the expertise and legitimacy of ICRW, which had once served a critical role in the foundation's transition to focusing on adolescent girls. When the foundation began its work with girls in 2004–2005, it was completely reliant on the expertise and legitimacy of development organizations with a track record in the field. Within five years, the foundation became a key expert in the field as a result of its branding, marketing, and public relations savvy; resources to hire the most creative, efficient professionals available; and its ability to convene powerful actors. As Laura explained to me in our interview in June 2009, "They have a whole set of special initiatives that are very high profile. They are given resources or people from other parts of the corporation for getting the messages out. They have lots of PR firms that work with them on their advertising. It is indistinguishable from their product advertising. It is issue rather than product advertising." This resulted in videos, banners, exhibitions, celebrity allies, and highly publicized events at global forums that secured girls a spot on the world stage and the Nike Foundation as the most recognizable girl expert in the world. The combination of these factors brought the corporate foundation legitimacy in the eyes of both the corporate world and the development world. Its M&E program was critical to enacting this broader strategy in its first five years of development.

Jessica, a Nike Foundation senior staff member, described the relationship between the M&E program and the foundation's theory of change relationship to me in an interview:

> What the foundation is trying to do is catalyze a theory of change we call the Girl Effect. And we describe that as being what happens when you have girls who are empowered across different dimensions. They are educated, they are healthy, wealthier, etc., and because of that they are able to participate in society in new and different ways. And that catalyzes the change in that society so that society itself again is healthier, wealthier, more dynamic, you know, and, ultimately, drives prosperity. What we are trying to figure out is how do you most effectively empower girls in order to unlock that process. In terms of the monitoring and evaluation, it is both

> an exercise in understanding whether that Girl Effect theory of change is true and why it's true. So [we're] looking at all of the potential pathways that girl might set into motion that Girl Effect phenomenon and also looking at all the different ways you can go from disenfranchised girls to empowered girls.

Even though the foundation operated on the assumption the Girl Effect was true in its marketing and communications strategies, it developed a methodology for collecting data on girls that framed them in economistic, market-based terms. As described by Sarah, this occurred on two levels. The first level focused on the adolescent girls' level of social, human, and financial capital vis-à-vis her family and community:

> We measure outcomes for girls. So is she more educated, is she healthy as she transitions through adolescence, is she HIV-free, what confidence gaining skills has she obtained as a result of different programs that are in place, how many more friends does she have, is she more mobile? There are all of those questions that really look at, has her *social capital* increased? Has her *human capital* increased by education and skills acquisition? And then has her *financial capital* actually increased through access to savings or access to credit? Or even access to inheritance. So we look at those three aspects at the level of the girl to see whether just her asset level has increased across those dimensions. . . . We know that when she has assets earlier in life she does all of these great things with it because she is an excellent resource manager.

The foundation then developed a system for examining how this acquisition of assets occurs, and how girls use these assets for themselves, their families, and communities:

> So we measure those outcomes for girls, but we also try and measure the Girl Effect, which is once she has those assets, what does she do with them? So, we have set up measurement and evaluation methodologies, at least, to try and track, when she has resources under her control, what does she do? Does she reinvest in the community? Does she reinvest in her family?. . . You can go into a community and you can see it. And you know what she does when she has, say for example, she has a small little business. She earns an income from that business. She puts herself back into school. She puts her brother back into school. She pays her brother's tuition. You can see what she does with her resources to know that the phenomenon exists.

To specifically measure these outcomes, the Nike Foundation employed a set of data collection technologies it created.

Universal Indicators

The foundation developed a set of "universal indicators"—age of first pregnancy or first birth, the age of marriage, and level of education—for understanding adolescent girls in all the countries across Latin America, Africa, and Asia where the foundation funded programs. As Jessica explained, "We have the universal set but then for each investment and for the purpose of those investments, then we would add on others that we are specifically trying to test for." Jessica described the foundation's understanding of those universal indicators as follows:

> The age of pregnancy or first birth, the age of marriage, and secondary school education, those three are the most robust by a long shot. The sense is that if one or more of those is good, that is pretty much all you need to know about the situation of girls in that country. If you knew nothing about the country situation but that there was a 95 percent school graduation rate, you probably wouldn't need to know more to know that girls are in a great position. If the age of marriage is twenty-five and not fifteen, you already know that you are in a subset of countries.

Within the Nike Foundation's vision, those universal indicators served as proxy measures for the ultimate measures of income rates and accumulated assets, both financial assets and material goods, as outlined in the foundation's overall strategic plan that Sarah shared with me in 2009. As described by Rachel, a Nike Foundation staff member, those measures were part of positioning the Girl Effect as "an economic equation." That equation was critical to making the foundation's strategy relevant to Nike, Inc. and for other institutions, such as the World Bank and WEF. In an interview, Sarah described the specific relationship of the "universal indicators'" to the Girl Effect:

> Then if the Girl Effect really sets into motion then what you should see, just to cut through everything, you should see indicators like graduating from secondary school, those rates going up. You should see age at first birth, hmmm, increasing from 12 and 13, like the lowest ages of first birth increasing to the ages of when she might finish secondary school. Basically, if she

> can get through secondary school, and then there is access to credit markets and the financial economic markets are opened up to her then she is kind of on the path to unleash the Girl Effect.

To understand if and how these indicators contribute to the larger economic equation on girls' value for development, the foundation developed an M&E plan with its grantees for each program it funded in the Economic Empowerment Portfolio. A critical part of this plan was a tailored questionnaire that the girls were to complete at the beginning and end of the programs. With a degree of variation, all three of the NGOs funded by the Nike Foundation in Brazil collected data on the same universal indicators during the time period of the study. While my interviewees at Nike Foundation who ran the M&E program at that time presented the approach of using universal indicators as the foundation's overall M&E approach as of 2010, and the strategic plan that was shared with me mirrored this, Nike Foundation to me in their feedback to the manuscript in 2017 says it was only used with "a very small subset of Nike Foundation grantees." The foundation explained to me it later discontinued this M&E strategy. As described by the foundation, "The evolution of the M&E approach was informed by the recognition that a more bespoke approach to each grantee's project would be more useful. The approach going forward allowed for a range of methodologies."[5]

Questionnaire

The questionnaire AFD develoved, in collaboration with Nike Founation, ICRW, and GJO was aligned with the universal indicators the Nike Foundation sought to measure. The questionnaire included sections focused on the following areas: basic demographic information, levels of educational attainment, family, forms of documentation, labor and employment history, personal and family income, material goods, attitudes regarding gender norms, affective and sexual experiences, experiences with motherhood, levels of social integration and friendships, sports, levels of violence, and levels of self-efficacy and self-confidence.[6]

The section on basic demographic information sought information on their age, race and ethnicity, and religion, and inquired about their levels of educational attainment and their educational aspirations for higher education and/or further training. The questionnaire asked about the configuration of family members they live with, the educational levels of their parents, the type and level of support they receive from family members, overall family income level, and the contributions of different family members to household income and resources. They were also asked about their forms of documentation, including if they have a birth certificate, identity card, CPF (Brazilian identification number), and work card, and if they are registered voters.

The section on their labor and employment history focused on the informal and formal labor market including their experiences with internships, self-employment, and paid formal labor. It also asked about the amount and usage of their salary, household expenditures, and status of savings and checking accounts, including amounts and percentage of salary deposited per month. There were also detailed questions on the material goods they own. For example, it included questions on whether they or their families have a refrigerator, microwave, TV, stereo, video player, DVD, desktop or laptop computer, or cell phone. The questionnaire also asked a series of questions relating to whether they paid in part or full for the goods, and whether or not they had autonomy to sell the goods.

A portion of the questionnaire focused on attitudes regarding gender norms and affective and sexual experiences. For example, it asked which forms of sex they have engaged in, including vaginal, oral, and anal sex; the age of first sexual experience; contraception use; and relationship and marital status. Furthermore, the questionnaire asked about their experiences with motherhood, specifically whether they have children, how many they have, and the age of their first pregnancy. Other questions included levels of social integration and friendships; experiences with different types of violence; sports practices, including which sports they play, why or why not, and how frequently; and their levels of self-esteem and self-confidence.

According to AFD's procedures, before completing the baseline questionnaire, the participants eighteen years or older must have signed an informed consent form agreeing to participate in the interviews, and those under age eighteen needed their parent's or guardian's signature. Based on communication with the Nike Foundation, "the survey that was approved by this partner organization's Institutional Review Board and reviewed by the Nike Foundation did not ask about, list, or require responses to questions about specific forms of sex in which girls may have engaged."[7] Drafts of the questionnaire that were shared with me show that the Nike Foundation and their partner, International Center for Research on Women, edited various versions of the survey with the question included. I also have the final questionnaire that was distributed to the young women. Moreover, the results from the question regarding forms of sex were outlined in the baseline report on the survey results that I translated from Portuguese to English for the NGO to send the Nike Foundation as part of the organization's required M&E documents.

GIRLS AS DATA

Through the foundation's M&E program, the young women in the programs became research subjects in a social experiment. In this sense, building on Paul Rabinow, the educational programs and their classrooms became a laboratory and the young women became sources of data.[8] This process of seeing "people as data,"[9] as Thomas Popkewitz explains, was part of the development of a "modern way of knowing" as governments shifted from focusing on their subjects to governing the population.[10] This focus on population originates in the field of power Michel Foucault identifies as government or "the conduct of conduct."[11] For Foucault, the purpose of "modern" government is to ensure "the welfare of the population, the improvement of its condition, the increase of its wealth, longevity, health, etc."[12] As a result, variables such as fertility and health become critical to the management of a population.[13] In this way, government as a field of power directed at adolescent girls by the entire apparatus of the Girl Effect aims to "empower" the population to ensure its health, improvement, and well-being, and, correspondingly, to secure the economic prosperity of nations and the world.

As observed in this study, according to Popkewitz, "Data required a double reflexivity." It necessitated "the objectification of the self so that the inner characteristics of the person could be known as data and used for change."[14] It also involved what Popkewitz describes as "the re-inscription of the data into positive strategies by which groups and individuals would become agents of change."[15] In this way, girls were objectified as research subjects in the Nike Foundation's M&E program. They became disembodied data for proving the Girl Effect's efficacy as a theory of change in which girls are the primary agents for ending poverty. The educational interventions were critical to implementing positive strategies for girls to unleash the Girl Effect as a method of change. The aggregated M&E data created a universalized portrayal of heterogeneous subjects that was then re-inscribed on participants through programmatic interventions.

While various subjects, including pregnant girls, older women, and boys and young men, were excluded from participation in the program, as the "categorical complications" in the category of adolescent girl suggest, a diversity of young women were included.[16] For example, contrary to homogenized portrayals of girls in the Girl Effect and assumptions about their sexual and affective lives, not all of the young women were heterosexual. A group of five young women who actively participated in the program identified as lesbians. Yet, their bodies and experiences were not reflected in the homogenized, heteronormative portrayals of Third World girls, who are frequently depicted as child brides or hyperreproductive during their adolescence. The effect was that the actual girls and young women in the program were not seen, while a set of consequential assumptions was made about them, their lives, and their future potential.

GIRL EXPERTS

The process of collecting data on girls and disseminating these forms of authoritative knowledge depended on an ever-changing, varied constellation of experts the Nike Foundation identified as "girl experts" and "girl champions." There is nothing new or unusual about experts and their knowledge of development subjects. They are constitutive of liberal forms of government, and they play a defining role in modern institutions and individuals' behavior in them.[17] In the case of the Girl Effect, these experts proclaim the "will to empower,"[18] "will to know," or they "share in the will to improve."[19] As Tania Li explains, these experts are "trustees"—those who "claim to know how others should live, to know what is best for them, to know what they need."[20] Although experts desire to do good to others, their "claim to expertise in optimizing the lives of others is a claim to power."[21]

These girl experts and champions were individuals and institutional actors internal and external to the foundation who came together around the category of adolescent girl as objects of knowledge, and participated in structuring interventions in their name. The foundation drew on content experts who focused on the relationships of girls to poverty, education, health, and economic development. In particular, it built on the expertise of individuals and institutions that have long promoted the benefits of investing in girls' education for development.[22] Despite the foundation's claims that there wasn't sufficient data on girls, it used the evidence of these experts to make strong claims about the benefits of investing in girls for the purposes of development.

In doing so, it overlooked critiques of the instrumental use of girls' education for poverty alleviation and development.[23] Moreover, it disregarded decades of critical feminist concerns regarding the racialized nature of seeking to control the reproductive lives of particular girls and women.[24]

One set of experts provided the content knowledge for the creative marketing, advertising, brand management, and public relations experts—those who supported the packaging, selling, and distribution of expertise to the public through brand campaigns, viral videos, and other promotional materials. These experts were critical to disseminating the universalized images of Third World girls and their imagined potential—without their diverse forms of representation, the discourse would have limited circulation.

Another set of experts were powerful figures whose expertise normally does not focus on gender or target girls and women, such as heads of multilateral banks, ministers of finance, and CEOs.[25] These influential figures, such as Robert Zoellick, former president of the World Bank, and Ngozi Okonjo-Iweala, former managing director of the World Bank, bring economic authority to the cause of girls, as this is often seen as a soft development issue. They enabled the Girl Effect to become a legitimate model for economic development. Yet, in communicating to those powerful actors, the foundation often further rendered the social, cultural, political, and ethical nuances of gender, education, and development invisible.

The Nike Foundation also frequently drew on celebrity philanthropists and political celebrities, whose desirability lies in their ability to capture public attention through media outlets ranging from Twitter to popular magazines.[26] These included actress Anne Hathaway, who attended the AGI launch at the World Bank, and Queen Rania of Jordan, who has attended and participated in panels on the circuit of global forums, including CGI and WEF.

Together, this constellation of experts contributed to the production and distribution of the Girl Effect, generating the authoritative and convincing knowledge upon which it hinges. Yet, those different sets of actors rarely, if ever, visited the programs and almost never directly encountered the actual young women in programs Nike Foundation funded.[27] Their expertise was contingent upon the deployment of particular M&E technologies for understanding the population in and through the Nike Foundation portfolio and influenced how these technologies came to bear on the lives, educations, and futures of girls and young women.

THE IMPLICATIONS OF GIRLS AS DATA

This iterative process of knowledge production and educational intervention was predicated on the logic of the Girl Effect. The logic is based on the relationship between the presumed reproductive capacities and imagined economic potential of Third World girls. The relationship between the foundation's universal indicators and its ultimate measures revealed this underlying logic. Girls' bodies must be heterosexually protected to push back the age of childbearing and marriage as part of the strategy for realizing their economic potential, as measured by income rates and accumulated assets. Those were the ultimate measures of economic empowerment from the foundation's perspective. The logic is dualistic in that it attempts to "push back" childbearing and marriage to unleash their future economic potential. If the girls delay childbearing and marriage, they are more likely to stay in school longer. As the foundation described, this results in "empowering her potential for future opportunities, and enabling her to get better jobs."[28] This intimate relationship between heterosexuality and economics enables the production of the returns—real or imagined—that investments in adolescent girls purportedly create.

Technologies deployed by the Nike Foundation and its partners, such as the questionnaire, standardized the messy labor of monitoring and evaluating how effective programs were at unleashing this logic. The very system of measuring and evaluating the educational programs was not based on if, how, what, and to what extent adolescent girls were learning or what they saw as meaningful education or change in their lives; rather, it was based on if, how, and to what extent they were acquiring "assets" and avoiding "pitfalls," such as marriage and pregnancy, that would limit their role as an economic resource for development. The universal indicators and ultimate measures informed the content of the questionnaires I reviewed from AFD and the other NGO in Brazil that was part of Nike Foundation's Economic Empowerment Portfolio. As such, there were lengthy, quasi-standardized sections in the questionnaires that captured: (1) education level and aspirations; (2) intimate sexual and affective experiences, pregnancy, and motherhood; and (3) marriage. Beyond these indicators, the sections on "ultimate measures" of economic empowerment included questions about their labor and employment experience, their personal and family income, amounts in savings and checking accounts, and material possessions. Together, the universal indicators and the ultimate measures mirrored the dualistic logic of the Girl Effect.

Regulating adolescent girls' sexuality and affective relationships was core to the logic of the Girl Effect. In theory, knowledge on sexual practices could potentially enable more effective regulation of their current and future sexual practices. Collecting knowledge on the sexuality of Othered bodies is a practice with a long history in colonial and development interventions.[29] And just as progress of empire has been measured in relation to the colonized female body, today, the status of development is measured against female bodies in the Global South.

Created in the image of this logic, the questionnaire reflected who these adolescent girls supposedly were, what mattered to them, and what they needed before they were even recruited for the program. It was a universalizing technology. It took the embodied, situated experiences of young women throughout the world and fed them into a universalizing model of knowledge production. In turn, this model used the universalized idea of them to gather particular knowledge on their lives, their families, and their communities.

But the actual lives and experiences of the girls often contradicted the logic of the Girl Effect. For example, pursuing higher education and future employment were central to the goals of Regina, a young mother in the program with a three-year-old daughter. Thus, rather than destroying her future, as in the discourse of the Girl Effect, motherhood gave her an important reason to pursue her aspirations. One day in class, she pulled all of her diplomas out of her purse, including her high school equivalency degree and her computer course certificate, to show them to me and others in our conversation. We all joked that she better leave them at home lest she get robbed, a humor reflective of everyday life in the neighborhoods in Rio de Janeiro.[30] On another day, toward the end of the session, Regina was the only young women to show up for the program. She diligently worked alone in the computer lab on her assignment. Years later as I write this book, nothing about Regina's life fit the Girl Effect's trajectory of an adolescent girl who falls into a trapdoor due to adolescent pregnancy. As of December 2016, she was employed as a professional hairstylist, and is the mother of a healthy, growing daughter.

Yet, the particular experiences of the young women and situated context of this knowledge was erased as the data on young women like Regina were fed into standardized forms of analysis that contributed to creating a composite, universalized portrait of a Third World girl as an instrument of development. It was a portrait created in the Nike Foundation's own image. The universal served as a technology for indexing development at the level of the adolescent girl's body. It measured all of the elements considered necessary for ending poverty at that level.[31] The Nike Foundation's M&E strategy crystallized the logic of the Girl Effect as an instantiation of the "feminization of responsibility and obligation" in development.[32] As such, the girls' bodies became the site where poverty could be managed through them even though the Girl Effect's logic is predicated on their interrelations with others, as Sarah's example of the sister paying for her brother's tuition reflects.

The construction and implementation of questionnaires across geographical and cultural locations was highly contested both internally and externally. As Deborah, a Nike Foundation staff member, explained, "Some of us were skeptical." She explained that externally there were "grantees that pushed back" on the universal indicators. In particular, "There was a lot of pushback on the idea of sexual debut . . . It was just too personal." Moreover, she explained, there are "other proxies" for understanding this, including "marriage, contraception, and pregnancy." In Brazil, there was contestation between the NGOs and the Nike Foundation regarding the relevance and application of those indicators in their context. For example, Candida, an AFD staff member, argued that early marriage is simply not relevant in Brazil. Nevertheless, program-specific M&E plans still focused on these universal indicators. Interestingly, as Jessica explained, over time the foundation realized those universal indicators were not relevant for measuring program performance of individual projects as they frequently do not change in a six-month program cycle. Nevertheless, during the period I observed, the NGOs experienced intense pressure to meet the goals those universal indicators measure, and consequently M&E occupied a significant amount of their time and resources. It imbued the everyday of the program and created an aura of anxiety among staff and the young women alike.

The universal indicator of pregnancy, in particular, infused the everyday at AFD. As João, the researcher from GJO, critically noted in our conversation on AFD's uptake of the Nike Foundation's indicator, this reflected, "The Nike Foundation's obsession with pregnancy. It's called social control." The goal of pushing back pregnancy entered classroom curriculum and pedagogy and influenced how staff members related to the young women. As Susana explained in an informal conversation in the office, "Last session a girl became pregnant despite our talking about it. This time, we are talking about it in 'Gender,'" a short course developed in the program. Through this incorporation of the goal in the formal curriculum and pedagogy, education became the means for regulating (hetero) sexual bodies.

As such, success or failure of the educational intervention depended on effective regulation of the young women's sexuality through formalized curricula. In the words of Luciana, one of the participants, the gender course focused on "everything about men and women, sexuality, and pregnancy." These interventions resulted in the young women being monitored for fear of programmatic failure (i.e., pregnancy). Toward the end of my fieldwork, during a long, late afternoon staff meeting, I observed how the goal of pushing back pregnancy materialized in practice. As the previous conversation ended, Susana lowered her eyes, gently shaking her head. She uttered, "I have something sad." She paused. "Again, there is a young woman in the program who is pregnant. We didn't meet our goal, our indicator." Susana turned to another staff member to ask, "How many months is she?" The staff member responded, "Three months, and after the Gender class." For Susana, the pedagogical and curricular interventions were insufficient. Successful management of the young woman's heterosexuality had failed. Her perception of failure was palpable. As this example reflects, this indicator resulted in ongoing anxiety around the ever-present possibility of pregnancy.

Yet, pregnancy was not the only site where this regulation of sexuality occurred. Queer lives and bodies were disciplined as well, in ways that usually linked to the labor market. In recruitment sessions, the program staff members often described the program's goal of educating the young women to fit the "profile" the labor market seeks: "The objective of the course is qualification for the labor market. The course prepares you with the profile companies are looking for. With the *jeito* the market looks for." *Jeito* signifies one's way of being in Portuguese. In this respect, the market desires or is imagined to desire heterosexual bodies. In preparing the young women with this profile, queer bodies were also regulated. It was the other side of the obsessive focus on pregnancy.

An interaction among two staff members and myself reflected the ongoing tension surrounding this form of preparation for the labor market. Late one afternoon, I walked into Leticia's classroom as she cleaned up from her Portuguese language class. She held a set of "personal flags" decorated by the young women during her classroom activity. The assignment asked them to represent answers to a series of questions on themselves using symbols. Susana encouraged the young women to practice this, as it was purportedly a common activity in job interviews. Leticia leafed through the flags, showing us one young woman's. In the top left corner, there was a yellow soccer ball with a blue Nike "Swoosh" drawn on it. Below it was a heart colored with a rainbow of colors. Inside the heart, the world "girl" was written in English. Leticia appeared upset by the flag.

She told us, "She cannot use this for a selection process interview. If she uses this, no. . . .," her voice trailing off. This resulted in a tense encounter among Leticia, Juliana, another staff member, and me, arguing about whether or not the program should mold the young women to conform to the labor market. I immediately interjected, "I don't agree with you. It is her personal flag." Juliana told her, "This is her identity. It is important for her." My level of frustration rose as she continued with her position. I said, "You cannot teach the young women to conform to the labor market." Juliana told us how she had spoken with a queer-identified young woman from the last group. She explained, "I asked her if she would work somewhere where she couldn't be herself. She said never." She commented further, "She went to her interview dressed as a man, as a man," describing the shirt, jacket, and shoes the young woman had worn. I said, "The young women are going to encounter multiple barriers in seeking employment associated with their race, class, gender, and sexuality. You need to discuss this with them. But you cannot educate them to conform to the labor market." Continuing to debate into the common space of the office, we gradually settled down.

For Foucault, "The chief function of the disciplinary power is to 'train.'"[33] In this sense, disciplining the young women's bodies served educative function. While the means of disciplining may differ based on the different perceived threats of heterosexual and queer sexuality, the end goal was employable subjects. In this example, Leticia's desire to censor the young women's presentation of self represented an attempt to educate an employable subject. This occurred with all of the young women regardless of their sexual orientation, often in conversations on their sartorial choices or complementary remarks on their professional-appearing hair and make-up style; however, with the queer young women, it focused on a particular (hetero)sexual fashioning of the self. In a conversation with Susana regarding a young woman in the program who was depressed, she told me, "She says that she is not happy being with women. But she *chooses* to be with women. If she isn't happy, she should paint a new picture for herself." Like removing the flag, painting a new picture of oneself requires modifying the self, including one's desires and choices. In the end, both young women I refer to slowly over time stopped attending the program despite their early enthusiasm and dedication. They were not alone as attendance was very sparse by the program's end. When João asked the AFD leadership if his research team could look for established patterns in the attendance data, he was quickly silenced. He was told the inquiry was not relevant for the program focus.

THE CONSEQUENCES OF ACCOUNTABILITY

Through the process of proving the Girl Effect, the Nike Foundation made the NGOs "accountable," as Sarah explained. Yet, as the story of the flag reveals, it was accountable to the foundation, not to the young women it served. It did so through the creation of rigorous M&E plans, ongoing deadlines, and pressure—perceived or real—to produce the desired results. Laura, a Nike Foundation partner, reflected this idea more broadly in our conversation in June 2009. As she explained:

> They are very demanding as a partner. Again because they come from the corporate sector they are impatient and arrogant. And sometimes they don't understand that you are doing a rural survey in Ethiopia, you just aren't going to get this. I like their high standards, but they are immature in the development arena. It definitely influences the quality of their relationships with their grantees. Annoyed and disgruntled. Excited to partner with them but that they need to spend a lot of money to jump into a lot of extra hoops. They are very detailed and demanding, more so than other donors. So in terms of time and effort they are a very costly for grantees. They give a big load of money for M&E. For the long term, for some grantees, it actually increases their capacity. Grantees never had a donor who made them do these things.

For AFD, the development of its M&E plans took almost a year, pushing back actual program implementation. After being regulated by the corporate foundation, AFD, in turn, regulated the young women through its educational program. Despite the fact that the Nike Foundation did not mandate the young women's participation in M&E, in practice their education became contingent on becoming research subjects. Their participation in the program and their graduation from it was predicated on their participation in the baseline and endline questionnaires. Yet, who demanded this practice and why? During lunch one day in a nearby restaurant, I brought up the question with two staff members, Juliana and Gisele. I asked, "If the young women don't participate in the baseline questionnaire, they cannot participate in the program?" Juliana responded, "They can choose not to answer specific questions, but they have to do the baseline. If they don't, they cannot participate." I followed-up, "Is that a Nike Foundation rule?" "Yes," Juliana responded. Laughing, she further explained, "There was a young woman at the *aula magna* (inaugural class) who had attended class before completing the baseline. I had told her she could, but another staff member said that she couldn't."

Correspondingly, the young women's graduation from the program was conditioned on participation in the endline questionnaire. Concerned with their low numbers, AFD's staff members tried to convince the young women to complete the questionnaire. Yet, cajoling them into participating proved a challenge since they were already familiar with the content of the questionnaire. During snack-time one afternoon, I stood in the kitchen with the young women and staff members. Mareli, a senior staff member, asked the young women, "Who will be here tomorrow?" to complete the endline questionnaire that was to be administered that day. There was an awkward pause. One of the young women in the group said she'd be there. Various others were noncommittal. One young woman said, "No," shaking her head. Mareli emphasized that it would be short. Noting their lack of response, she stated quietly, yet with an anxious tone, "We need you all to be here tomorrow."

By the graduation ceremony later that month, many of the young women had not completed the endline questionnaire. It was a ceremony without certificates. They were distributed to the young women upon completion of the M&E process rather than at the ceremony. The Nike Foundation claims that it did not mandate this;[34] AFD may have felt so much pressure to have sufficient numbers in the study that it made the young women's completion of the program contingent upon their participation in the research process. As I sat in the office one day, Juliana answered the phone. It was months after the graduation ceremony. She told a young woman from a previous session, "To get a certificate, you need to do an interview with the researchers. What time would work? The researchers will be here all day. There is no way to do it another day. You have to come. If you don't do it, you are not going to be certified. I don't know what they are going to do with the girls who don't come." When Marcela mentioned that they had withheld the certificates in a conference call I participated in with AFD, GJO, and the Nike Foundation, its staff members Erica and Jennifer interjected to convince AFD otherwise.

Thus, in practice—intended or unintended—the young women's free education became contingent upon becoming a research subject. In the human subjects' sense, they consented to participate. Yet, there are questions as to whether consent to participate as a human subject in this experiment is possible. Consent is predicated on the notion of a choice; yet, if that choice is directly linked, in practice, to an educational opportunity for which they will be refused entrance, or denied a certificate if they do not participate in the entirety of the experiment, it does not seem as though the young women are being given a legitimate, ethical choice. If they were to refuse initial participation, they were not presented with an educational alternative, and if they discontinued their participation in the research, yet actually completed the program, they did not receive a certificate. Lastly, the young women were not informed about the larger experiment in which they consented to participate, where their data would travel, who would have rights to it, and how it would be used. The experiment—its intervention and data collection—was thus predicated on the constraints of vulnerable subjects for whom choice is constrained.

The observed practice of withholding a certificate even though a young woman completed the program could impact their lives and futures in profound ways. They received no credit for their participation in a five-month course despite the time, resources, and dedication they and their families committed. Moreover, it foreclosed employment opportunities that the program might have secured for them in the future. The power of the certificate in their lives should not be underestimated. Denying them a certificate for their failure to participate in this social experiment could have profound consequences for their uncertain futures.

Measuring "Success"

The purpose of the young women's participation in the Nike Foundation's massive data collection project was not internal to the foundation or to its grantees. As Jessica explained, the foundation focused on a "systems change" approach to development with the aim of changing the agendas of more powerful development institutions and governments. In her language, "We are trying to figure out how to change everyone else's billion dollar endowments to be more girl-friendly." As Sarah described, "success" was thus measured as follows:

> So let's not call success co-funding by the Gates Foundation for one of the programs that we run, which can be a measure of success. Let's call success that DFID and the World Bank actually re-engineer significant portions of their economic development program to more consciously look at the needs of girls in their strategies and incorporate those needs in the ordinary course of doing their economic development programs or health programs or whatever.

Success, as explained by Sarah, was defined as influencing more powerful institutions. The foundation did so in order to leverage these institutions' power/knowledge/capital in the service of its development vision. In contrast, success could have been defined as educating the young women as an end in and of itself and/or developing long-term relationships with the young women or the communities in which they live. In addition to funding on larger scales, in the later years of the foundation's work on the Girl Effect, it continued to fund a select group of smaller organizations, as the foundation noted in correspondence with me in 2013.

Within the foundation's model, the actual young women in the program I studied became instruments for creating relationships between the Nike Foundation and bigger players. As such, they were critical to generating the knowledge base necessary for advocating for a systems change approach within these institutions. As the foundation sought to reach these national governments and international aid players, it gathered evidence before disseminating its findings. The number of girls the interventions targeted therefore depended on a "formula" derived from which particular aspect of the theory it was testing. As Jessica further described:

> What we are investing in is not simply to know that we have reached 1,000 girls. It is that we have learned something in that process that will change the behavior of another institution. And if that is the criteria, then if investing in a 10-year-long program that reaches 10,000 girls is perceived to be an important part of that formula, then we would do that. If it is

> something else in which it is shorter, but more targeted, that is just testing something, there are lot of different ways we can use the information with our own branding and marketing skills and the rest to drive that influence and mobilization agenda.

Thus, in the end, the actual young women in this program and the others in the portfolio became the means for proving the foundation's theory of change and, ultimately, for reaching the institutions who will bring the intervention to "scale." In this way, M&E as a learning process was not about the girls themselves, but about how knowledge about the girls would enable the foundation to market itself and its theory of change.

Understanding this approach helps to explain why none of the Latin American grantees in the Economic Empowerment Portfolio were refunded after their three-year grants, regardless of whether the programs succeeded or failed to produce their desired outcomes. The executive director of another NGO grantee in the Economic Empowerment Portfolio explained this realization to me in a tone of confusion and frustration in October 2011: "I thought they really cared about adolescent girls. We proved it. We economically empowered girls. They won't even talk to me now. They want nothing to do with me." While the NGO director thought the goal was to prove the Girl Effect in order to support adolescent girls in the communities they serve, it became clear to me that the Nike Foundation's goal was to gather evidence, brand and disseminate it, and, thus, scale-up interventions through partnerships with bigger players. In this sense, the corporation and foundation were successful, as Jessica defined it earlier, on an unprecedented scale through their large-scale partnerships with the World Bank and DFID.

Disjunctures in Knowledge Production

One late afternoon in 2010, I sat in the office of Marcela, a senior AFD staff member, prior to a conference call with the Nike Foundation and other grantees in the Economic Empowerment Portfolio. She began telling me a story:

> It's the story of the man who is searching on the ground under the street light. You ask him, 'Are you okay?' He says, 'I have had a little too much to

> drink, and I lost my keys.' You say, 'You lost your keys here?' He says, 'No, but that is where the light is.' The Nike Foundation may shine the light, but that may not be where the issues are.

Before I could ask her why she and her colleagues did not attempt to redirect this light, she looked directly at me. "But you can be critical. Your sustenance does not depend on them."

In this chapter, I have argued that in multiple educative realms, from classrooms to global forums, the Girl Effect shapes knowledge production, it educates, and it influences the social relations of educational programs focused on girls and young women. As I observed, on one level, the knowledge funded and produced through the Nike Foundation's M&E program informed and was informed by the educational interventions funded by the foundation. That recursion occurred through the young women as their bodies were simultaneously sources of knowledge and objects of regulation. On another level, the foundation actively disseminated that knowledge in their videos, websites, exhibits, and other promotional materials as they advocated a "girl-centered" approach to development. Those materials attempted to educate different publics about what the Nike Foundation thought they should know about adolescent girls, why it mattered, and how they should act upon it. Yet, as with the man under the streetlight, there was often a disjuncture between the knowledge the Nike Foundation produced and disseminated through M&E and the bodies, lives, and futures of the young women in the programs it funded and beyond.

6 Negotiating Corporatized Development

Large black stick figures of an assortment of bodies drawn on white butcher paper lined the hallway of a state-administered high school. The school was just over the bridge from Rio de Janeiro, along the Guanabara Bay at the bottom of a favela. As I walked down the hall during a visit in May 2010, I noticed the figure of a pregnant female body. It stood out amidst the other figures. Unlike the discourse on pregnant bodies I was accustomed to encountering through the Girl Effect, this figure symbolized the pregnant female body as a legitimate body in the school rather than a body to be hidden or a population to be controlled. The simple, yet stark black-and-white image worked against the local, national, and globalized discourses on adolescent pregnancy that I had encountered in my research.

In the months prior to our visit, heavy rains and landslides had devastated the area, destroying homes and communities. Hundreds of people died in the destruction. The school had served as a shelter for displaced families. The visit to the school with staff members from the Gender Justice Organization (GJO) had been postponed several times due to the school's closure. To visit the school, I accompanied Olivia, a female program manager, João, a researcher, and a female college intern

Figure 11. Photograph of stick figure depicting a pregnant body on the wall of a school outside of Rio de Janeiro. The quote by Walt Whitman written in Portuguese translates, "If anything is sacred, the human body is sacred," April 2010. Photograph by the author.

from the United States. It was my second month conducting fieldwork at GJO where I served as a volunteer during the latter portion of fieldwork in the city, supporting Olivia and João with the Nike Foundation–funded programs they were implementing and evaluating. They both had master's degrees in the social sciences and many years of experience in the field of gender and sexuality.

Over the past two years, the teachers in this high school had been working to incorporate questions of gender and sexuality into the curriculum, pedagogy, and structure of the school. They began with a "problem with adolescent pregnancy"; however, through their collective work, they decided to take a less common approach to addressing it than schools and organizations usually do. They sought GJO's support to change the structure of the school in order to effectively include pregnant young girls in the school rather than targeting them as individuals or pushing them out as commonly occurred. To support this work, they would address questions of gender and sexuality with all of the young people in their school. As Olivia explained to me, they were working to "incorporate questions of gender in a big and profound way in the school." She emphasized, "The body is important in this." And the stick figures lining the hallway illustrated her observation.

The school's and GJO's approaches to adolescent pregnancy ran contrary to the discourse of the Girl Effect that I had come to Brazil to study. Within the Girl Effect, adolescent pregnancy represents the loss of adolescent girls' imagined potential to end poverty and promote development. As demonstrated with AFD, pregnant young women were excluded from the program's selection process whereas the figure of the assumed fertile, yet non-pregnant female adolescent body was configured as the intervention site for delaying pregnancy and reducing the number of births.[1]

When I first arrived at GJO, I was struck that no one was discussing adolescent pregnancy or young women in instrumental ways. In fact, it seemed I was the only one talking about the Girl Effect. This was evident in the way that the organization theoretically imagined and practically designed and implemented their programs. This was puzzling to me as the Girl Effect influenced the conceptualization and everyday practices of AFD, the other organization where I conducted research. I wondered how

GJO could ignore the logic, goals, and practices of the Girl Effect while AFD adopted them, although awkwardly and never fully, as its own. What were the consequences of that for the organizations in terms of their relationships with the foundation, and for the ways in which girls and young women were understood and interacted with?

In this chapter, I examine the power relations underlying the NGOs' uneven negotiations of the Girl Effect and the Nike Foundation's power/knowledge/capital regime. For insight into the nature of those dynamics, I consider the conditions that enabled GJO to theorize and act beyond the terms of the Nike Foundation while AFD was constrained by them. I focus on the material and nonmaterial resources the NGOs mobilized, and I examine the boundaries of possibility that resulted from a curricular, pedagogical, and relational perspective.

I argue that given the inherently uneven power relations in the funding relationship between grantees and corporate foundations, if an NGO is to successfully negotiate the power/knowledge/capital regime of corporatized development, it must mobilize material and nonmaterial resources to its advantage. These include expertise and authority, education and training, administrative and financial independence, as well as time and space. If the NGO is unable to do so, as I observed in the case of AFD, the corporate foundation's logic, goals, and measurements of success limit and/or take over the NGO's agency. As this chapter demonstrates, because GJO successfully mobilized these resources to its benefit, it was able to disregard the Girl Effect and maneuver around the Nike Foundation, while AFD was constrained by both.

NGOS AND THE CORPORATE EFFECT

Within the Girl Effect apparatus, NGOs funded by the Nike Foundation were key political sites where the policies and practices of the foundation were negotiated, particularly in the foundation's first five years focused on girls. Without the NGOs, the foundation didn't have the space to execute its original development interventions. Moreover, given the timing of the foundation's entrance into Brazil, the foundation was in search of legitimizing partners. As I will show, GJO served this role. Yet, at the same time, as feminist scholars remind us, NGOs are often caught in a "double bind," as they are "situated between the powerful forces dominating them and the disenfranchised communities they intend to serve."[2] How the NGOs navigated that terrain, particularly through their access to material and nonmaterial resources, determined, in large part, their relationship to the Girl Effect as a structuring logic, and thus, the types of gendered, sexualized, and racialized subjects their pedagogical and curricular practices worked to produce.[3]

As Victoria Bernal and Inderpal Grewal describe, the "NGO form" has "come to make sense through an articulation of a negative form: it is defined by something that it is not."[4] As they theorize, it is understood as "not the state." But, as the case of the Girl Effect reveals, the NGO's negative form takes on additional meaning in the context of corporatized development. It is also defined as not the corporation, or, in other words, non-corporate space. It is the perception of the NGO's negative form that enables, in part, the power of corporatized development. Building on Timothy Mitchell's notion of "state effect,"[5] Bernal and Grewal explain that NGOs "make the state visible by emphasizing that they are not the state, even as forms of governmentality proliferate within them."[6] In the same way, the perceived independence of NGOs from corporations is what enables them to produce their "corporate effect"[7]—to make Nike, Inc. and Nike Foundation visible by highlighting that the NGOs are not the corporation. Without this perception, NGOs could not do the work of legitimizing corporate power and extending the reach of corporations into new populations and geographies without it being highly politicized. NGOs serve as an "anti-politics machine,"[8] in the language of James Ferguson, enabling corporations to disarticulate their development interventions in poor girls and women in the Global South from their labor exploitation of the same population and to neutralize their attempts to control girls' and women's fertility in order to shape economic futures.

ADOLESCENT PREGNANCY AS A CONTESTED SITE

Adolescent pregnancy provides a unique site for examining how the Girl Effect is negotiated. Across geographies and scales, it is a contested issue that reflects hierarchical power relations among social actors and between institutions. In this way, adolescent girls' bodies become, in the language of Lata Mani, a "ground"[8] upon which institutions negotiate the power/knowledge/capital regime of the Girl Effect.

The Girl Effect's adoption of the globalized, pathologizing discourse on adolescent pregnancy converges with localized discourses in Rio de Janeiro and national discourses in Brazil that view adolescent pregnancy as a problem with grave social, health, and economic consequences for girls *and* society.[9] In both cases, interventions in their reproductive lives are proposed as a way to contain poverty and violence.

This is based on a long history of controlling the reproduction of poor girls and women of color in the country.[10] In the later portion of the twentieth century, foundations and NGOs were complicit in perpetuating that history.[11] The Ford Foundation has a well-documented history of funding organizations, such as *Bem-estar familiar no Brasil* (The Brazilian Society for Family Welfare), known as BEMFAM, that promoted reproductive control, including sterilization. BEMFAM, which is a member of the International Planned Parenthood Federation (IPPF), was one of the first grantees of the Ford Foundation's population program, between 1967 and 1978. In total, the organization received US$5.4 million from the Ford Foundation for "research on the side effects of contraception, studies on the commercial distribution of contraceptives in Brazil, training, and information and education in the area of family planning."[12] As Ford Foundation's direct funding for BEMFAM decreased, IPPF, which continued to be supported by the Ford Foundation, funded BEMFAM. As reported by the Ford Foundation, BEMFAM was criticized for participating in "the sterilization of low-income women, for implanting IUDs without providing sufficient information or securing patient consent, and for inadequate follow-up and counseling."[13] BEMFAM currently runs a not-for-profit condom and lubricant business, generating approximately US$4 million for the NGO, to finance its family planning and sexual and reproductive health programs. Along with GJO, International Planned Parenthood Federation/Western Hemisphere Region was an initial grantee of Nike Foundation, and BEMFAM was a subgrantee. Based on communication with the Nike Foundation, it "supported the organization in coordinating a program that brought together young people to promote dialogue around sexual and reproductive health and rights within the perspective of the Millennium Development Goals at national-level decision making forums."[14]

While systematic sterilization and forced contraception is no longer a pervasive issue in Brazil, as reflected in the broader global transformation from reproductive control to reproductive hegemony, racialized efforts to control fertility, particularly among poor girls and women, still exist on multiple scales. In the context of Brazil, in 2007 then governor of Rio de Janeiro Sergio Cabral defended the legalization of abortion as a way to contain urban violence. Drawing on Steven Levitt and Stephen J. Dubner, the authors of *Freakonomics*, who discuss a purported relationship between legalized abortion and violence reduction in the United States, Cabral explained that the fertility rates among women living in favelas in Rio de Janeiro create a "factory that produces marginality." Fertility, he claimed, "has everything to do with violence. You take the number of children per mother in the Lagoa Rodrigo de Freitas, Tijuca, Meier and Copacabana," majority white, middle- to upper-class neighborhoods in the city, "it is the Swedish standard. Now take Rocinha," a poor favela with a majority mixed race and Afro-Brazilian population. "It is the standard of Zambia and Gabon," he said, making a derogatory racialized reference to the fertility rates of these African nations.[15]

Anthropologist Maria Luiza Heilborn, the coordinator of the national research project *Gravidez na adolescência* (adolescent pregnancy), referred to as GRAVAD, calls Cabral's claim that "the reproduction of the poor is equal to the invasion of hordes of criminals plaguing the big Brazilian cities" a reductionist cause/effect equation.[16] Demographer George Martine and the anthropologist Sonia Corrêa similarly claim that his simplistic logic "seduces public opinion, sidesteps the main causes of complex social problems, such as violence, and makes the poor, especially women, their scapegoats."[17] As they explain, "It is also worth noting that, historically, fertility control policies that led to the instrumental use of abortion, either for eugenic purposes or as a way of solving complex social problems, were not only condemned as an abuse of rights, but did not have the expected results."[18] Cabral is not alone in his racialized and classed position on female fertility, nor is it in any way isolated to the Brazilian context. The targeting of Black and Brown women's reproduction has long been used as a way to blame them for the "structural inequities" that they inhabit and, correspondingly, as a method of social and population control in Brazil and throughout the world.[19]

GJO'S HISTORY

In contrast to AFD and the other organizations in Latin America that began working in this area to catch the new corporate funding stream, GJO has worked on gender justice and violence prevention since its inception in 1997. The organization transformed from one that focused on HIV/AIDS in Brazil in the late 1990s into a global organization dedicated to gender justice and equity. It is currently one of the leading international NGOs working on gender and sexuality, particularly through its work with men and boys. Its authority grew, in part, due to its leadership by one of the world's foremost experts on men and boys, who publishes widely, presents at conferences, and serves in leadership positions in and has founded a number of transnational networks. With these credentials came a tremendous amount of linguistic, cultural, and networking capital. Even when the directorship changed, the directors who succeeded him were each well regarded nationally, regionally, and internationally. Beyond its international stature, GJO is also considered a local, Brazilian organization. This so-called native status gives it another form of authority that operates at the local, national, and international level. When it is facing Brazilian NGOs, networks, or national ministries, it is considered a local or national organization; this native status also increases its credibility, authenticity, and authority on the international stage when funders or international NGOs are looking for local or national on-the-ground organizations with whom to partner or fund. It was the particular combination of local, national, and international authority, and significant representation on each scale, that other organizations based in Brazil, but run by Brazilians, or based in the United States but directed by Brazilians in Brazil, did not and could not attain.

During my fieldwork, I observed the ways in which the organization's expertise was widely called upon on a local, state, national, and international level. I accompanied its staff into local community-based organizations throughout the city and state of Rio de Janeiro, and attended workshops it conducted for state and municipal secretariats of education and health in Rio de Janeiro and Salvador, Bahia, in northeastern Brazil. Moreover, its staff members presented at academic conferences I attended, including, but not intentionally, participating on a panel I organized on gender and sexuality in education. On an international scale, I also attended the CGI annual meeting in New York City with its executive director in 2010, which was the NGO's first year attending the forum. While I initiated the introduction through my role on CGI's Girls and Women's team, the organization was invited back in future years with its leadership playing an increasingly visible role.

GJO'S GENDER PRAXIS

GJO employs a gender lens to understand young people's lives and practices in specific cultural contexts, and uses its own research to design interventions and campaigns at different scales to promote gender equity and violence prevention. Underlying this work is a belief that contesting hegemonic gender norms and power relations, as well as heteronormativity, needs to be at the heart of approaches to gender equity. GJO takes the perspective that we are socialized into hegemonic gender and sexual identities throughout our lives. These are durable identities reinforced by multiple institutions, including the family, religions, schools, and the state. Young people live out their gender and sexuality in these institutions in complex and contradictory ways. Drawing on these ideas, GJO seeks to promote an integrated understanding of gender and sexuality in an effort to guarantee the rights of youth to be true to their gender and sexuality. As described by Olivia, these hegemonic identities work to place "people in boxes"; in contrast, as she explains, GJO seeks "to break rigid norms" around gender and sexuality. This represents an entirely different conceptualization of young people's lives and futures than that of the Girl Effect.

GJO used the Nike Foundation funding it received in 2005–2011 to strengthen its established research, programming, and advocacy on gender equity. As one senior manager described to me in conversation, in addition to working with young men, "We thought it was important to work with young women." Its programming for young women, ages fifteen to twenty-four, was carried out in conjunction with its existing programming for young men—rather than by ending its programming with young men and/or targeting young women in isolation, as occurred with the Brazilian NGOs in the foundation's Economic Empowerment portfolio. Nevertheless, the Nike Foundation described the project as working with girls in isolation: "To use social marketing and to create innovative group educational activities for girls in three slums in Rio de Janeiro to address their sexual and reproductive health and empowerment in sexual relationships."[20] In practice, however, there was no distinction between GJO's curricular and pedagogical approach with young men and women in the schools and communities in which they worked.

GJO developed the program curriculum and methodology by working with thirty young people in three communities in Rio de Janeiro, with five young women and five young men coming from each community. During this first phase of the program, GJO involved the community in its efforts by distributing, testing, and evaluating their materials in places occupied by young people—from beauty salons to Internet cafes. My observations began during the second phase of the program when it expanded into schools in and around Rio de Janeiro and in Salvador, Bahia. As Olivia described to me, through this endeavor, GJO served as "a base of support in schools that want to focus on questions of gender and sexual reproduction." She further explained, "We are attempting to address the question of sexual and reproductive health as a right of the young people." In each school, there was a different focus and curriculum. In this way, the GJO team sought to co-constitute the projects with students and teachers based on their needs and desires. Drawing on an understanding of students and teachers as unique social actors and knowledge holders within the school, it utilized participatory methodologies based on dialogue to develop its programs. Olivia explained, "In the political context of public schooling in Brazil, the process of co-construction is critical, as school leadership and teachers are often resistant to ready-made projects coming from outside of the school." As she described, GJO felt that the process of developing the program with individuals at different levels of the school hierarchy was essential to authentically integrating the work into the structure of the school and to ensuring its long-term sustainability after the pilot project's completion.

GJO's program was framed within the political context of Brazilian public education. This context is grounded in the constitution of 1988, which guaranteed rights to all citizens regardless of race, sex, skin color, age, or any other form of discrimination. The National Curricular Parameters, developed between 1995 and 1997, represent an important advance for promoting gender equity, as they guarantee a political opening for integrating work on gender and sexuality into Brazilian public schools. Nevertheless, the promotion of gender and sexuality in schools, as well as by most private organizations and government-based programs, is often limited to the area of health. Initiatives frequently focus on avoiding sexually transmitted diseases (STDs) and pregnancy as opposed to promoting a gender-based approach to guaranteeing sexual and reproductive rights. In this way, GJO's approach to taking up the Brazilian curricular parameter in a holistic way set them apart from other institutions focusing on gender and sexuality.

GJO'S PROGRAM IN SALVADOR

After developing its methodology in Rio de Janeiro, GJO identified the school in Salvador, Bahia, on the northern periphery of the city, where it would implement the program, and a control school through the Secretariat of Education of the state of Rio de Janeiro, which introduced Olivia to the Secretariat of Education of the state of Bahia. The Bahian secretariat proposed state-administered high schools for the implementation and control school. The implementation high school was recommended for its openness around gender and sexuality and for its willingness to partner with outside organizations to enhance the learning environment of the school. When I asked Olivia about the school, she explained that it had an HIV/AIDS prevention project and a small project sponsored by the secretariat, but it needed more support to work in a way that was, in her language, "connected to gender and human rights."

While the program began with volunteer student facilitators, following their first facilitation, the students, teachers, and Olivia decided that it was better if the teachers led the facilitation and the students supported the teachers and Olivia with the promotion of the workshops and the school's gender equity campaign. As Olivia explained, the students "were fearful they would not be respected" by the other students. Because Olivia could only visit Salvador once per month, two teachers took the place of the students in facilitating on a weekly basis. While she didn't prepare them in terms of the subject area, they met together and worked on the curriculum, chose relevant activities, and established the important aspects of each theme and activity. In total, there were eighteen activities and ten workshops. As we discussed the teachers' facilitation, over time Olivia emphasized that their approach was different than she ideally desired. She was concerned that they did not sufficiently focus on the "question of gender, with respect to difference and sexual and reproductive rights." As she explained, "This was difficult because each time I said something, they didn't want to listen." They would say, "Everything's okay." Yet, as she spoke, her body moved back as she drew in her breath and gently shook her head to demonstrate that clearly everything wasn't okay from her perspective.

Within the workshops, it appeared that the teacher facilitators and the other teachers had not moved beyond a restrictive understanding of gender and sexuality grounded in a prevention-based approach. This approach, which was in line with their training and work in this area, was focused on avoiding STDs and pregnancy as opposed to a gender-based approach which promotes sexual and reproductive awareness and rights.

As Olivia explained, the two lead teachers had "a habit of scaring the young people into using condoms to prevent pregnancy and avoid STDs." They would focus their lessons on "young women who had become pregnant." In a threatening, fear-inducing way, the young women became "the example of why the students have to use a condom." In contrast, she explains, "They have a right to their sexual life. That is not a problem. The students must be respected." She continues, "People have a right to live their sexual life and their choices. We need to advance those questions. But because [the teachers] were so used to this perspective, they didn't hear these ideas." As Olivia and I continued discussing the program, she reflected on how João, GJO's director of research, observed that there was "very little debate in the classroom. The teachers didn't prioritize debate and reflection." For her, this reflected the traditional role of the "authoritarian professor." Yet, as she explained, GJO's "goal of promoting gender equity" necessitated that they also "question vertical power relations" that were deeply entrenched in formal schooling. Nevertheless, at moments during the workshop it appeared as though GJO's work was reinforcing this structure through a top-down approach to working with the teachers on integrating questions of gender and sexuality into their teaching practice.

With regard to the question of pregnancy, she says, rather than just "thinking about preventing the pregnancy, we support them to choose the best time" and "to make conscious decisions in accordance with the expectation of each person." As she explained, "You need to think about rights, desires, and commitments." She expanded, "What are their rights to be a mother or father? What is it to be a mother or father, in terms of questioning the naturalness of it? Are you prepared to be one? What are the resources that you have in relation to your pregnancy?" For her, all of this is part of the choice. As she explained, "When I was doing my master's research was when I learned the most about adolescent pregnancy." She observed that in the community where she conducted her fieldwork in Rio de Janeiro, "When young women don't have a set career path, it may not matter if they became mothers at age 18 or not. Just because they pushed back pregnancy did not mean that they would have a different career future." To the contrary, she explains, "In this case, the fact of being a mother did not destroy their future, but bettered it. They wanted to be examples for their children so they oftentimes returned to school or went to work." As she further contrasted, this experience was "very different than girls who don't have a baby. So, how is it that we say that pregnancy interferes or doesn't in a girl's future, or that this girl is going to lose her life when some of them begin to structure, organize their life as a result of the pregnancy?" In response, I commented that this example went against the discourse of the Nike Foundation with regard to pregnancy, which regarded adolescent pregnancy as the death of the development[21] subject. As we discussed the Nike Foundation's approach, which she was still relatively unfamiliar with, she said it reminded her of the Ford Foundation's funding of BEMFAM in the 1960s and 1970s.

GJO'S TEACHER WORKSHOP

After Olivia and I arrived in Salvador in late May 2010, we took a taxi to the high school. Turning off the highway, the taxi slowly made its way on small road alongside a stone wall and pulled into an opening with a gate. There was no sign outside the high school, which sat on an expansive dirt field. On the rusty-red colored school wall, there was a small placard with the school name on it. When we entered the school door, there were murals depicting different African countries. The first one showed Ghana in green, red, and yellow colors with 1957, the date of its independence from England, written on the wall. As we later learned, the school was to be featured at the midday local news report for its focus on Afro-Brazilian and African cultures. Whereas the majority of the students, teachers, and administrators at the school were Afro-Brazilian, only one staff member at GJO at the level of program manager or on the executive team was Afro-Brazilian at the time of my fieldwork in 2010.

Olivia worked with the school principal, a middle-age Afro-Brazilian man, to hold a workshop for the teachers that would help them to begin thinking about how to integrate new ways of approaching gender and sexuality into their subject areas and mentoring. They agreed the teachers had to embrace the program as intended. When the principal introduced Olivia, hugging her, he explained, "There are few professors directly involved in this project. We have to have everyone involved. These are very, very complicated questions" about gender and sexuality. In the workshop's morning session, Olivia stood in front of the blackboard to introduce the teachers to GJO and the broader project, which until this point had only been supported by the two lead teachers. She explained that GJO was working to adapt methodologies it had developed in community-based locations in conjunction with young people in Rio de Janeiro for teaching and learning about gender and sexuality in schools. She explained, "The school is an interesting space of socialization and a place where the young people spend most of their lives." Yet, while there is a political mandate to incorporate the question of sexuality in schools through the National Curricular Parameters, "There aren't tools for teachers to work with." GJO's goal, she states, is "to attempt to think more structurally about these issues" in the context of schools. She emphasized to the teachers, "This is not a ready-made project. It is not a capacity training." A few professors let out a sigh of relief. She explained, "The purpose of the work on gender and sexuality is to think about our lives in relation to these questions."

At the beginning of the afternoon session, she opened with a slide titled, "Gender Norms." She provided a series of examples, including "Women are taught to be sensual at the same time they are taught not to be sexually easy." Drawing on her own life, she explained how her friends have reacted to her being single at thirty years old. "They feel badly for me," she shared. As another example, she mentioned the idea that "A pregnant adolescent girl loses her life," referring to popularized, circulating discourses on the issue. These gender norms are part of "our daily performance of gender. We are capable of change. We need to think a little about identity in order to denaturalize these norms." She continued, "We lose a lot of potential when we try to fit ourselves or other people in a box. It is a form of power. It is important that sex and gender are not understood as rigid or dichotomous identities. There are people, such as transgenders and transsexuals, who question these categories." As she continued the conversation with the teachers, she asked, "People are singular. We categorize them in an attempt to normalize. There are excluded people. The issue is, what are the policies to include the excluded?" She used the example of the gains of the *Movimento Negro* (Black Movement), including affirmative action, to discuss the idea of substantive inclusion. As she explained, "Inclusion is not bringing every person in, but enabling people to express their potential through the movements that bodily practices enable." Echoing Foucault, whom she frequently read, she stated, "Schools bring everyone into the norm. We don't want a school for everyone, but for each one." She gave the example of "homosexual men having feminized characteristics that are devalorized." She created a scenario for the group. "A physical education teacher desires for all of the feminine males to play *futsal* (soccer with five players). The question is why?" She noted, "Inclusion does not mean having everyone in the same boat."

As she explained using an intersectional lens, there are always "other categories that are involved—social class, race/ethnicity, age, and sexual orientation. It is necessary to deconstruct these hierarchical categories." She further explained, "Look at people who are invisible, particularly in the area of social class . . . If these questions are mixed together, they compound into unequal relations of power. If you are poor, Black, female, and homosexual, you are often invisible." She noted, "If we don't work on questions of gender together with race and questions of homosexuality, it is more difficult to make a change."

The conversation shifted to discussing the role and responsibility of teachers and the schools in promoting sexual and reproductive rights. Olivia emphasized the need for young people to have access to information in order to ensure they have "the right to pleasure, but not to purify the population," which is frequently the approach in schools and society. "Young people have a right to live pleasure," she emphasized. One of the young female teachers explained, "They have a lot of shame. The majority prefer to buy a condom in the pharmacy and not bring it home," rather than take it home from school. As Olivia emphasized, "The school has an important function in facilitating these questions. It's an important space."

GJO's Nike Foundation–funded program was its first program in public schools in Brazil. Previously, it had always worked in community-based settings. During my fieldwork at GJO, I was responsible for writing a program report for the Nike Foundation on the organization's pilot work in the school in Salvador. Together with the executive leadership and program and research staff, I worked on the report, which ended with a set of questions that were central to GJO's own inquiry. They reflect their concern with how to meaningfully transform the structures of schooling. In the conclusion of the evaluation, I wrote: "These reflections on learning processes, how to evaluate these processes, and the impacts of the project necessitate we consider what types of structures can be developed and reinforced to facilitate equitable social practices in schools, particularly along the lines of gender, sexuality, race, and age, and to promote critical learning in the areas of gender, sexuality, and broader human rights. First, how do we ensure that teachers are reflective of themselves as gendered, sexualized subjects and are aware of their own practices in the context of the school, their homes, and their broader community? Second, since gender is a relation of power, how do we foster an environment in public schools that encourages teachers and the school leadership to think about hierarchical relations of power in the classroom and the broader school structure and to analyze their own participation in consciously and unconsciously (re)producing these unequal relations of power through their everyday practices? Third, how do we support the development of classrooms and schools that transform rather than reproduce inequitable social practices?"

These questions, which defined GJO's approach to working on gender and sexuality provided a far more holistic, transformative approach than the Girl Effect's approach to intervening in the lives of adolescent girls. Its theoretical approach and methodology of transformation of structures went against the Nike Foundation's instrumentalization of individuals. Yet, what enabled GJO to work in this way, while AFD anxiously managed its participants' gender and sexuality through its adoption of the foundation's discourse on adolescent pregnancy and gender empowerment? In the sections that follow, I examine the material and nonmaterial resources that influenced the relationships among the NGOs and Nike Foundation.

LEGITIMACY IN THE FIELD

When the foundation first approached GJO, it was just beginning its work with adolescent girls. GJO received the Nike Foundation's first grant in 2005. As GJO's executive director, Jeff, described to me in a 2007 interview, "We were their first grant. They needed to get funding out the door. They told us, get a proposal to us in 10 days." The person Nike Foundation hired to set up its portfolio was from a prestigious US foundation. As Jeff further explained, it was "the seal of confidence from [that foundation] that led to the opening" with Nike Foundation.

GJO helped the foundation establish its legitimacy in the country and more broadly in the field, and as a result, GJO held the expertise in the funder-grantee relationship. To illuminate this, a senior manager at GJO contrasted the difficulty of obtaining funding from the Brazilian government with the ease of getting funding from the Nike Foundation. I asked if the organization had to go through the RFP process, as the other Brazilian NGOs did. He looked confused. He and others confirmed that GJO's funding was not contingent on that process.

Similarly, Nike, Inc. approached the Brazilian office of an established US-based international foundation in a similar fashion when it was still in the process of deciding upon a specific focus for the Nike Foundation. In addition to its external reputation, this foundation had developed a strong reputation in Brazil for supporting reproductive health, gender and racial equity, and human rights. As a senior program manager at that foundation explained to me, Nike, Inc. wanted the foundation to fund its publication on women in sports in Brazil because of the foundation's "prestige in the city." As she remarked, they wanted "the support of the [. . .] Foundation as a type of political recommendation. They wanted the mark of the foundation. It would open doors for Nike . . . I decided not to do that." She carefully explained her reasons for not providing Nike, Inc. with the foundation's legitimizing authority. "It does not need our money because it is a company. I was thinking of Nike asking for money from us, not as an expansion of our work, but as a diversion of funds." She also explained, "Sports is not where we put money, even though it may be an important area." Lastly, it was "very clear they were supporting organizations focused on sports because it was related to business . . . I thought it was a bit complicated for the [. . .] Foundation to be attached to the strategy. I was not sure about the difference between the foundation and the corporation. It was not a priority [for me] to understand that at that moment."

While asking a prestigious foundation to fund the corporation's new focus was different than the Nike Foundation seeking to fund a prominent NGO in the field, the underlying motivations were similar. The corporation, and later the Nike Foundation, needed well-established organizations to give it legitimacy in Brazil and in the field of gender and sexuality, particularly since many were bound to question the corporation's intentions.

TRANSLATIONAL ABILITY

Like other well-established, powerful NGOs across fields, including human rights, public health, and the environment, GJO also had strategic translational abilities for defining and enacting its mission across scales.[22] Rooted in an anchoring mission, it tightly bound its work around the promotion of gender equality, around which it organizes its programming, research, and advocacy. Using the lens of gender as a social relation of power, it understood how gender inequality functions across sites and scales, and, accordingly, intervenes in these different spheres. In this way, I observed the way it sees state secretariats, national ministries, and the transnational networks in which it engages as just as integral to its mission as its community-based partners in Rio de Janeiro or Salvador.

While the Nike Foundation had developed its focus on unleashing the Girl Effect, it was so inexperienced in the world of gender and development that it could not move across scales in meaningful ways. It didn't have GJO's translational ability to fluidly move between international, regional, national, and local arenas. That resulted in insecurities that persisted long after it began to gain legitimacy in the field, leading to self-aggrandizing and aggressive behaviors toward others in the field. I witnessed that on multiple occasions at CGI when the foundation would try to force its agenda on a planning meeting or program event. Laura, a partner of the Nike Foundation, explained the potential effects of this behavior in an interview with me in June 2009: "I think it might affect their relationship with some grantees, some that are very committed to working with girls, especially the bigger ones who don't need Nike funding. I think they could potentially think twice. In fact, I have said they need to be careful not to burn their social capital with others. In terms of managing their relationships, they have to stumble through it." As she further elaborated, one grantee expressed, "Enough is enough, we could toss this grant aside. If you want to partner with us then we have some requirements. There is some learning happening. It's a grantee that they cannot afford to lose."

EDUCATION AND EXPERTISE

GJO's employees were highly educated, trained, and experienced in the area of gender and sexuality. In particular, staff on the programs and research teams had extensive training in gender, feminist, and queer theory as well as psychology and public health. In their everyday practice, I observed how this translated into employees actively drawing on these bodies of knowledge, including understandings of gender as a social construction, as a performance, and as culturally, socially, and historically embedded.

As a result of their education and training, GJO's employees perceived their colleagues and the organization as a whole to be highly qualified. As one senior manager explained to me, "We ask for a lot [of financial compensation], but we are very qualified. What differentiates GJO is that we have a research unit." As he explained, not only did GJO execute programs, similar to many NGOs, it also had a research unit that conducted M&E studies on its own work and was routinely contracted to conduct research for other organizations.

In contrast, AFD's employees were very new to working with young women, and, with one exception, they were entirely unfamiliar with the field of gender and sexuality. Their understanding of working with girls and young women came via the Nike Foundation's knowledge and expertise, when, ironically, the majority of Nike Foundation staff had almost no prior experience with gender and sexuality or with girls as a population on either a theoretical or practical level. During the time of my primary interviews at the foundation (2009–2010), only one senior staff member at Nike Foundation had a degree in women's studies, and she managed the creative division that developed the Girl Effect rather than working with programs or the M&E unit. In addition, while a number of the program managers had experience in the field of international development, only two program managers I encountered had significant experience working with girls or girls' education prior to working at the foundation. The remainder of the senior management and program managers had significant corporate experience, with many of them holding MBAs, but very little experience in international development. For example, one senior manager worked on shoes in China for the corporation before moving over to the foundation. Thus, for most of the employees, as with the staff of AFD, this was their first time working in the area of gender and sexuality. As a result, as Laura explained to me, "They are far from stale because they are coming from the corporate side for a short period, focusing on the issue and bringing their bright ideas to bear."

GJO was thus the expert vis-à-vis the Nike Foundation. It had the knowledge and experience on the topic and in the country. As a senior manager at GJO once exclaimed, "We have a new contact [at Nike

Foundation]. She doesn't know anything." This perception led GJO to have a fundamentally different power/knowledge relationship with the Nike than AFD. GJO had the power to operate independently of the Nike Foundation from an intellectual perspective whereas AFD was dependent on them. For GJO, this translated into a practical independence in their everyday work and M&E reporting to the foundation. For example, in the research report I wrote for GJO to send to the foundation, I critiqued various aspects of the Girl Effect's underlying logic, including its approach to adolescent pregnancy. When I asked GJO's leadership if they were concerned with the fact that I was critical, they shrugged it off as insignificant. To my knowledge, the foundation never responded to the report.

Moreover, given its expertise in M&E, the Nike Foundation requested that GJO oversee AFD's M&E process. This signaled that the Nike Foundation perceived AFD to be less competent, creating a complex, often tense relationship between the two NGOs. For example, João often grew frustrated by AFD's lack of expertise and experience in the field and by the dynamic between AFD and the Nike Foundation in a way I didn't observe with his M&E work for GJO. João explained:

> Nike Foundation has a recipe that comes from the context of Africa. The indicators don't make sense here in Brazil. But pregnancy and motherhood have to be indicators because Nike thinks that pregnancy can affect work. Yes, while she is pregnant it will be difficult to get a job, as no one hires pregnant women, but afterwards it won't be. Why is it that Nike doesn't want girls to get pregnant? For Nike Foundation, it is seen as evil. It's a really big thing for Nike Foundation.[23]

In working on the participant questionnaire for AFD, he explains that he did not want to ask the young women if they have children or if they are pregnant. "Nike said AFD had to ask. But we have other ways to discover that." João was constrained in his work on the AFD project in a way that he wasn't when evaluating GJO's projects. This went beyond the question of pregnancy, as he was similarly frustrated with the Nike Foundation's focus on entrepreneurship for young women in precarious financial and personal situations, as it could subject them to further precarity and indebtedness.

Nevertheless, while GJO's work moved beyond the instrumentalist focus on gender and sexuality deployed through the Girl Effect, it also employed practices that reproduced hegemonic logics of development. As I observed, its authority on national, regional, and transnational scales where it was praised and rewarded for its progressive politics on gender equality translated in local settings into a more top-down approach to gender equality than the organization and its staff seemed to imagine for itself. When encountering teachers and communities that were not privy to the knowledge that circulated in these elite state and private spheres, I observed the ways in which the organization reproduced uneven power dynamics between itself and those with whom it was partnering. In particular, this occurred through presentations or workshops on the ways teachers and administrators should be thinking and acting on gender equity, such as the teacher workshop I described. Rather than co-constructing the program with the teachers, as Olivia had ideally sought to do through the partnership, the teachers' perceived inability to move beyond rigid gender norms, homophobia, or public health perspectives on adolescent pregnancy led to a traditional pedagogical approach that mirrored the very one which Olivia herself critiqued. Thus, in practice, its embodiment of its mission varied across scales.

The research arm of GJO, for example, under the leadership of João, also employed M&E practices to measure the success of their programs and those of others, including AFD, using the same technologies the Nike Foundation promoted, such as baseline and endline surveys to measure changes in behavior, thinking, and conditions. In this way, the young women and men in the schools where GJO was implementing its program unknowingly became research subjects in a transnational experiment. GJO administered its surveys without parents or students consenting to participate, following what they explained to me as a new law allowing a principal to authorize research in schools without parental consent.[24] While perhaps legal, it raised questions for me about practices of consent among vulnerable subjects and the ethics of testing new methodologies and programs on young people and their communities.

Moreover, following common silences on race in the field of development,[25] GJO worked through a similar colorblind logic. In conversation with a GJO staff member, he explained that the executive leadership had responded in recent years to a survey from the Ford Foundation on whether it was investing in racial diversity. He stated, "I told them you cannot say that we are. What racial diversity? Let's be honest."

ADMINISTRATIVE AND FINANCIAL INDEPENDENCE

Administrative and financial independence were also critical factors enabling GJO to remain unrestrained by the Nike Foundation's logic and expectations. At the time I conducted my research, GJO was an independent organization founded and headquartered in Rio de Janeiro. Soon after, it opened a Washington, DC, office to manage its operations outside of Brazil. In comparison, AFD was a Brazilian organization affiliated with a Washington, DC–based NGO. This administrative distinction mattered on two levels. First, GJO had deep roots in the city. It had significant ties to local universities, foundations, corporations, NGOs, and local- and state-level secretariats. While AFD was also located in Rio de Janeiro, most of the organization's connections to local organizations, corporations, and government entities were relatively dependent on the executive director or on the organization's relationship with its Washington, DC, office and other Latin American affiliates. Second, since GJO didn't have to report back to an external authority, the executive director and senior leadership team could execute plans and make financial decisions without asking permission from, or answering to, a larger governing and financial body. In contrast, AFD's DC office secured the Nike Foundation grant, and held the contract with the Nike Foundation. The Brazilian affiliate then had a contractual agreement with the DC office to administer the grant. The DC office, in large part, had control over the affiliate's financial resources. As I observed, control over financial resources leads to control over discourses, decision-making, and other factors that constrain an organization's ability to act independently.

In contrast, GJO had multiple sources of ongoing funding at the time it was approached by the Nike Foundation. Those funders included well-known progressive international foundations and bilateral and multilateral organizations. That financial security ensured that GJO did not need the Nike Foundation's funding to exist or to continue its programming, which freed the organization from the constraints the other NGOs working with the Nike Foundation experienced. It could simply use the foundation's funding to complement its ongoing programing. Most important, its financial security ensured that it didn't have to worry about being re-granted. One of the most anxiety-producing aspects of AFD's relationship with the foundation was whether they would receive another grant. That created a feeling of dependency based on the fact that their ability to succeed according to the Nike Foundation's criteria and framework for success was perceived to determine their future.

At the time of the Nike Foundation's RFP, AFD held a grant from a prestigious regional funding source for its program for young men and women, but this was ending, necessitating the NGO securing funding to remain operational. Along with many other NGOs, it rushed to catch the new funding stream dedicated to girls to ensure funding for three years. Yet, even after receiving the funding and transforming their focus, the organization was not meeting the foundation's ongoing expectations. That grew paralyzing as the fear of not having funding in the future became more and more real as time passed. AFD began to act in ways that it otherwise might not have if it had not been concerned with re-granting. AFD ultimately did not get refunded when the Nike Foundation shifted its focus away from NGOs and toward the more important development institutions like DFID. AFD then had difficulty securing new funding. After receiving a small grant to hold it over, the program ended and AFD's Rio office shuttered its door. The employees lost their jobs, and had to struggle to receive pay for time they had worked. When I spoke with them in 2013, they were still attempting to resolve this issue with the Washington, DC, office.

Targeting girls has become a common financial practice for NGOs. It is a strategy for generating funds and for ensuring the survival of an organization. By changing their population focus, AFD, along with two other NGOs in Latin America funded through the Economic Empowerment Portfolio, were able to successfully secure millions of development dollars, but the consequences were significant. With their funding came the discourse of the Girl Effect, which impacted the ways in which AFD targeted and interacted with adolescent girls and young women and excluded adolescent boys and young men, who had previously been included.

Given the radically uneven power dynamics underlying corporate investment in girls, NGOs are in a position to benefit from, yet are simultaneously constrained by, corporate funders. Given the corporation's financial power and broader influence in the field of development, NGOs were weary of potential backlash, and thus careful regarding the character, depth, and public nature of their criticism. Nevertheless, the quiet critiques continued throughout my fieldwork, even if they only came in whispers and private conversations.

TOWARD AN UNDERSTANDING OF NGOS IN THE GIRL EFFECT

As this chapter demonstrates, understanding the power relations infusing the negotiations between the corporate foundation and the NGOs is essential for revealing how the Girl Effect was constructed, in part, through NGOs. They served as a linchpin in corporatized development. Without them, corporate foundations, such as the Nike Foundation, would not have been able to enact their forms of corporate benevolence and social responsibility.[26]

As the cases of GJO and AFD reveal, NGOs were incorporated within the Nike Foundation's corporatized development practices even if they ignored or rejected its logic. By GJO agreeing to partner with Nike Foundation, it provided the foundation with legitimacy and a platform in Brazil even after the more prestigious US foundation operating in Brazil declined to partner with it.

In this way, the "NGO form" provides the very objects of benevolence, expertise, capacity, relationships, and space that enable corporatized development to occur in non-corporate spaces, such as classrooms and communities.[27] Thus, "enacting the corporation,"[28] to borrow Marina Welker's concept, occurs, in part, in the context of these noncorporate spaces—from community-based spaces in favelas to NGO offices in the *centro* of Rio de Janeiro. These become part of the continually shifting geography of corporatized development.

Yet, at the same time, the NGO partnerships also reveal the very limits of corporatized development. In different ways, the stories of both AFD and GJO demonstrate that the project of the Girl Effect was never complete in the sphere of NGOs. The power of corporations and their foundations is ultimately limited by access to material and nonmaterial resources and conditions beyond the financial resources of philanthropy. In the case of GJO, the NGO used its expertise, translational ability, and financial and administrative independence to exert its power in relation to the corporate foundation. It rejected the foundation's logic whereby exposing the boundaries of possibility. Whereas in the case of AFD, the NGO failed to properly take up and prove the corporate foundation's logic. In both cases, the limits of the project of corporatized development were revealed.

Conclusion

ACCELERATING AND FREEING THE GIRL EFFECT

This book began on the New York Stock Exchange in the heart of Wall Street as prominent US transnational corporations declared poor, racialized girls and women to be an "emerging market." Even though the Third Billion Campaign itself has fizzled in strength and momentum, it represented, even if only for a moment, the ways in which "doing good" and "doing well" have become inextricably entangled around the bodies of Third World girls and women, blurring the lines between benevolence and profit. This occurred as US transnational corporations promoted the business case that gender inequality stymies economic growth and corporate profits. It has become the dominant rationale for urging corporations to invest in this population and for corporate foundations and CSR departments to justify their company's investments to their executives, boards of directors, and shareholders.

The Nike Foundation's Girl Effect brand represented the most prominent example of that form of corporatized expertise. It branded the common sense discourse that investing in girls' education, health, and economic empowerment is the most efficient solution for ending poverty and promoting economic growth. In this way, the Girl Effect reveals the ways in which these corporate investment practices simultaneously seek to position poor girls and women as instruments of poverty alleviation and as new frontiers for capitalist accumulation. Over almost a decade, the Nike Foundation used the knowledge and legitimacy it developed through its NGO partnerships with organizations like AFD and GJO, together with its marketing and branding power, to scale up the Girl Effect beyond the reach of the grassroots, national, and international NGOs. The foundation's targets became the World Bank and DFID, two of the most powerful development agencies in the world.[1] Yet, by 2014 it was clear that traditional development partners were not operating at the speed or providing the return the foundation sought.

ACCELERATING THE GIRL EFFECT

Moving beyond the world of development, the Nike Foundation set its sights on the entrepreneurial innovations and fast capital of Silicon Valley. Its breakthrough concept was the Girl Effect Accelerator. An accelerator is the start-up community's notion of a program that puts seed capital and mentoring into new for-profit ventures. The accelerator launched by Nike Foundation in partnership with the Unreasonable Group was an "intensive two-week program for entrepreneurs leading wildly innovative start-ups that are positioned to benefit millions of girls in poverty."[2] It was the first accelerator targeting businesses that focus on girls in their business plans, particularly on those who live on less than $2 per day. The accelerator represented a significant move beyond the perceived limitations of traditional development channels and into the world of market-driven enterprise. As Shaifali Puri, an Indian American woman and then executive director of global innovation at Nike Foundation, explained at the early November 2014 accelerator launch event in San Francisco, venture capitalists, angel investors, and entrepreneurs represent the foundation's next frontier for allocating far more capital than development donors have historically dedicated or had the capacity to invest.

Prior to the launch, entrepreneurs leading ten ventures in India and on the African continent, including in Nigeria, Uganda, Zambia, and Kenya, gathered at a luxury tent camp in Napa Valley for the two-week Girl Effect Accelerator. Since history demonstrates that nothing Nike, Inc.

or the Nike Foundation does is small, the foundation boldly approached the valley's top venture capital funds from Sand Hill Road (famous for its concentration of high-net worth funds) and tech designers from Google and Stanford University's Institute of Design (known as the d. school) to mentor the entrepreneurs in venture development. The Nike Foundation and the Unreasonable Group, its primary partner, described the ventures in the accelerator as the "true 'black swans' of our time: startups that have significant market traction, are working in the world's fastest emerging markets, and are positioned to measurably benefit millions of girls in poverty."[3] The entrepreneurs, who included both citizens of the countries and white US citizens living and working in those countries, presented their business plans and growth strategies for their bottom-billion ventures. They received intensive feedback from the mentors on how to target girls, take their businesses to scale, and, ultimately, profit while doing good.

Following the accelerator's program in Napa Valley, Nike Foundation and the Unreasonable Group hosted a launch in San Francisco for hundreds of techies, venture capitalists, and entrepreneurs at the beautiful Palace of Fine Arts. The show opened in the usual way Nike Foundation opens their events—with its viral Girl Effect video. The lights dimmed as the other participants and I settled into our chairs in the auditorium. As the screen in the front of the room went black I thought about how many events I had attended that began with this video or the 2.0 version. There was never any discussion of the video afterward. It was as if a video about a girl who will end poverty for herself and the world needs no explanation.

The idea of girls' potential to end poverty, as reflected in the video, was evident throughout the launch. Yet, unlike previous events I had attended or language I had become accustomed to hearing from its staff over the past nine years, the accelerator rapidly moved the crowd from the idea of investing in girls to end poverty to investing in their potential market value.[4] In this way, the return that was described was no longer the potential on GDP; it was a hard and fast bottom line. The crowd gathered to understand the profit potential of these for-profit enterprises. In her opening remarks, Shaifali Puri described how the foundation ended up in Silicon Valley:

> So you might ask yourself, what are we doing here, in the heart of San Francisco rather than walking the corridors of power in DC or in Davos or at the United Nations. Well, we've done that, and we will continue to do that, but the reality looks like this. In 2013, global aid flows were $136 billion. And despite the clear evidence of the multiplier effect, only an estimated 1% of those aid flows are targeted towards adolescent girls. But by way of contrast, a recent G8 task force estimated that the total amount invested by strategic impact investment funds on the planet is forecast to increase by 20% this year. And even outside impact investing, in more mainstream pools of capital, $45 trillion dollars has been publicly committed to be allocated towards social and impact returns as well as economic ones.
>
> So, this is what we know. We cannot stop the clock or keep the clock ticking for those 250 million adolescent girls if we do not unlock new actors, new models, and new market-led resources to work on their behalf. We know we must harness the talents, resources, the time, and attention of entrepreneurs, investors, and private capital that resides in innovation cradles around the world.
>
> Silicon Valley often describes itself as the nexus of dreaming, of doing. And many people have done big and dreamed even bigger in Silicon Valley, but I defy anyone in this room to find bigger dreams or doers than the entrepreneurs in our inaugural cohort of the Girl Effect Accelerator. They are building rapidly growing, scalable, successful businesses that are delivering education, energy, financial services, health, and livelihood to people, to millions of people living on less than $2 a day. Some of them are even generating revenue, which is an unusual term in these parts. But more importantly, they are committing that as their businesses continue to grow, continue to expand, continue to enter new markets, and new geographies, they will ensure that their products, their services, and their impact delivers innumerable benefits for adolescent girls living in poverty.

Given that the audience was filled with venture capitalists and entrepreneurs rather than the development actors and philanthropists that are more typical of most Girl Effect events, Puri's final point was emphasized again and again to this audience throughout the event—poor adolescent girls present substantial market potential and economic opportunity for those who dare to invest. As she explained, "Indeed Ban Ki Moon earlier this year at the World Economic Forum declared that affecting adolescent girls is the single biggest multiplier effect for global development because doing so creates clear pathways to new markets and new economic opportunity." Reflecting these dual notions of "doing good" for girls and "doing well" through girls, Mara Abrams, the former Nike Foundation's global partnerships manager, explained on the Girl Effect website ahead of the event, "I'm excited for these startups to show the world that it is possible to build a successful company that is both profitable and able to impact girls' lives on a massive scale."

As Puri noted, to talk about girls as a billion-dollar market is uncomfortable, particularly for traditional development audiences. Yet, this is, in part, why the Nike Foundation moved into the for-profit sector. She insists this language is necessary:

> All of these entrepreneurs are doing something huge and real in the for-profit sector. And they are not doing it by being niche or having a niche mindset. They are doing it with the same scale of ambition that any entrepreneur anywhere in the world who can fix it themselves as a game-changer and a world-changer is doing it. They're just doing it for problems that really, really matter. And not just that matter, but as one of our great mentors pointed out to us just yesterday, or the day before, in markets that are *billions of dollars in potential size, scope and opportunity.*
>
> And it feels strange sometimes to talk about an issue as morally, viscerally, culturally, and socially penetrating as the marginalization of adolescent girls in these kinds of terms. But I honestly believe that it is necessary because what these entrepreneurs are really showing you is that none of us in this eco-system, this for-profit, market-based, market-led, venture-driven, venture-backed eco-system can wash our hands of this problem. . .
>
> These entrepreneurs are leap-frogging the absence of electricity, the absence of schools and the absence of banks to do what they do. So, they're doing it, and showing us and blazing us a trail. I'm here today to say that frankly anyone of us can and *none of us can afford not to.*

The message to the investors was clear. Not only can they not avoid the problems facing adolescent girls, as they limit economic growth and profit potential throughout the world, they cannot afford not to invest in girls because there are profits to be made at the bottom of this pyramid.

As Mohanjit Jolly, an Indian American partner at the venture capital firm DFJ, whose investments include Twitter, Tumblr, Skype, and Solar

City, explained, "I am here to basically do my part as what I call, the do good, do well investor. So, we are not a philanthropic entity. We are a venture capital firm, but I am here as hopefully some proof that you can actually do social good to tens of millions, maybe hundreds of millions of people around the world and do it profitably, which is the angle that I take."

Following the launch, in which images of girls and the ventures targeting them were on exhibition, a self-selected, small group of investors, entrepreneurs, and Nike Foundation staff met the following day at the private investor gathering in the city. The event cost $675 per person. As a result, there were only approximately fifteen to twenty paying individuals who attended the event, including myself (using research funds). The other attendees were entrepreneurs and staff from the Nike Foundation and Unreasonable Group. Here, both the investors and the entrepreneurs seeking their capital spoke with ease about profiting from adolescent girls as a bottom billion market.

After a "deep dive" session with one of the entrepreneurs, a white, US male, I stood in the hallway outside the bathroom with Jeff, a white angel investor, who invests capital in start-ups. Jeff and I, along with another attendee and a Nike Foundation staff member, had just spent two hours with the founder as he extolled his bottom of the pyramid model. The entrepreneur was attending the Girl Effect Accelerator to develop a plan for targeting girls in its expansion and to seek an additional round of funding. Jeff turned to me saying, "I hope they go public, and make their investors a boat load of money." While the raw calculus of these investors' interest in educating girls through this for-profit model was evident—they were in it for the economic returns—they also had other visions and underlying motivations.

Jeff had explained in the earlier session that he was concerned about the impact of population growth on wildlife, or in his language, with "saving the critters." Thus, as an environmentalist and a capitalist, he was drawn to the Girl Effect on two fronts. First, he was investing in the Girl Effect to reduce fertility rates among Black and Brown girls in the Global South in order to limit the impact of population growth on animal life, deforestation, and climate change, and, second, to generate economic returns for his investments. Underlying both of these motivations is the racializing, neo-Malthusian logic of population control where some human life must be reduced in order to ensure healthy wildlife and profit. This begs the question of what it means for one to care more for animals and profit than for Black and Brown lives and futures.

One of the other start-ups reflected the foundation's proficiency at harnessing benevolence in the service of profit. I attended a "deep dive" session with the two senior executives of the company, along with a few others, including a private equity employee, a Skoll Foundation employee, and a Nike Foundation employee. After they described their business model, I asked, "Why the sudden interest in girls?" The business model they had just described did not target girls. As young, upper-class men from the African continent educated at elite universities and trained at companies in the United States and Europe, they explained that they had grown concerned about the condition of girls in their country. At the same time, they received an invitation from the Nike Foundation and the Unreasonable Group to attend the accelerator. The confluence of these events led them to accept the invitation with the intention of participating in the accelerator to "help" girls in their country. As the CEO remarked, "We came here thinking, what can we do to help girls?" The two entrepreneurs recounted their mentoring sessions during the accelerator program with a Nike, Inc. executive who encouraged them to bridge their benevolent focus with the market potential of girls for their business. As the CEO explained, "[The executive] told me, 'Think of girls as a target market for you some day. How do you unlock that market?'" In response to the executive's urging, the other individual remarked, "Girls become women, and women become our customers. So obvious, but I didn't see it." He further relayed their conversation with the executive, as he explained her response to his line of inquiry: "When [the executive] was with us, I asked specifically, 'What is Nike, Inc. doing about the Girl Effect?' She told us, 'It is squarely about their supply chain. You gotta get the supply chain right. This is the only thing we do. Because that is where the business case is. And it is the most sustainable because it's not based on an individual.'" As they further explained this realization, the CEO considered how they might bring about this transformation in their business model:

> Can we unlock the Girl Effect through our business model? . . . But the why has to be aligned with our business case. We had a conversation about it

> with our board. This is a huge investment. Aside for my own personal investment, I was raised by a single-mother. I've concluded that women are more productive than men. But that is not going to win the day. There is a target market and a real business case. We are going to measure what is going on in our agent network. How productive are the women agents in comparison to male agents? Develop the case. What is the business case to go after schools? Then we measure it. If there is a business case, no one will question.

Through the girl-focused mentoring the entrepreneurs received, along with the broader conversations in the accelerator, they shifted their understanding of working with girls as a benevolent possibility to girls as a future accumulation strategy. Based on communication with Nike Foundation, this quote "does not represent the executive's full perspective." As the foundation explained, her intention was "to help entrepreneurs think more broadly about adolescent girls and to look at their approach from different angles."[5]

The accelerator supported the entrepreneurs to make the business case for investing in girls in two ways. The first was the intimate one-on-one work the accelerator was doing with companies in emerging markets to make them understand the potential of girls as a new market and to restructure their business models to target them. But, as a social relation, a market only exists if there are both investment opportunities (i.e., businesses) and capital (i.e., investors). Thus, in the second way, the foundation moved into Silicon Valley, and created inspiring, personalized environments for individuals and firms with capital to become "girl investors," a new class of investors the foundation initiated, in part, if not fully. In bringing together potential businesses and investors, and transforming them through carefully curated and choreographed work, the foundation was working to create a new market where it did not already exist. By doing so, the foundation worked to bring ventures and investors together to actively construct poor girls as a new frontier market. While this only lasted for a year, the accelerator enabled the foundation to move from talking about girls as engines of development and an emerging market and investing in programs and policies targeting them based on this assumption, to being intimately involved in the making—the labor and funding—of girls as a new capitalist frontier.

AND ONWARD WE GO: FREEING THE GIRL EFFECT

The moment was fleeting, however. The foundation's focus on targeting for-profit ventures through the accelerator was still in its nascent stages when the Girl Effect was declared independent of Nike, Inc. and the Nike Foundation on September 1, 2015, less than one year after the accelerator launch. Girl Effect was founded as a social business based in London. Unlike the Nike Foundation, it operates both a charitable and a business arm. In this way, the Girl Effect may be freer to promote for-profit endeavors focused on girls than were allowed under the foundation's 501(c)(3) status.[6] This shift came after a decade of building, legitimizing, and developing its focus on adolescent girls in collaboration with other partners. In coordination with a press release from the new Girl Effect organization, Maria Eitel, former president and CEO of the Nike Foundation and now co-chair of the Nike Foundation, chairman of Girl Effect, and Nike, Inc. executive, wrote an e-mail to Nike Foundation grantees and partners.[7] She wrote:

> Over the past decade, we have touched millions of girls' lives. And every ounce of insight, and hard work, and effort you have made to the Girl Effect matters. It matters to the girl. It matters to Nike. It matters to me. And, I know, it matters to you.

Her focus on the value of the work to girls, the company, herself, and each of the grantees and partners who have committed to the Girl Effect, was an attempt to reinforce the notion that the work mattered despite Nike, Inc. and the Nike Foundation's decision to reduce its institutional commitment to the issue by becoming independent from the Girl Effect. She reassured the recipients of the e-mail that although the path has been challenging, it "has all been in the service of learning, and then applying our highest talents to make good on an insight: When a girl rises up, she lifts everything—and everyone—around her." As this book has narrated, the project of the Girl Effect is a recursive process of knowledge production and educational intervention based on "an insight" about Third World girls developed and branded by the foundation.

In minimal detail, Eitel explained the nature of the Nike Foundation's future relationship with the Girl Effect.

> I am proud to share that after being incubated at the NIKE Foundation, fueled by our collective hard work, Girl Effect is now becoming its own entity outside of NIKE. Girl Effect the movement, will now also be an organization that will pursue all the relationships in the private, public, and social sectors that are required to now take the Girl Effect to scale and reach all 250 million adolescent girls living in poverty. The NIKE Foundation remains a committed supporter of the work.

How, and to what extent, Nike, Inc. will continue to provide financial and logistical support for Girl Effect was not clear in the e-mail or the press release to the public. Based on personal communication with Nike Foundation, it "continues to champion and support Girl Effect's mission."[8] During its first year as an independent organization, Nike Foundation gave $15,400,000 to support Girl Effect's charitable activities.[9] Yet, beyond charitable work, the Girl Effect is now positioned to engage in for-profit business pursuits, which the foundation was previously constrained from doing due to its 501(c)(3) status as a tax-exempt foundation.

THE GENDER EFFECT

Regardless of the vagueness of the corporation's decision or its manner of extracting itself from its commitment, what is clear is that Nike, Inc.'s moment of crisis had passed. When the corporation made the decision to focus the foundation on adolescent girls in 2005, it was still recovering from being the target of the anti-sweatshop movement in the 1990s. This process of recovery was part of reconstructing consent for its consumer brand and the corporation itself. For Nike, Inc., the Girl Effect was a concrete manifestation of its process of imagining itself to be a socially responsible corporation.

Nike, Inc.'s commitment to adolescent girls accompanied the corporation's other efforts to make its ethical and unethical practices explicit[10] by marketing the greening of its production and disclosing its contract factories.[11] Together with the work of the foundation, these efforts have been part of restoring the company's image in the public imagination. With the exception of brief media attention for labor unrest in contract factories and campaigns by activists, such as Jim Keady's No Sweat campaign and the efforts of United Students against Sweatshops, the anti-sweatshop movement is no longer influential in the United States, and Nike, Inc. is no longer a global pariah.

Despite purportedly responsible practices, the Nike Foundation's investment in the Girl Effect over the past ten years occurred even as Nike, Inc.'s business practices continued to exacerbate conditions of vulnerability for the same population they claimed to be serving. Rather than deal with its own role in pioneering and perpetuating practices of outsourcing poor, racialized female labor in its supply chain, the company committed to economically empowering individual girls who would ideally pursue their own self-interests as new participants in employment and consumer markets in the global economy. In doing so, it developed an individualized solution to ameliorating the effects of its systemic corporate abuses of Third World girls and women as outsourced laborers and its perpetuation of the structural problems of flexible, transnational capitalism.

Thus, the far most successful "gender effect" has been Nike Foundation's extension of the corporation's legitimacy, authority, and reach without the corporation having to deal with the contradictions in its business practices and in capitalism itself. That has had the effect of de-politicizing girls and women's demands for fair corporate labor practices and a just global economy and disarticulating poverty's persistence from the historical, structural conditions that produce it and for which corporations such as Nike, Inc. are often partially responsible.

As a result of its efforts to contain its external and internal crises since 1998, regardless of whether its underlying contradictions were resolved or not, Nike, Inc. no longer needs the foundation's focus on girls to legitimize it as a good corporate citizen. As this history of Nike, Inc. demonstrates, the emergence and hegemony of CSR in the first decade of the new millennium, as a discourse and paradigm through which business functions, was critical to the recovery of corporate capitalism from the anti-globalization attacks in the 1990s, the financial crisis of 2008, and ongoing environmental crises. It enabled corporations to incorporate activist demands for socially responsible companies into its corporate practices without substantively shifting their forms of profit maximization.[12]

The case of Nike, Inc.'s story with adolescent girls ultimately reveals how the corporate focus on poor girls and women of color in the Global

South is constituted through the reactionary *and* expansionary tendencies of corporate capitalism. It demonstrates how one company recuperated from the critique waged against it while investing in the economic potential of girls and women on the edges of its supply-chain and consumer geographies.

In that way, the reactionary and expansionary practice of investing in girls and women has become part of the making of frontier capitalism. In the case of Nike, Inc., the Girl Effect Accelerator marked the clearest expression of these racialized and gendered economistic desires. It revealed the expansionary tendencies of corporatized development's focus on girls and women in a way no other moment in Nike, Inc.'s decade-long commitment to adolescent girls did. It was a concrete illustration of imagining and investing in Third World girls as a potential billion-dollar market and, thus, a valuable new capitalist frontier.

CORPORATE FUNDING FOR FEMINIST FUTURES?

Corporatized development is a power/knowledge/capital regime negotiated between corporations, corporate foundations, and their grantees and partners. In order for a grantee or partner to successfully negotiate this regime, I showed how it must mobilize material and nonmaterial resources to its advantage; the cost of an inability or failure to negotiate is dependency on the corporation or corporate foundation. In this way, the corporation or corporate foundation becomes sovereign over the organization and its future as the corporate logics, goals, and measures of success work to constrain the organization's practices.

As Nike, Inc. and Nike Foundation shift the focus of the foundation away from adolescent girls, there is a proliferation of corporations entering the field on local, national, regional, and transnational scales. I am interested in how other corporations are negotiating their development practices with progressive, transnational feminist and women's organizations, in particular. Some of these companies have realized the complexities of working with girls and women on the ground, and are challenging Nike Foundation's manner of engagement. Rather than plow forward with their instrumentalist economic agendas and limited knowledge of the issues facing girls and women, a number of corporations are moving toward a more holistic approach where they seek the expertise of feminist and women's organizations that have long worked with girls and women. This is evident in relationships between a small group of corporations and progressive, transnational women's rights and feminist organizations that often rejected corporate funding yet are now cautiously engaging corporations to capture this funding stream and to advocate for more progressive feminist understandings of girls' and women's well-being and futures. In August 2015, the Win-Win Coalition was launched after almost two years of efforts by these women's and feminist organizations, including Association of Women in Development (AWID), Global Fund for Women, Mama Cash, and Fundo Elas, their "bridge builder" allies that move between the women's rights and corporate sectors, and a small group of companies, including PepsiCo, C&A, and Symantec, to support these "cross-sector partnerships." How these new partnerships are negotiated, and to whose benefit, is critical to understanding how this phenomenon will continue to play out in the future.

As documented in this book, corporations overwhelmingly pursue the "business case" for girls' and women's empowerment, which translates, in most cases, into a narrow economic focus detached from a women's rights agenda. Corporations tend to avoid the language of women's rights, and human rights more broadly, given potential contradictions with their own business practices. Instead, they frame girls and women as "resources" for poverty alleviation and development, the language and meaning of which is often contested by women's rights and feminist organizations who resent this framing.

With time, this most recent moment of transnational corporate investment in girls and women will reveal the possibilities, tensions, and contradictions of these awkward engagements, as the relationships among philanthropic benevolence, corporate profit, and feminism are articulated with gender, sexuality, race, and poverty across diverse institutions in uneven geographies. The women's rights and feminist organizations who engage in these corporate partnerships may have to negotiate the often conflicting, if not explicitly antagonistic, agendas of their corporate donors and grassroots grantees, many of whom live with and work against exploitative corporate labor, and environmental, consumer, and militaristic practices in their communities and countries.

Continuing to examine this phenomenon is important for understanding how the ongoing, yet subtly transforming processes of the feminization of capitalism are shaping the terrain of feminist struggle against social, cultural, political, and economic exploitation, particularly as progressive, transnational feminist and women's organizations are seeking funding and the ability to influence how these investments in girls and women are structured, and for whom.

What does it mean for the hegemony of corporate capitalism when feminist and women's organizations long involved in holding corporations accountable and transparent are now partnering with them? Is this another example of a "corporate effect" where corporations not only need mainstream NGOs and liberal feminist organizations but also progressive feminist and women's organizations to legitimize their corporate power by neutralizing critique against them and to extend their reach into new frontiers?

Or are feminist and women's organizations defining the terms of engagement and perhaps even creating partnerships that move "beyond the business case," as Suzanne Bergeron and Stephen Healy describe, toward a more just conceptualization of gender, development, and the global economy?[13] As explained to me by one feminist activist who had long been a critic of feminist engagement in corporate spaces, these are attempts to command a "seat at the table rather than under it." If this is possible, what is gained, and what is lost in this strategic maneuver?

Throughout this study, my interlocutors across diverse locations in the development regime have consistently called for increased transparency and accountability for corporations in their relationships with Third World girls and women as laborers in their factories, agricultural fields, and retail stores as well as purported beneficiaries of their philanthropic and socially responsible endeavors. Yet, in these complicated transnational relationships, to whom and for what are these corporations responsible? And who and what can hold them accountable for their effects on girls' and women's lives and futures as well as on labor, the environment, and communities around the world? As progressive, transnational feminist and women's organizations become increasingly important actors in this phenomenon, critical feminist scholars and activists must contend with whether, how, and to what extent corporate capital can be used for progressive feminist purposes, and whether these actors can, in turn, hold corporations accountable to the girls and women their capital supposedly benefits, and shape, if not transform, the hegemonic discourse on the Third World potential of girls and women. Or, as evidenced thus far, will corporate capital continue to remake itself, incorporating progressive feminist claims into its new hegemony, as it shapes the terrain of struggle in its own image and further entrenches relations of exploitation that put poor, racialized girls and women in increasingly precarious positions as the frontiers of capitalism expand?

Sources to Timeline of Nike, Inc. and Nike Foundation History and Public Response

1964 Knight, Phil. *Shoe Dog: A Memoir by the Creator of NIKE.* New York, London, Toronto, Sydney, New Delhi: Scribner, 2016

1971 Strasser, J.B., and Laurie, Becklund. *Swoosh: The Unauthorized Story of Nike and the Men who Played There.* NY: HarperCollins Publisher, 1991

Goldman, Robert, and Stephen, Papson. (1998). *Nike Culture: The Sign of the Swoosh.* London, California, New Delhi: SAGE Publications Ltd, 1998

1977 Strasser, J.B., and Laurie, Becklund. *Swoosh: The Unauthorized Story of Nike and the Men who Played There.* NY: HarperCollins Publisher, 1991

1988 Peter, Jeremy W. "The Birth of 'Just Do It' and Other Magic Words." *The New York Times,* August 19, 2009. http://www.nytimes.com/2009/08/20/business/media/20adco.html

1991 Jeff, Ballinger. "Inside the Vienna Consensus." *CounterPunch,* January 11, 2008. https://www.counterpunch.org/2008/01/11/inside-the-vienna-consensus/

1992 Jeffrey, Ballinger. "The New Free-Trade Heel; Nike's Profits on the Backs of Asian workers." *Harper's Magazine,* August 1992. https://harpers.org/archive/1992/08/the-new-free-trade-heel/

Prakash, Sethi. *Setting Global Standards: Guidelines for Creating Codes of Conduct in Multinational Corporations.* Hobken, New Jersey: John Wiley & Sons, Inc., 2003

1993 Locke, Richard M. *The Promise and Perils of Globalization: The Case of Nike.* Cambridge: MIT Working Paper Series, July 2002. https://ipc.mit.edu/sites/default/files/documents/02-007.pdf

Atkinson, Michael. *Battleground Sports.* Westport, Connecticut, London: Greenwood Press, 2009.

1994 Locke, Richard M. *The Promise and Perils of Globalization: The Case of Nike.* Cambridge: MIT Working Paper Series, July 2002. https://ipc.mit.edu/sites/default/files/documents/02-007.pdf

1996 Sydney, Schanberg H. "Six Cents an Hour." *Life Magazine,* June 1996. https://www.laborrights.org/in-the-news/six-cents-hour

Jeff, Jensen. "Marketer of the Year: Nike." *AdAge,* December 16, 1996. http://adage.com/article/news/marketer-year-nike/30663/

Daniel, Tsang C. "Just Do It! The Boycott Nike Campaign." *Stern Publishing, Inc. OC Weekly,* December 13, 1996. https://www.saigon.com/nike/news/Oc1.html

1997 Dana, Canedy. "Nike Appoints Andrew Young to Review its Labor Practices." *The New York Times,* March 25, 1997." http://www.nytimes.com/1997/03/25/business/nike-appoints-andrew-young-to-review-its-labor-practices.html

Laura, Hartman P. *et al.* (eds.). *Rising Above Sweatshops: Innovative Approaches to Global Labor Challenges.* Westport, Connecticut, London: Praeger, 2003

Russell, Mokhiber, and Robert, Weissmann. "Multinational Monitor's 10 Worst Corporations of the Year." *Multinational Monitor,* December 30, 1997. http://multinationalmonitor.org/focus/focus.9708.html

World Bank Group. "Nike in Vietnam: The Tae Kwang Vina Factory." *WorldBank.Org.* http://siteresources.worldbank.org/INTEMPOWERMENT/Resources/14826_Nike-web.pdf (accessed December 28, 2017).

Dana, O'Rourke. "Smoke From a Hired Gun: A Critique of Nike's Labor and Environmental Auditing in Vietnam as Performed by Ernst & Young." *Transnational Resource and Action Center,* November 10, 1997. http://nature.berkeley.edu/orourke/PDF/smoke.pdf

Peter, Dreier. "The Campus Anti-Sweatshop Movement." *The American Prospect,* September – October 1999. "http://prospect.org/article/campus-anti-sweatshop-movement

Tim, Connor. "Clinton's 'No Sweatshop' Agreement: A Small Step or a Great Leap Forward for the Rights of Workers. *CorpWatch,* September 12, 1997. http://www.corpwatch.org/article.php?id=3032

1998 John, Cushmand, J. Jr. "International Business: Nike Pledges to End Child Labor and Apply U.S. Rules Abroad." *The New York Times,* May 13, 1998. http://www.nytimes.com/1998/05/13/business/international-business-nike-pledges-to-end-child-labor-and-apply-us-rules-abroad.html

Holman, Jenkins W. Jr. "The Rise and Stumble of Nike." *The Wall Street Journal,* June 3, 1998. https://www.wsj.com/articles/SB896820560693432500

Laura, Hartman P. *et al.* (eds.). *Rising Above Sweatshops: Innovative Approaches to Global Labor Challenges.* Westport, Connecticut, London: Praeger, 2003

1999 Kevin, Quigley F.F. "Global Alliance Aims to Improve Factory Workers' Lives." *Alliance Magazine.* March 01, 2001. http://www.alliancemagazine.org/analysis/global-alliance-aims-to-improve-factory-workers-lives/

Matt, Wilsey, and Scott, Lichtig. The Nike Controversy. *Stanford.edu,* May 12, 1998. https://web.stanford.edu/class/e297c/trade_environment/wheeling/hnike.html

2000 Steven, Greenhouse. "Nike's Chief Cancels a Gift Over Monitor of Sweatshops." *The New York Times,* April 25, 2000. http://www.nytimes.com/2000/04/25/us/nike-s-chief-cancels-a-gift-over-monitor-of-sweatshops.html

2001 Tim, Connor. "Still Waiting for Nike To Do It: Nike's Labor Practices in the Three Years Since CEO Phil Knight's Speech to the National Press Club." *The Global Exchange,* May 2001. https://archive.cleanclothes.org/documents/01-05NikeReport.pdf

Julia, Day. "Nike: 'no guarantee on child labour.'" *The Guardian,* October 19, 2001. https://www.theguardian.com/media/2001/oct/19/marketingandpr

2003 Adweek Staff. "Nike's Knight is Advertiser of the Year." *AdWeek,* February 2003. http://www.adweek.com/brand-marketing/nikes-knight-advertiser-year-61714/

2004 Simon, Zadek. "The Path to Corporate Responsibility." *Harvard Business Review,* December 2004. https://hbr.org/2004/12/the-path-to-corporate-responsibility

2005 Nike, Inc., "Investor News Details: Nike Foundation Steps on to new field." *Nike News.* March 08, 2005. http://investors.nike.com/investors/news-events-and-reports/investor-news/investor-news-details/2005/Nike-Foundation-Steps-on-to-New-Field/default.aspx

Nike, Inc., "Nike Issues FY04 Corporate Social Responsibility." *Nike News.* April 13, 2005. https://news.nike.com/news/nike-issues-fy04-corporate-responsibility-report

Nike, Inc. "Nike Publishes List of Global Contract Factories in Push for Greater Transparency and Collaboration to Improve Footwear and Apparel Industry Labor Conditions." *CSRWire,* April 13, 2005. http://www.csrwire.com/press_releases/24956-Nike-Publishes-List-of-Global-Contract-Factories-in-Push-for-Greater-Transparency-and-Collaboration-to-Improve-Footwear-and-Apparel-Industry-Labor-Conditions

Ruth, Levine, *et al.* "Girls Count: A Global Investment & Action Agenda." *The Center for Global Development,* 2009. https://novofoundation.org/wp-content/uploads/2012/07/Girls_Count_2009.pdf

Nike, Inc. "Nike Publishes List of Global Contract Factories in Push for Greater Transparency and Collaboration to Improve Footwear and Apparel Industry Labor Conditions." *CSRWire,* April 13, 2005. http://www.csrwire.com/press_releases/24956-Nike-Publishes-List-of-Global-Contract-Factories-in-Push-for-Greater-Transparency-and-Collaboration-to-Improve-Footwear-and-Apparel-Industry-Labor-Conditions

2008 CBS News. "Vietnamese Shoemakers Walk Out on Nike." *Associated Press,* April 1, 2008. https://www.cbsnews.com/news/vietnamese-shoemakers-walk-out-on-nike/

Foundation Center. "NIKE, NoVo Foundation Commit $100 Million to the Girl Effect." May 28, 2008. http://philanthropynewsdigest.org/news/nike-novo-foundation-commit-100-million-to-the-girl-effect

Nike, Inc. "Adolescent Girls Initiative Launched." *Nike News,* October 10, 2008. https://news.nike.com/news/adolescent-girls-initiative-launched

Nike, Inc. "Nike Foundation Launches New girleffect.org." *Nike News,* December 11, 2012. http://news.nike.com/news/nike-foundation-launches-new-girleffectorg

2009 A Berkshire Company. "World Economic Forum Gives Adolescent Girls a Voice on the Global Stage." *BusinessWire,* James 30, 2009. http://www.businesswire.com/news/home/20090130005608/en/World-Economic-Forum-Adolescent-Girls-Voice-Global

Nike, Inc. "Nike Foundation Joins Cross-Sector Leaders in Gender Equality Symposium." *Nike News,* March 30, 2009. https://news.nike.com/news/nike-foundation-joins-cross-sector-leaders-in-gender-equality-symposium

2010 Steven, Greenhouse. "Pressured, Nike to Help Workers in Honduras." *The New York Times.* July 26, 2010. http://www.nytimes.com/2010/07/27/business/global/27nike.html

Feminist.com. "The Girl Effect 2010 Video 'The Clock is Ticking' Receives Premiere at Clinton Global Initiative. http://www.feminist.com/activism/girleffect.html (accessed December 28, 2017).

2011 John, Braddock. "Nike Faces Allegations of Worker Abuse in Indonesia." *World Socialist Web Site,* September 08, 2011. https://www.wsws.org/en/articles/2011/09/nike-s08.html

Bart, King. "Mattel, HP, Nike Ranked Among Top Ten by Corporate Responsibility Magazine. *Sustainable Brands,* March 4, 2011. http://www.sustainablebrands.com/news_and_views/articles/mattel-hp-nike-ranked-among-top-ten-corporate-responsibility-magazine

Herrera, Tilde. "Nike's Sustainability Report Takes Top Ceres-ACCA Award." *GreenBiz,* May 11, 2011. https://www.greenbiz.com/news/2011/05/11/nikes-sustainability-report-takes-top-ceres-acca-award

2012 Locke, Richard M. *The Promise and Perils of Globalization: The Case of Nike.* Cambridge: MIT Working Paper Series, July 2002. https://ipc.mit.edu/sites/default/files/documents/02-007.pdf

2014 Unreasonable Group. "The Girl Effect Accelerator." *GirlEffectAccelerator.* https://unreasonablegroup.com/portfolio/girl-effect/ (accessed December 28, 2017).

Mike, Ozanian. "The Forbes Fab 40: The World's Most Valuable Sports Brand 2014." *Forbes,* October 7, 2014. http://www.forbes.com/sites/mikeozanian/2014/10/07/the-forbes-fab-40-the-worlds-most-valuable-sports-brands-2014/#4f2a71751676

2015 Nike, Inc. "Girl Effect News: Girl Effect Embarks on New Chapter." *Nike News,* September 01, 2015. http://news.nike.com/girl-effect

Notes

PREFACE

1. *The Girl Effect*, The Girl Effect, 2008, www.girleffect.org/media?id=3453.

2. "CGI 2009 Annual Meeting," Clinton Global Initiative, n.d., ,https:/www.clintonfoundation.org/clinton-global-initiative/meetings/annual-meetings/2009/webcasts/day-2

3. Nike Foundation, "Investor News Details: Nike Foundation Steps on to New Field," Nike News, March 8, 2005, http://investors.nike.com/investors/news-events-and-reports/investor-news/investor-news-details/2005/Nike-Foundation-Steps-on-to-New-Field/default.aspx.

4. "United Nations Millennium Development Goals," United Nations, n.d., www.un.org/millenniumgoals/.

5. "International Women's Day Marked around the World," an interview between Amy Goodman and Kavita Ramdas, Democracy Now, March 8, 2010, accessed March 13, 2012, www.democracynow.org/2010/3/8/international_womens_day_marked_around_the.

6. "International Women's Day: History of the Day," United Nations Women, n.d., accessed August 14, 2017, www.un.org/en/events/womensday/history.shtml.

7. These include development institutions, such as the World Bank and USAID, private foundations, such as the Gates Foundation, nongovernmental organizations, such as CARE and Plan International, and global forums, such as the World Economic Forum and the Clinton Global Initiative.

INTRODUCTION

1. "Third Billion Seeks to Empower Women, Brooke Says," Bloomberg TV, accessed February 1, 2012, www.ustream.tv/recorded/20156941.

2. Booz & Co. was acquired by PricewaterhouseCoopers in 2014, and its name was changed to Strategy&.PricewaterhouseCoopers,- accessed January 31, 2017, www.pwc.com/us/en/press-releases/2014/pwc-completes-its-acquisition-of-booz-and-company.html.

3. "The Third Billion," strategy + business, accessed December 28, 2017, https://www.strategy-business.com/article/10211?gko=98895

4. Ibid.

5. Ibid.

6. Ibid.

7. "The Third Billion," The Third Billion, accessed July 17, 2013, https://web.archive.org/web/20130625122005/http://thethirdbillion.org/.

8. Ibid.

9. Ibid.

10. Mulher360, "Corporate Movement for Women's Economic Development," Walmart Brasil, 2015, 9, www.walmartbrasil.com.br/wm/wp-content/uploads/2015/08/Movimento-Mulher-360-En.pdf.

11. "O Movimento," Movimento Mulher 360, n.d., accessed September 5, 2017, http://movimentomulher360.com.br/institucional/o-movimento/.

12. For reports by development institutions and corporations, see the following: Kristin Lewis, "The Gender Dividend: A Business Case for Gender Equality," UN Women, 2011, www2.unwomen.org/~/media/headquarters/media/publications/en/unwomenthegenderdividend.pdf?v=1&d=20140917T100949; "The Business of Empowering Women: Where, Why, and How," McKinsey&Company, January 2010, http://mckinseyonsociety.com/the-business-of-empowering-women/; "The Business Case for Women's Economic Empowerment: An Integrated Approach," International Center for Research on Women, Oak Foundation, and Dalberg and Witter Ventures, 2014, www.icrw.org/publications/business-case-womens-economic-empowerment-integrated-approach.

For more critical accounts of the "business case," see the following: Suzanne Bergeron and Stephen Healy, "Beyond the Business Case: A Community Economics Approach to Gender, Development and Social Economy" (draft paper prepared for the UNRISD Conference on Potential and Limits of Social and Solidarity Economy, Geneva, 2013, 6–80; Juanita Elias, "Davos Woman to the Rescue of Global Capitalism: Postfeminist Politics and Competitiveness Promotion at the World Economic Forum," *International Political Sociology* 7, no. 2 (June 1, 2013): 152–69, doi:10.1111/ips.12015; Elisabeth Prügl and Jacqui True, "Equality Means Business? Governing Gender through Transnational Public-Private Partnerships," *Review of International Political Economy* 21, no. 6 (2014): 1137–69, doi:10.1080/09692290.2013.849277; Adrienne Roberts, "The Political Economy of 'Transnational Business Feminism,'" *International Feminist Journal of Politics* 17, no. 2 (January 28, 2014): 209–31.

13. "The Global Economy: Strengthening Growth and Job Creation—Statement at G20 Leader's Summit," *OECD* (remarks by Angel Gurria, secretary-general, OECD, Brisbane, 2014), www.oecd.org/g20/summits/brisbane/the-global-economy-strengthening-growth-and-job-creation.htm.

14. Ibid.

15. "Be What's Possible, Gap, Inc., n.d., accessed September 5, 2017, www.bewhatspossible.com/pace.

16. *10,000 Women*, Goldman Sachs, accessed December 22, 2011, www.goldmansachs.com/citizenship/10000women/.

17. C. K. Prahalad, *The Fortune at the Bottom of the Pyramid: Eradicating Poverty through Profits* (London: Pearson FT Press, 2009) 6.

18. Paul Collier, *The Bottom Billion: Why the Poorest Countries Are Failing and What Can Be Done about It* (Oxford: Oxford University Press, 2007).

19. C. K. Prahalad and Stuart L. Hart, "The Fortune at the Bottom of the Pyramid," Strategy+Business, January 10, 2002, www.strategy-business.com/article/11518?gko=9a4ba.

20. Ananya Roy, "Ethical Subjects: Market Rule in an Age of Poverty," *Public Culture* 24, no. 1 (2012): 106.

21. Thank you to Dinak Rajak for her suggestions on this topic and to Selah Agaba for her work on this section.

22. Another example is Hinustan Unilever's Fair and Lovely whitening cream that markets whiteness to girls' and women's aspirations, which are predicated on (post)colonial desires rooted in notions of colorism for light skin tones, "social hierarchy based on gradations of skin tone within and between racial/ethnic groups". These desires are often linked to discrimination in marriage and job markets. As described by the company, the whitening cream has provided "hope to millions of women around the world, especially in Asia, who desired fairer and even-toned skin, for how it made them feel about themselves, and for how it made the world see them." See Glenn, Evelyn Nakano. "Yearning for Lightness: Transnational Circuits in the Marketing and Consumption of Skin Lighteners," *Gender & society* 22, no. 3 (2008): 281–302. Despite criticism, the company operates in over forty countries across Asia, Africa, and Latin America.

23. Avon, "Experience Avon's History," Avon: The Company for Women, n.d., September 5, 2017, http://www.avoncompany.com/aboutavon/history/index.html.

24. Linda Scott et al., "Enterprise and Inequality: A Study of Avon in South Africa," *Entrepreneurship Theory and Practice* 36, no. 3 (2012): 543–68.

25. Matthew Bishop and Michael Green, *Philanthrocapitalism: How Giving Can Save the World* (New York: Bloomsbury Press, 2009).

26. Linsey McGoey, "Philanthrocapitalism and Its Critics," *Poetics* 40, no. 2 (April 2012): 185–99.

27. Ibid.

28. Ibid.

29. Ibid., 197.

30. Kohl-Arenas, Erica, *The Self-Help Myth: How Philanthropy Fails to Alleviate Poverty* (Oakland: University of California Press, 2015).

31. "Gap and Walmart in Bangladesh: A History of Irresponsibility and Empty Promises," Clean Clothes Campaign, n.d., accessed September 5, 2017, https://cleanclothes.org/resources/background/history-gap-and-walmart-bangladesh/.

32. Melissa Fisher similarly examines how the first generation of women to work on Wall Street beginning in the 1960s produced what she identifies as "market feminism," bringing together market logics with the liberal feminist goals of achieving gender equality in education and the labor market. Melissa S. Fisher, *Wall Street Women* (Durham, N.C.: Duke University Press, 2012).

33. Elisabeth Prügl, "Corporate Social Responsibility and the Neoliberalization of Feminism," in *Gender Equality and Responsible Business: Expanding CSR Horizons*, ed. Kate Grosser, Lauren McCarthy, and Maureen A. Kilgour, (Sheffield, UK: Greenleaf Publishing, 2016), 46–54; Calkin, "Feminism, Interrupted? Gender and Development in the Era of 'Smart Economics,'" *Progress in Development Studies* 15, no. 4 (2015), http://journals.sagepub.com/doi/pdf/10.1177/1464993415592737; Roberts, "The Political Economy of 'Transnational Business Feminism'"; Prügl and True, "Equality Means Business? Governing Gender through Transnational Public-Private Partnerships."

34. Nancy Fraser, "Feminism, Capitalism, and the Cunning of History," *New Left Review*, no. 56 (April 2009): 97–117.

35. Coleman wrote this in *Forbes* during the days prior to her participation as co-chair of the Empowering Women and Girls track at the 2010 Clinton Global Initiative annual meeting, an event that I participated in for my research. Isobel Coleman, "Women Are the New Global Growth Engine," *Forbes*, September 15, 2010, www.forbes.com/2010/09/15/women-growth-globalization-leadership-citizenship-strategy.html.

36. Fraser, "Feminism, Capitalism, and the Cunning of History," 111.

37. Hester Eisenstein, *Feminism Seduced: How Global Elites Use Women's Labor and Ideas to Exploit the World* (Boulder, Colo.: Paradigm Publishers, 2009), 133.

38. Fraser, "Feminism, Capitalism, and the Cunning of History," 114.

39. Lucy Ferguson and Daniela Alarcon Moreno, "Gender Expertise and the Private Sector: Navigating the Privatization of Gender Equality Funding," in *The Politics of Feminist Knowledge Transfer: Gender Training and Gender*

Expertise, ed. Maria Bustelo, Lucy Ferguson, and Maxime Forest (Basingstoke, UK: Palgrave Macmillan, 2016).

40. Denise Ferreira da Silva, *Toward a Global Idea of Race*, vol. 27 (Minneapolis: University of Minnesota Press, 2007), xxx.

41. Joan W. Scott, "Gender: A Useful Category of Historical Analysis," *American Historical Review* 91, no. 5 (1986): 1053–75.

42. In chapter 4, I discuss the ways in which age and gender work together to produce the specific category of adolescent girl within the Girl Effect.

43. Chandra Talpade Mohanty, "Under Western Eyes: Feminist Scholarship and Colonial Discourses," in *Third World Women and the Politics of Feminism*, ed. Talpade Chandra Mohanty, Ann Russo, and Lourdes Torres (Bloomington: Indiana University Press, 1991).

44. Examples of texts that do this work include the following: Soujorner Truth, "Women's Rights," in Deborah K. King and Beverly Guy-Sheftall, *Words of Fire: An Anthology of African-American Feminist Thought* (New York: New Press, 1995): 36; Ida B. Wells-Barnett, *On Lynchings*. (Amherst, N.Y.: Humanity Books, (1892) 2002), www.aspresolver.com/aspresolver.asp?BLTC;S10224; Hazel V. Carby, *Reconstructing Womanhood: The Emergence of the Afro-American Woman Novelist* (New York: Oxford University Press, 1987); Patricia Hill Collins, *Black Feminist Thought: Knowledge, Consciousness, and the Politics of Empowerment* (Boston: Unwin Hyman, 1990); Kimberle Crenshaw, "Mapping the Margins: Intersectionality, Identity Politics, and Violence against Women of Color," *Stanford Law Review* (1991): 1241–1299; Evelyn Nakano Glenn, "The Social Construction and Institutionalization of Gender and Race: An Integrative Framework," in *Revisioning Gender*, ed. Judith Lorber, Myra Marx Ferree, and Beth B. Hess (New York: Sage, 1999); bell hooks, *Feminist Theory from Margin to Center* (Boston: South End Press, 1984); Paola Bacchetta, "Openings: Reflections on Transnational Feminist Alliances," (paper presented at the Conference Genre et Mondialisation, Ministère de la Recherche, Paris, March 23, 2007); Combahee River Collective, in *Home Girls, a Black Feminist Anthology*, ed. Barbara Smith (New York: Kitchen Table: Women of Color Press, 1983); Angela Y. Davis, *Women, Race, & Class* (New York: Random House, 1981); bell hooks, *Feminist Theory from Margin to Center* (Boston: South End Press, 1984); Cherie Moraga and Gloria Anzaldúa, *This Bridge Called My Back: Writings by Radical Women of Color* (New York: Kitchen Table: Women of Color Press, 1983); Gloria Anzaldúa, *Borderlands: The New Mestiza = La Frontera* (San Francisco: Spinsters/Aunt Lute, 1987); Trinh Minh-ha, *Women Native Other* (Bloomington: Indiana University Press, 1989); Norma Alarcón, "Theoretical Subjects of This Bridge Called My Back and Anglo-American Feminism," in *Feminist Theory Reader: Local and Global Perspectives*, ed. Seung-Kyung Kim and Carole R. McCann (New York: Routledge, 2003); Chela Sandoval, *Methodology of the Oppressed* (Minneapolis:

University of Minnesota Press, 2000); Audre Lorde, *Sister Outsider: Essays and Speeches* (Trumansburg, N.Y.: Crossing Press, 1984).

45. Paola Bachetta, "Openings: Reflections on Transnational Feminist Alliances," vol. 23 (paper presented at the Conference Genre et Mondialisation, Ministère de la Recherche, Paris, March 23, 2007).

46. Trinh T. Minh-Ha, *Woman, Native, Other: Writing Postcoloniality and Feminism* (Bloomington: Indiana University Press, 2009), 97.

47. Mohanty, "Under Western Eyes: Feminist Scholarship and Colonial Discourses," 335.

48. Ibid.

49. Ibid., 334.

50. Kathryn Moeller, "Searching for Adolescent Girls in Brazil: The Transnational Politics of Poverty in 'The Girl Effect,'" *Feminist Studies* 40, no. 3 (2014): 575–601.

51. *The Girl Effect: I Dare You to See I Am the Answer*, Nike Foundation, 2010.

52. See: "Nike Watch," Oxfam, n.d., accessed September 5, 2017, www.oxfam.org.au/what-we-do/ethical-trading-and-business/workers-rights-2/nike/; "Nike," Clean Clothes Campaign, March 31, 2014, https://cleanclothes.org/livingwage/tailoredwages/company-submissions/nike-submission.pdf/view; "Nike Campaign," Global Exchange, n.d., accessed November 3, 2010, www.globalexchange.org/fairtrade/sweatfree/nike; Richard Locke, "The Promise and Perils of Globalization: The Case of Nike," Industrial Performance Center, Massachusetts Institute of Technology, July 2002, https://ipc.mit.edu/sites/default/files/documents/02-007.pdf.

53. "Innovate for a Better World: Nike FY05-06 Corporate Responsibility Report," (Corporate Social Responsibility Report, Nike, Inc., Beaverton, Ore., 2006, 16.

54. Naomi Klein, *No Logo: Taking Aim at the Brand Bullies* (New York: Picador, 2000); Locke, "The Promise and Perils of Globalization: The Case of Nike."

55. John H. Cushman, "International Business: Nike Pledges to End Child Labor and Apply U.S. Rules Abroad," *New York Times*, May 13, 1998, www.nytimes.com/1998/05/13/business/international-business-nike-pledges-to-end-child-labor-and-apply-us-rules-abroad.html.

56. Accusations of abusive labor practices at its contract factories continue: Stephen Wright, "Nike Faces New Worker Abuse Claims in Indonesia," Huffington Post, July 2011, www.huffingtonpost.com/2011/07/13/nike-faces-new-worker-abuse-indonesia_n_896816.html; Jim Keady, "Are Nike's Factory Workers Paid a Living Wage? (video blog)," Huffington Post, accessed April 24, 2012, www.huffingtonpost.com/jim-keady/nike-sweatshops-wages_b_1021155.html; Nicholas Casey and Raphael Pura, "Nike Addresses Abuse Complaints at

Malaysia Plant," *Wall Street Journal*, August 4, 2008, www.wsj.com/articles/SB121779204898108093; James Hookway and Anh Thu Nguyen, "Vietnam Workers Strike: Factory Employees Seek Higher Wages as Inflation Soars," *Wall Street Journal*, April 2, 2008, www.wsj.com/articles/SB120704094273579965.

57. Ellen McGirt, "Meet the League of Extraordinary Women: 60 Influencers Who Are Changing the World," Fast Company, June 2012, www.fastcompany.com/1839862/meet-league-extraordinary-women-60-influencers-who-are-changing-world.

58. Ibid.

59. Ibid.

60. Ibid., emphasis in original.

61. Nike Foundation, "Investor News Details: Nike Foundation Steps on to New Field."

62. For more information on Nike, Inc.'s strategy over time in emerging markets, see the following: "Cricket Anyone? Sneaker Makers on Fresh Turf; Nike Has a New Rival in Developing Markets," *New York Times*, accessed August 14, 2017, http://query.nytimes.com/gst/fullpage.html?res=9E0CE4D7113FF93BA15752C0A9609C8B63&pagewanted=all; "Nike Inc. Makes Emerging Markets Top Priority (NKE, MCD, KO, DPZ)," Investor Place, accessed August 14, 2017, http://investorplace.com/2010/05/nike-inc-nke-emerging-markets-mcdonalds-mcd-coca-cola-ko-dominos-pizza-dpz/#.WZH_ciMrL0E; "Nike CEO: How we'll reach $50B in sales," CNBC, accessed August 14, 2017, www.cnbc.com/2015/10/14/nike-ceo-how-well-reach-50b-in-sales.html.

63. Casey and Pura, "Nike Addresses Abuse Complaints at Malaysia Plant"; Hookway and Nguyen, "Vietnam Workers Strike: Factory Employees Seek Higher Wages as Inflation Soars."

64. Nike Manufacturing Map, Nike, Inc., accessed August 29, 2017, http://manufacturingmap.nikeinc.com/.

65. Since I conducted my fieldwork and finished my dissertation in 2012, there has been a proliferation of publications on the Girl Effect. Michelle Murphy, *Seizing the Means of Reproduction: Entanglements of Feminism, Health, and Technoscience* (Durham, N.C.: Duke University Press, 2012); Emily Bent, "A Different Girl Effect: Producing Political Girlhoods in the 'Invest in Girls' Climate," in *Youth Engagement: The Civic-Political Lives of Children and Youth*, ed. Sandi K. Nenga and Jessica K. Taft (Bingley, UK: Emerald Group Publishing, 2013), 3–20; Heather Switzer, "(Post)Feminist Development Fables: The Girl Effect and the Production of Sexual Subjects," *Feminist Theory* 14, no. 3 (December 1, 2013): 345–60, doi:10.1177/1464700113499855; Jason Hickel, "The 'Girl Effect': Liberalism, Empowerment and the Contradictions of Development," *Third World Quarterly* 35, no. 8 (October 3, 2014): 1355–73, doi:10.1080/01436597.2014.946250; Sydney Calkin, "Post-Feminist Spectatorship and the

Girl Effect: 'Go Ahead, Really Imagine Her,'" *Third World Quarterly* 36, no. 4 (May 18, 2015): 654–69.

66. "The Girl Effect: What Do Boys Have to Do with It?," International Center for Research on Women, 2010, 1, www.icrw.org/wp-content/uploads/2016/10/The-Girl-Effect-What-Do-Boys-Have-to-do-with-it.pdf.

67. "Our Work," Nike, Inc., n.d., accessed October 10, 2009, http://nikeinc.com/pages/our-work.

68. Maria Eitel, "Day 1 at Davos: Girls, Economies and Green Innovation," Huffington Post, March 30, 2010, www.huffingtonpost.com/maria-eitel/day-1-at-davos-girls-econ_b_440715.html.

69. *Guardian*, March 23, 2012, accessed September 5, 2017, www.theguardian.com/global-development/poverty-matters/2012/mar/23/girl-hub-strength-weaknesses; *Guardian*, February 10, 2012, accessed September 5, 2017; *Slate*, August 26, 2016, accessed September 5, 2017.

70. Switzer, "(Post)Feminist Development Fables: The Girl Effect and the Production of Sexual Subjects"; Ofra Koffman and Rosalind Gill, "'The Revolution Will Be Led by a 12-Year-Old Girl': Girl Power and Global Biopolitics," *Feminist Review* 105, no. 1 (November 2013): 83–102; Michelle Murphy, "Economization of Life: Calculative Infrastructures of Population and Economy," in *Relational Architectural Ecologies: Architecture, Nature and Subjectivity*, ed. Peg Rawes (London: Routledge, 2013), 139–55; Farzana Shain, "'The Girl Effect': Exploring Narratives of Gendered Impacts and Opportunities in Neoliberal Development," *Sociological Research Online* 18, no. 2 (2012): 9.

71. For an ethnographic account of the corporate focus on girls, see: Lyndsay Hayhurst, "Corporatising Sport, Gender and Development: Postcolonial IR Feminisms, Transnational Private Governance and Global Corporate Social Engagement," *Third World Quarterly* 32, no. 3 (May 20, 2011): 531–49.

72. Bent, "A Different Girl Effect: Producing Political Girlhoods in the 'Invest in Girls' Climate."

73. Moeller, "Searching for Adolescent Girls in Brazil: The Transnational Politics of Poverty in 'The Girl Effect.'" Kathryn Moeller, "Investing in the Girl Effect in Brazil: Corporatized Development, Girls' Education, and the Transnational Politics of Poverty." (PhD thesis, University of California, Berkeley, 2012).

74. Michael Goldman, *Imperial Nature: The World Bank and Struggles for Social Justice in the Age of Globalization* (New Haven, Conn.: Yale University Press, 2005).

75. Ibid.

76. Richard Peet, *Unholy Trinity: The IMF, World Bank and WTO* (London: Zed Books, 2003).

77. Dinah Rajak, *In Good Company: An Anatomy of Corporate Social Responsibility* (Palo Alto, Calif.: Stanford University Press, 2011).

78. In education, for example, see the following: Stephen J. Ball, *Global Education Inc.: New Policy Networks and the Neo-liberal Imaginary* (London: Routledge, 2012); Susan Robertson, Karen Mundy, and Antoni Verger, eds., *Public Private Partnerships in Education: New Actors and Modes of Governance in a Globalizing World* (Cheltenham, UK: Edward Elgar Publishing, 2012).

79. Gillian Hart, *Disabling Globalization: Places of Power in Post-Apartheid South Africa* (Berkeley: University of California Press, 2003).

80. Rajak, *In Good Company.*

81. Ibid.

82. Tania Murray Li, *The Will to Improve: Governmentality, and the Practice of Politics* (Durham, N.C.: Duke University Press, 2007), https://books-google-com.ezproxy.library.wisc.edu/books/about/The_Will_to_Improve.html?id=U-7JGmMm3a4C.

83. Andrew Barry, "Ethical Capitalism," in *Global Governmentality: Governing International Spaces*, ed. Wendy Larner and William Walters (London: Routledge, 2004), 195–221.

84. Thomas Wuil Joo, "Corporate Governance: Law, Theory and Policy," Social Science Research Network, October 10, 2004.

85. Barry, "Ethical Capitalism."

86. Ibid., 201.

87. Ibid., 196.

88. Ibid., 196.

89. Ibid.

90. Anke Fleur Schwittay, "Digital Citizens, Inc: Producing Corporate Ethics, Flexible Networks and Mobile Entrepreneurs in the Global Marketplace" (PhD thesis, University of California, Berkeley, Calif., 2006); Rajak, *In Good Company.*

91. Schwittay, "Digital Citizens, Inc: Producing Corporate Ethics, Flexible Networks and Mobile Entrepreneurs in the Global Marketplace," 12.

92. Ibid.

93. Sophia Muirhead, "Corporate Contributions: The View from Fifty Years," (research report, Conference Board, New York, June 1999), www.conference-board.org/publications/publicationdetail.cfm?publicationid=429.

94. "The Good Company: Is Corporate Philanthropy Worthwhile?," *Economist*, February 23, 2006, www.economist.com/node/5517678.

95. Dinah Rajak, "'HIV/AIDS Is Our Business': The Moral Economy of Treatment in a Transnational Mining Company," *Journal of the Royal Anthropological Institute* 16, no. 3 (August 5, 2010): 568.

96. Fernanda Duarte, "What Does a Culture of Corporate Social Responsibility 'Look' Like? A Glimpse into a Brazilian Mining Company," *International Journal of Business Anthropology* 2, no. 1 (April 2011): 106–22; Rajak, *In Good Company*; Jessica Smith and Frederico Helfgott, "Flexibility or Exploitation?

Corporate Social Responsibility and the Perils of Universalization," *Anthropology Today* 26, no. 3 (June 2010): 20–23, doi:10.1111/j.1467-8322.2010.00737.x.

97. The UN Global Compact was developed in 2000. It "asks companies to embrace, support, and enact, within their sphere of influence, a set of core values in the areas of human rights, labour standards, the environment, and anti-corruption." UN Global Compact, "The Ten Principles," *United Nations Global Compact*, n.d., accessed September 5, 2017, www.unglobalcompact.org/what-is-gc/mission/principles.

98. WBCSD was founded prior to the 1992 Rio Earth Summit "to ensure the business voice was heard at the forum." WBCSD, "WBCSD—World Business Council for Sustainable Development," n.d., accessed September 5, 2017, www.wbcsd.org/home.aspx.

99. CGI was founded in 2005 by former President Clinton "to inspire, connect, and empower a community of global leaders to forge solutions to the world's most pressing challenges." "Clinton Global Initiative," Clinton Foundation, n.d., accessed September 5, 2017, www.clintonfoundation.org/clinton-global-initiative.

100. Rajak, *In Good Company*, 1.

101. Thomas Piketty, *Capital in the Twenty-First Century*, trans. Arthur Goldhammer (Cambridge, Mass.: Belknap Press of Harvard University Press, 2014); Kathryn Moeller, "A Critical Feminist and Race Critique of Thomas Piketty's Capital in the Twenty-First Century," *British Journal of Sociology of Education* 37, no. 6 (2016): 810–22, doi:10.1050/01425692.2016.1165085.

102. Suzana Sawyer, "Disabling Corporate Sovereignty in a Transnational Lawsuit," *PoLAR: Political and Legal Anthropology Review* 29, no. 1 (May 2006): 23–43, doi:10.1525/pol.2006.29.1.23.

103. ICRW was one of the Nike Foundation's first NGO partners, originally contracted to design the foundation's initial monitoring and evaluation strategy, before differences between the institutions led to a change in this relationship.

104. The event was hosted by the International Center for Research on Women in Washington, D.C., March 7, 2012.

105. Moeller, "A Critical Feminist and Race Critique of Thomas Piketty's Capital in the Twenty-First Century."

106. Jennifer Bair, "Signs," *Journal of Women in Culture and Society*, 36, no. 1 (2010): 203.

107. Silvia Federici, *Caliban and the Witch: Women, the Body and Primitive Accumulation* (Brooklyn, N.Y.: Autonomedia, 2004), 12.

108. Ibid., 61.

109. Colette Guillaumin, *Racism, Sexism, Power and Ideology* (London: Routledge, 2002); Anibal Quijano, "Coloniality of Power, Eurocentrism, and Latin America," *Nepantla: Views from the South*, 1, no. 3 (2000): 533–80; Stuart Hall, "Europe's Other Self," *Marxism Today*, no. 25 (August 1991): 18–19; Cedric

J. Robinson, *Black Marxism: The Making of the Black Radical Tradition* (Chapel Hill: University of North Carolina Press, 1983).

110. Guillaumin, *Racism, Sexism, Power and Ideology*, 70–71.

111. Robinson, *Black Marxism: The Making of the Black Radical Tradition*, xiii.

112. Ibid., 2.

113. See for example: Jodi Melamed, "Racial Capitalism," *Critical Ethnic Studies*, 1, no. 1 (2015): 76–85; Ramon Grosfoguel, *Colonial Subjects: Puerto Ricans in a Global Perspective* (Berkeley: University of California Press, 2003); Ramon Grosfoguel and Margarita Cervantes-Rodriguez, eds., *The Modern/Colonial/Capitalist World-System in the Twentieth Century: Global Processes, Antisystemic Movements, and the Geopolitics of Knowledge* (Westport, Conn.: Praeger Publishers, 2002).

114. Quijano, "Coloniality of Power, Eurocentrism, and Latin America," 533.

115. See earlier discussion on the categories of Third World women and girls.

116. Ferreira da Silva, *Toward a Global Idea of Race*, xxix–xxx.

117. Ibid., xxx.

118. Maria Lugones, "Heterosexualism and the Colonial Modern Gender System," *Hypatia* 22, no. 1 (2007): 186.

119. Ibid.

120. Ibid.

121. Ibid., 187.

122. Ferreira da Silva, *Toward a Global Idea of Race*, xxx.

123. Angela Y. Davis, *Women, Race, & Class* (New York: Vintage Books, 1983), 23–24.

124. Ibid., 29.

125. Bachetta, "Openings: Reflections on Transnational Feminist Alliances."

126. Ibid., 2.

127. Ibid.

128. Ferreira da Silva, Toward a Global Idea of Race, xxxi.

129. Uma Kothari, "Critiquing 'Race' and Racism in Development Discourse and Practice," *Progress in Development Studies* 6, no. 1 (2006): 1–7; Uma Kothari, ed., *A Radical History of Development Studies: Individual, Institutions, and Ideologies* (London: Zed Books, 2006), http://journals.sagepub.com/doi/pdf/10.1191/1464993406ps123ed; Sarah White, "Thinking Race, Thinking Development," *Third World Quarterly* 23, no. 3 (2002): 407–19.

130. Sarah White, "Thinking Race, Thinking Development," 407.

131. Kothari, "Critiquing 'Race' and Racism in Development Discourse and Practice," 1.

132. Gayatri Chakravorty Spivak, *A Critique of Postcolonial Reason: Toward a History of the Vanishing Present* (Cambridge, Mass.: Harvard University Press, 1999), 200.

133. Mary Beth Mills, "Gender and Inequality in the Global Labor Force," *Annual Review of Anthropology* 32, no. 2003 (2003): 41–62, doi:10.1146/annurev.anthro.32.061002.093107; Jane L. Collins, "Mapping a Global Labor Market: Gender and Skill in the Globalizing Garment Industry," *Gender & Society* 16, no. 6 (December 2002): 921–40, doi:10.1177/089124302237895; Aihwa Ong, "The Gender and Labor Politics of Postmodernity," *Annual Review of Anthropology* 20, no. 1991 (1991): 279–309.

134. David Harvey, *Spaces on Neoliberalization: Towards a Theory of Uneven Geographical Development* (Stuttgart, Germany: Franz Steiner Verlag (1656), 2005); Collins, "Mapping a Global Labor Market: Gender and Skill in the Globalizing Garment Industry"; June C. Nash and Maria P. Fernandez-Kelly, eds., *Women, Men, and the International Division of Labor* (Albany: State University of New York Press, 1984).

135. Harvey, *Spaces on Neoliberalization: Towards a Theory of Uneven Geographical Development.*

136. Bair, "On Difference and Capital: Gender and the Globalization of Production," 205.

137. Collins, "Mapping a Global Labor Market: Gender and Skill in the Globalizing Garment Industry," 921.

138. Jane L. Collins, *Threads: Gender, Labor, and Power in the Global Apparel Industry* (Chicago: University of Chicago Press, 2003), 14.

139. David Harvey, *Spaces of Hope* (Berkeley: University of California Press, 2000), 108.

140. Melissa W. Wright, *Disposable Women and Other Myths of Global Capitalism* (New York: Routledge, 2006), 2.

141. Ibid., 150.

142. Mills, "Gender and Inequality in the Global Labor Force"; Ong, "The Gender and Labor Politics of Postmodernity"; For specific ethnographic examples, see: Pun Ngai, *Made in China: Women Factory Workers in a Global Workplace* (Durham, N.C.: Duke University Press, 2005); Lisa Rofel, *Other Modernities: Gendered Yearnings in China after Socialism* (Berkeley: University of California Press, 1999).

143. Leslie Salzinger, *Gender in Production: Making Workers in Mexico's Global Factories* (Berkeley: University of California Press, 2003).

144. For a perspective on the benefits of outsourcing and sweatshops on poverty, see Nicholas Kristof, "Where Sweatshops Are a Dream," *New York Times*, January 14, 2009, www.nytimes.com/2009/01/15/opinion/15kristof.html.

145. Dina M. Siddiqi, "Do Bangladeshi Factory Workers Need Saving? Sisterhood in the Post-Sweatshop Era," *Feminist Review* 91, no. 1 (2009): 154–74, doi:10.1057/fr.2008.55.

146. Manisha Desai, "Transnational Solidarity: Women's Agency, Structural Adjustment, and Globalization," in *Women's Activism and Globalization: Linking Local Struggles and Transnational Politics*, ed. Nancy A. Naples and Manisha Desai (New York: Routledge, 2002), 17.

147. Desai, "Transnational Solidarity: Women's Agency, Structural Adjustment, and Globalization."

148. "Just Pay It: Wage Compensation for Indonesian Nike Workers," Clean Clothes Campaign, January 12, 2012, https://cleanclothes.org/news/2012/01/12/just-pay-it-wage-compensation-for-indonesian-nike-workers.

149. Desai, "Transnational Solidarity: Women's Agency, Structural Adjustment, and Globalization."

150. Siddiqi, "Do Bangladeshi Factory Workers Need Saving? Sisterhood in the Post-Sweatshop Era."

151. Ibid.

152. Lata Mani, *Contentious Traditions: The Debate on Sati in Colonial India* (Berkeley: University of California Press, 1998).

153. Lata Mani, "Production of an Official Discourse on Sati in Early Nineteenth-Century Bengal," in *Women and Social Reform in Modern India: A Reader*, ed. Sumit Sarkar and Tanika Sarkar (Bloomington: Indiana University Press, 2008), 38–57; Mani, *Contentious Traditions: The Debate on Sati in Colonial India*.

154. Mani, "Production of an Official Discourse on Sati in Early Nineteenth-Century Bengal," 55.

155. Mani, *Contentious Traditions: The Debate on Sati in Colonial India*, 79.

156. Ibid.

157. Gillian Hart, "From 'Rotten Wives' to 'Good Mothers': Household Models and the Limits of Economism," *IDS Bulletin* 28, no. 3 (July 1997): 14–25, doi:10.1111/j.1759-5436.1997.mp28003002.x.

158. Gillian Hart, *Disabling Globalization*; Drucilla K. Barker and Edith Kuiper, eds., *Toward a Feminist Philosophy of Economics* (London: Routledge, 2003).

159. Gary S. Becker, "Altruism in the Family and Selfishness in the Market Place," *Economica* 48, no. 189 (February 1981): 1–15, doi:10.2307/2552939.

160. Hart, "From 'Rotten Wives' to 'Good Mothers': Household Models and the Limits of Economism."

161. Barker and Kuiper, *Toward a Feminist Philosophy of Economics*; Hart, "From 'Rotten Wives' to 'Good Mothers': Household Models and the Limits of Economism"; Gillian Hart, "Gender and Household Dynamics: Recent Theories and Their Implications," in *Critical Issues in Asian Development: Theories, Experiences and Policies*, ed. M.G. Quibria (New York: Oxford University Press, 1995), 39–74.

162. Naila Kabeer, *Gender Mainstreaming in Poverty Eradication and the Millennium Development Goals: A Handbook for Policy-Makers and Other Stakeholders* (London: Commonwealth Secretariat, 2003).

163. Cecile Jackson, "Rescuing Gender from the Poverty Trap," *World Development* 24, no. 3 (March 1996): 489–504.

164. Sylvia Chant, "Re- thinking the 'Feminization of Poverty' in Relation to Aggregate Gender Indices," *Journal of Human Development* 7, no. 2 (July 2006): 206, doi:10.1080/14649880600768538.

165. Ananya Roy, "Millennial Woman," in *International Handbook of Gender and Poverty: Concepts, Research, Policy*, ed. Sylvia Chant (Cheltenham, UK: Edward Elgar, 2010), 548–553.

166. Shahra Razavi, "Fitting Gender into Development Institutions," *World Development* 25, no. 7 (July 1977): 1111–1125, doi:10.1016/S0305-750X(97)00023-5.; Christine Ewig, "Hijacking Global Feminism: Feminists, the Catholic Church, and the Family Planning Debacle in Peru," *Feminist Studies* 32, no. 3 (2006): 632–660.

167. Elaine Unterhalter, *Gender, Schooling and Global Social Justice: Foundations and Futures of Education* (London: Routledge, 2007).

168. Razavi, "Fitting Gender into Development Institutions," 1112.

169. Frances Katherine Vavrus, *Desire and Decline: Schooling amid Crisis in Tanzania, Society and Politics in Africa* (Bern, Switzerland: Peter Lang Publishing, 2003); Regina Cortina and Nelly P. Stromquist, eds., *Distant Alliances: Promoting Education for Girls and Women in Latin America* (New York: RoutledgeFalmer, 2000); Christine Heward and Sheila Bunwaree, eds., *Gender, Education and Development: Beyond Access to Empowerment* (London: Zed Books, 1998); World Bank, *Priorities and Strategies for Education: A World Bank Review* (Washington, D.C.: The International Bank for Reconstruction and Development/World Bank, 1995).

170. Vavrus, *Desire and Decline: Schooling amid Crisis in Tanzania*, 33.

171. Barbara Knapp Herz and Gene B. Sperling, *What Works in Girls' Education: Evidence and Policies from the Developing World* (Washington, D.C.: Council on Foreign Relations Press, 2004); George Psacharopoulos and Harry Anthony Patrinos, "Returns to Investment in Education: A Further Update," (scholarly paper, Social Science Research Network, Rochester, N.Y., September 30, 2002).

172. Jackie Kirk, "Impossible Fictions: The Lived Experiences of Women Teachers in Karachi," *Comparative Education Review* 48, no. 4 (2004): 374–95; Regina Cortina, "Global Priorities and Local Predicaments in Education," in *Distant Alliances: Promoting Education for Girls and Women in Latin America*, ed. Regina Cortina and Nelly P. Stromquist (New York: RoutledgeFalmer, 2000), 179–200.

173. Lamia Karim, *Microfinance and Its Discontents: Women in Debt in Bangladesh* (Minneapolis: University of Minnesota Press, 2011); Ananya Roy, *Poverty Capital: Microfinance and the Making of Development* (New York: Routledge, 2010); Katharine N. Rankin, "Governing Development: Neoliberalism, Microcredit, and Rational Economic Woman," *Economy and Society* 30, no. 1 (2001): 18–37, doi:10.1080/03085140020019070.

174. Jamie Peck, "Geographies of Policy from Transfer-Diffusion to Mobility-Mutation," *Progress in Human Geography* 35, no. 6 (February 21, 2011): 773–97, doi:10.1177/0309132510394010; Mercedes González de la Rocha, "Gender and Ethnicity in the Shaping of Differentiated Outcomes of Mexico's Progresa-Oportunidades Conditional Cash Transfer Programme," in *The International Handbook of Gender and Poverty: Concepts, Research, Policy*, ed. Sylvia Chant (Cheltenham, UK: Edward Elgar Publishing, 2010), 248–53; Jamie Peck and Nik Theodore, "Mobilizing Policy: Models, Methods, and Mutations," *Geoforum* 41, no. 2 (March 2010): 169–174; Maxine Molyneux, "Mothers at the Service of the New Poverty Agenda: Progresa/Oportunidades, Mexico's Conditional Transfer Programme," *Social Policy & Administration* 40, no. 4 (July 19, 2006): 425–49, doi:10.1111/j.1467-9515.2006.00497.x.

175. Summers, "The Most Influential Investment."

176. Jackson, "Rescuing Gender from the Poverty Trap."

177. Eisenstein, *Feminism Seduced: How Global Elites Use Women's Labor and Ideas to Exploit the World*; Vavrus, *Desire and Decline: Schooling amid Crisis in Tanzania*.

178. From a policy and practice perspective rather than a theoretical perspective, the term frontier market was first coined in 1992 by Farida Khambata of the International Finance Corporation (IFC), the World Bank's arm focused on the private sector in developing countries. The IFC defines frontier markets as: "the 82 poorest countries supported by the World Bank's International Development Association (IDA), and the frontier regions of middle-income countries. These include many fragile and conflict-affected states." The IFC explains that "frontier markets face difficult conditions, lacking the private investment needed to create jobs, improve services, and reduce poverty. But while incomes may be low, with the right support they can produce fast-growing, competitive companies that drive economies forward." International Finance Corporation, "Private Sector Solutions in Development: Frontier Markets," International Finance Corporation, accessed September 3, 2017, www.ifc.org/wps/wcm/connect/corp_ext_content/ifc_external_corporate_site/ifc+news/pressroom/frontiermarkets.

179. Derek Gregory, *The Colonial Present: Afghanistan. Palestine. Iraq* (Malden, Mass.: Blackwell Publishing, 2004), 17, https://middleeastgeographies.files.wordpress.com/2014/12/gregory-the-colonial-present.pdf.

180. Hiba Bou Akar, "Contesting Beirut's Frontiers," *City & Society* 24, no. 2 (August 23, 2012): 150–72, doi:10.1111/j.1548-744X.2012.01073.x.

CHAPTER 1

1. I am drawing on the work of James Ferguson, Michael Goldman, Tania Li, and Ananya Roy, among others, who have looked at development as an apparatus, drawing on Foucault's notion of the apparatus.

2. Michel Foucault, *Power/Knowledge: Selected Interviews and Other Writings, 1972–1977*, ed. Colin Gordon (New York: Harvester Press, 1980).

3. Michel Foucault, *Discipline and Punish: The Birth of the Prison*, trans. Alan Sheridan (New York: Vintage Books, 1977); Foucault, *Power/Knowledge: Selected Interviews and Other Writings, 1972–1977*.

4. Giorgio Agamben, *The Signature of All Things: On Method*, trans. Luca D'Isanto and Kevin Attell (Cambridge: MIT Press, 2009).

5. Personal communication with Nike Foundation, August 11, 2017.

6. Verisk Maplecroft, "Risk Calculators and Dashboards," accessed September 3, 2017, https://maplecroft.com/about/news/child_labour.html.

7. Goldman, *Imperial Nature: The World Bank and Struggles for Social Justice in the Age of Globalization*, 156; italics in original.

8. Foucault, *Discipline and Punish: The Birth of the Prison*.

9. James Ferguson, *The Anti-Politics Machine: Development, Depoliticization, and Bureaucratic Power in Lesotho* (Minneapolis: University of Minnesota Press, 1994), 255.

10. My first ethnographic observations began in 2007 and continued until 2014.

11. Stuart Kirsch, *Mining Capitalism: The Relationships between Corporations and Their Critics* (Berkeley: University of California Press, 2014); Jill P. Koyama, *Making Failure Pay: For-profit Tutoring, High-stakes Testing, and Public Schools* (Chicago: University of Chicago Press, 2010); Rajak, *In Good Company*; Sawyer, "Disabling Corporate Sovereignty in a Transnational Lawsuit"; Marina Welker, *Enacting the Corporation: An American Mining Firm in Post-Authoritarian Indonesia* (Berkeley: University of California Press, 2014).

12. Goldman, *Imperial Nature: The World Bank and Struggles for Social Justice in the Age of Globalization*; Karim, *Microfinance and Its Discontents: Women in Debt in Bangladesh*; Roy, *City Requiem, Calcutta: Gender and the Politics of Poverty*.

13. Laura Nader. "Up the Anthropologist: Perspectives Gained from Studying Up," in *Reinventing Anthropology*, ed. Dell Hymes, (New York: Pantheon, 1972), 284–311.

14. Welker, *Enacting the Corporation: An American Mining Firm in Post-Authoritarian Indonesia*; Rajak, *In Good Company.*

15. Chris Ballard and Glenn Banks, "Resource Wars: The Anthropology of Mining," *Annual Review of Anthropology* 20, no. 15 (May 15, 2003): 294.

16. Kirsch, *Mining Capitalism: The Relationships between Corporations and Their Critics*; Peter Benson and Stuart Kirsch, "Capitalism and the Politics of Resignation," *Current Anthropology* 51, no. 4 (2010): 459–86; Ballard and Banks, "Resource Wars: The Anthropology of Mining."

17. Welker, *Enacting the Corporation: An American Mining Firm in Post-Authoritarian Indonesia.*

18. The names of the NGOs are pseudonyms to protect the anonymity of the individuals and organizations in my study. The word *empoderamento* has been borrowed from the English word *empowerment* and adopted in Portuguese.

19. Roy, *City Requiem, Calcutta: Gender and the Politics of Poverty*, 39.

20. Doreen Massey, *Space, Place and Gender* (Cambridge, UK: Polity Press, 1994).

21. Roy, *City Requiem, Calcutta: Gender and the Politics of Poverty.*

22. Goldman, *Imperial Nature: The World Bank and Struggles for Social Justice in the Age of Globalization*, 24.

23. Roy, *City Requiem, Calcutta: Gender and the Politics of Poverty*, 189.

24. Hart, *Disabling Globalization.*

25. Moeller, "A Critical Feminist and Race Critique of Thomas Piketty's Capital in the Twenty-First Century"; Moeller, "Searching for Adolescent Girls in Brazil: The Transnational Politics of Poverty in 'The Girl Effect.'"

26. Akhil Gupta and James Ferguson, *Anthropological Locations: Boundaries and Grounds of a Field Science* (Berkeley: University of California Press, 1997), 37.

27. Donna Haraway, "Situated Knowledges: The Science Question in Feminism and the Privilege of Partial Perspective," *Feminist Studies* 14, no. 3 (1988): 589.

28. Haraway, "Situated Knowledges: The Science Question in Feminism and the Privilege of Partial Perspective."

29. Bachetta, "Openings: Reflections on Transnational Feminist Alliances."

30. Haraway, "Situated Knowledges: The Science Question in Feminism and the Privilege of Partial Perspective," 589.

31. Spivak Gayatri Chakravorty and Sneja Gunew, "Questions of Multiculturalism," in *The Cultural Studies Reader*, ed. Simon During (London: Routledge, 1993), 197.

32. George E. Marcus, "Ethnography in/of the World System: The Emergence of Multi-Sited Ethnography," *Annual Review of Anthropology* 24 (1995): 95–117.

33. Ibid.

34. Ibid., 100.

35. Jean Lave and Etienne Wegner, *Situated Learning: Legitimate Peripheral Participation* (London: Cambridge University Press, 1991).

36. Marcus, "Ethnography in/of the World System: The Emergence of Multi-Sited Ethnography," 100.

37. Peter McLaren, "The Ethnographer as Postmodern Flaneur: Critical Reflexivity and Posthybridity as Narrative Engagement," in *Representation and the Text: Re-Framing the Narrative Voice,* ed. William G. Tierney and Yvonna S. Lincoln (Albany: State University of New York Press, 1997), 143–78.

CHAPTER 2

1. Antonio Gramsci, *Selections from the Prison Notebooks of Antonio Gramsci,* trans. Quentin Hoare and Geoffrey Nowell Smith (London: Electric Book Company, 1999), 625, http://abahlali.org/files/gramsci.pdf.

2. Antonio Gramsci, *Selections from the Prison Notebooks of Antonio Gramsci,* ed. and trans. Quintin Hoare and Geoffrey Nowell Smith (New York: International Publishers, 1971), 630.

3. Stuart Hall, "The Problem of Ideology: Marxism without Guarantees," *Sage Publications,* Fall 1986, 42.

4. Gramsci, *Selections from the Prison Notebooks of Antonio Gramsci,* 1999, 630.

5. For example, for a discussion of the reconstruction of common sense in US education, see: Michael W. Apple, *Educating the "Right" Way: Markets, Standards, God, and Inequality* (Abingdon, UK: Taylor & Francis, 2006).

6. Gramsci, *Selections from the Prison Notebooks of Antonio Gramsci,* 1971, 400.

7. Stuart Hall, *The Hard Road to Renewal: Thatcherism and the Crisis of the Left* (New York: Verso, 1988), 130.

8. Hart, *Disabling Globalization,* 27.

9. The World Bank Group is comprised of the International Bank for Reconstruction and Development (IBRD) and the International Development Association (IDA).

10. For additional information on this history, see www.un.org/esa/ffd/ffd3/wp-content/uploads/sites/2/WBG-UN-Brochure.pdf, accessed February 23, 2017.

11. Goldman, *Imperial Nature: The World Bank and Struggles for Social Justice in the Age of Globalization*; Karen Mundy, "Retrospect and Prospect: Education in a Reforming World Bank," *International Journal of Educational Development* 22, no. 5 (September 2002): 483–508.

12. To collect the documents, I specifically searched the World Bank's Documents and Reports using the following keywords: *education, men, women, girls, girls' education, gender, poverty,* and *economic growth.* "Documents

and Reports," World Bank, accessed October 23, 2011, www-wds.worldbank .org/WBSITE/EXTERNAL/EXTWDS/0,,detailPagemenuPK:64187510~menuPK :64187513~pagePK:64187848~piPK:64187934~searchPagemenuPK:64187283~site Name:WDS~theSitePK:523679,00.html.

13. "World Bank Group Historical Chronology," World Bank: Chronology, n.d., www.worldbank.org/en/about/archives/history/chronology.

14. The UNGEI archives are available online by date, theme, region, or title from 1999–2014. I reviewed all included documents for this period. The UNFPA electronic archive begins in 2000 and includes all documents to the present day, searchable by thematic area, publication type, or title. I selected the thematic categories "gender equality," "human rights," "ICPD," "population," and "development" and reviewed all available findings. The UNDP website, which does not specify the parameters of its archive by date, offers the option of sorting documents by theme or through an open search. I ran open searches for the following keywords: *girls' education, the girl effect, population and education, girls' education and fertility*, and *women's empowerment*. UNESCO offers a database of resources called UNESDOC, although many sources are only accessible in physical form at the organization's IBE library in Geneva. Others link from UNESDOC to scholarly journals or the World Bank. I ran both basic and advanced keyword searches for *population* and *women's empowerment*, as each term yielded thousands of results from advanced search options. Finally, UNICEF's Office of Research offers a basic search by keyword, an advanced search by thematic area, author, or geographic region, as well as the option to browse publications by year (between 1989 and 2014). I used the same keyword search at UNICEF as at UNESCO for all available resources. Lastly, I used documents from the UN Women website that holds documents focused on women from the inception of the CSW in 1944 until the present, including products of the UN Conferences on Women.

15. Hart, *Disabling Globalization*, 15.

16. The IBRD is one of the institutions under the World Bank Group.

17. Goldman, *Imperial Nature: The World Bank and Struggles for Social Justice in the Age of Globalization*, 60.

18. For a critique of the notion on progress, see Teodor Shanin, "The Idea of Progress," in *The Post-Development Reader*, ed. Majid Rahnema and Victoria Bawtree (Chicago: The University of Chicago Press, 1997), 65–71, http://pages .uoregon.edu/aweiss/intl422_522/The%20Idea%20of%20Progress.pdf.

19. W. W. Rostow, *The Stages of Economic Growth. A Non-Communist Manifesto* (Cambridge, UK: Cambridge University Press, 1960), 167.

20. Ibid., 29.

21. Ibid.

22. Mundy, "Retrospect and Prospect: Education in a Reforming World Bank," 484.

23. Mundy, "Retrospect and Prospect: Education in a Reforming World Bank."

24. Theodore W. Schultz, "Investment in Human Capital," *American Economic Review* 51, no. 1 (May 1961): 1.

25. Jerome Karabel and A. H. Halsey, eds., *Power and Ideology in Education* (Oxford: Oxford University Press, 1977), 12.

26. Schultz, "Investment in Human Capital," 1.

27. Karabel and Halsey, *Power and Ideology in Education*, 15.

28. Auturo Escobar, *Encountering Development: The Making and Unmaking of the Third World* (Princeton, N.J.: Princeton University Press, 1995).

29. Ibid., 2.

30. The IDA is the International Development Association. It is the "second multilateral lending facility" of the World Bank. Created in 1960, it provides "long term and highly concessional (virtually interest free) loans to the poorest developing countries." Mundy, "Retrospect and Prospect: Education in a Reforming World Bank" Devesh Kapur, John P. Lewis, and Richard Webb, *Perspectives* (Washington, D.C.: Brookings Institution Press, 1997), http://documents.worldbank.org/curated/en/1997/01/13074578/world-bank-first-half-century-vol-2-2-perspectives.

31. World Bank, "World Bank Education Sector Working Paper 1971" (working paper, World Bank, Washington, D.C., 1971), 13, emphasis mine, http://documents.worldbank.org/curated/en/149071468338353096/Education-sector-working-paper.

32. Cited in Goldman, *Imperial Nature: The World Bank and Struggles for Social Justice in the Age of Globalization*, 297.

33. Thank you to Nancy Kendall for this insight. For an elaboration of how this occurred in Malawi, as an example, see Nancy Kendall, "Global Policy in Practice: The 'Successful Failure' of Free Primary Education in Malawi" (doctoral dissertation, Stanford University, Palo Alto, Calif., 2004).

34. Kabeer, *Gender Mainstreaming in Poverty Eradication and the Millennium Development Goals: A Handbook for Policy-Makers and Other Stakeholders*, 17.

35. Maria Mies, *Patriarchy and Accumulation on a World Scale: Women in the International Division of Labour* (London: Zed Books, 1986), ix.

36. Geeta Chowdhry, "Engendering Development: Women in Development (WID) in International Development Regimes," in *Feminism/Postmodernism/Development*, ed. Marianne H. Marchand and Jane L. Parpart (London: Routledge, 1995), 30.

37. Thank you to Nancy Kendall for this insight.

38. "Introducing UNESCO," UNESCO, accessed June 24, 2014, http://en.unesco.org/about-us/introducing-unesco.

39. "United Nations Educational, Scientific and Cultural Organization (UNESCO)," United Nations in Ethiopia, n.d., accessed August 17, 2017, http://et

.one.un.org/content/unct/ethiopia/en/home/resources/un-agencies-profiles/united-nations-educational—scientific-and-cultural-organization.html.

40. The other mandates of UNESCO were "building intercultural understanding," "pursuing scientific cooperation," and "protecting freedom of expression."

41. Karen Mundy, "Educational Multilateralism in a Changing World Order: UNESCO and the Limits of the Possible," *International Journal of Educational Development* 19, no. 1 (1999): 28.

42. The document, which would become the Universal Declaration of Human Rights, was first reviewed by the UN General Assembly in 1946, and later adopted in 1948. "The Universal Declaration of Human Rights," United Nations, December 10, 1948, www.un.org/en/universal-declaration-human-rights/index.html.

43. "Access of Girls and Women to Education in Rural Areas: A Comparative Study," UNESCO, 1964, http://unesdoc.unesco.org/images/0000/000013/001322eo.pdf.

44. "Short History of the Commission on the Status of Women," UNCSW, n.d., accessed August 17, 2017, www.un.org/womenwatch/daw/CSW60YRS/CSWbriefhistory.pdf.

45. "Access of Women to Out-of-School Education," UNESCO, accessed April 1, 2016, http://unesdoc.unesco.org/images/0012/001262/126287EB.pdf; UNESCO, "Access of Girls and Women to Education in Rural Areas: A Comparative Study" "Access of Women to the Teaching Profession," UNESCO, 1961, http://unesdoc.unesco.org/images/0012/001262/126291EB.pdf.

46. UNESCO, "Access of Girls and Women to Education in Rural Areas: A Comparative Study," 4.

47. Goldman, *Imperial Nature: The World Bank and Struggles for Social Justice in the Age of Globalization*, 69.

48. World Bank, "World Bank Group Historical Chronology."

49. Goldman, *Imperial Nature: The World Bank and Struggles for Social Justice in the Age of Globalization*, 69.

50. "World Bank Education Sector Working Paper 1974," 1 (working paper, World Bank, Washington, D.C.

51. World Bank, "World Bank Education Sector Working Paper 1974," 14–15, http://documents.worldbank.org/curated/en/868961468741007167/Education.

52. Ibid., 15.

53. Goldman, *Imperial Nature: The World Bank and Struggles for Social Justice in the Age of Globalization*, 71.

54. World Bank, "World Bank Education Sector Working Paper 1971," 15.

55. "General Conference, 15th Session: International Education Year," UNESCO, September 12, 1968, http://unesdoc.unesco.org/images/0016/001601/160197eb.pdf.

56. Jacqueline Chabaud, *The Education and the Advancement of Women* (Paris: UNESCO, 1970), preface.

57. Ibid., 10.

58. Ibid., 10.

59. Nelly P. Stromquist, "The Impact of Structural Adjustment Programmes in Africa and Latin America," in *Gender, Education and Development: Beyond Access to Empowerment*, ed. Christine Heward and Sheila Bunwaree (London: Zed Books, 1998), 17–32; Jane Parpart, "Deconstructing the Development 'Expert': Gender, Development and the 'Vulnerable Groups,'" in *Feminism/ Postmodernism/Development*, ed. Marianne H. Marchand (London: Routledge, 2003), 221–43.

60. Vavrus, *Desire and Decline: Schooling amid Crisis in Tanzania*; Parpart, "Deconstructing the Development 'Expert': Gender, Development and the 'Vulnerable Groups'" Stromquist, "The Impact of Structural Adjustment Programmes in Africa and Latin America."

61. Diane Elson, "Male Bias in Macro-Economics: The Case of Structural Adjustment," in *Male Bias in the Development Process*, ed. Diane Elson, 2nd ed. (Manchester, UK: Manchester University Press, 1995), 164–90.

62. Sally Baden, "The Impact of Recession and Structural Adjustment on Women's Work in Selected Developing Countries" Interdepartmental Project on Equality for Women in Employment, International Labour Office, December 1993, 45, www.bridge.ids.ac.uk/sites/bridge.ids.ac.uk/files/reports/re15c.pdf.

63. Commonwealth Secretariat, *Women and Structural Adjustment: Selected Case Studies Commissioned for a Commonwealth Group of Experts*, (London: Commonwealth Secretariat, 1991); UNICEF, *The Invisible Adjustment: Poor Women and the Economic Crisis*" (Santiago, Chile: UNICEF, 1989).

64. Desai, "Transnational Solidarity: Women's Agency, Structural Adjustment, and Globalization."

65. Eisenstein, *Feminism Seduced: How Global Elites Use Women's Labor and Ideas to Exploit the World*, 135.

66. UNICEF, *The Invisible Adjustment: Poor Women and the Economic Crisis*, 12.

67. Stromquist, "The Impact of Structural Adjustment Programmes in Africa and Latin America."

68. Joseph E. Stiglitz, *Globalization and Its Discontents* (New York: W. W. Norton & Company, 2003); Vavrus, *Desire and Decline: Schooling amid Crisis in Tanzania.*

69. Paul Streeten et al., "Poverty and Basic Needs" (working paper, World Bank, Washington, D.C., September 1, 1980), 3, http://documents.worldbank.org/curated/en/1980/09/6454349/poverty-basic-needs.

70. World Bank, "World Bank Group Historical Chronology."

71. Stromquist, "The Impact of Structural Adjustment Programmes in Africa and Latin America," 23.

72. Stromquist, "The Impact of Structural Adjustment Programmes in Africa and Latin America."

73. Across all of the UN sources, there is a gap between sources from the late 1970s and into the 1980s. Sources begin again in the late 1980s and early 1990s.

74. Karl Polanyi, *The Great Transformation: The Political and Economic Origins of Our Time* (Boston: Beacon Press, 1944).

75. George Psacharopoulos and Maureen Woodhall, *Education for Development: An Analysis of Investment Choices* (Oxford: Oxford University Press, 1986).

76. T. Paul Schultz, "Women and Development: Objectives, Frameworks, and Policy Interventions" (policy research working paper, World Bank, Washington, D.C., April 30, 1989), 1, http://documents.worldbank.org/curated/en/1989/04/437022/women-development-objectives-frameworks-policy-interventions.

77. Ibid., 96.

78. Elizabeth M. King, "Does Education Pay in the Labor Market? The Labor Force Participation, Occupation, and Earnings of Peruvian Women. Living Standards Measurement Study Working Paper Number 67" (working paper, World Bank, Washington, D.C., 1990), v, http://documents.worldbank.org/curated/en/174511468776408219/pdf/multi-page.pdf.

79. World Bank, "World Bank Group Historical Chronology."

80. Ibid.

81. Lawrence Summers' remarks at the 1992 annual meetings of the World Bank are published in the following book: Lawrence Summers, *Investing in All the People* (Eighth Annual General Meeting of the Pakistan Society of Development Economists) (Islamabad: World Bank, 1992), 1, www-wds.worldbank.org/servlet/WDSContentServer/WDSP/IB/1992/05/01/000009265_3961003011714/Rendered/PDF/multi_page.pdf.

82. Ibid., 15.

83. Ibid., 16.

84. Murphy, "Economization of Life: Calculative Infrastructures of Population and Economy," 146.

85. Elizabeth M. King and Anne Hill, eds., *Women's Education in Developing Countries: Barriers, Benefits, and Policies* (Baltimore: John Hopkins University Press, 1993), http://documents.worldbank.org/curated/en/1993/06/440603/womens-education-developing-countries-barriers-benefits-policies.

86. John Hobcraft, "Women's Education, Child Welfare and Child Survival: A Review of the Evidence," *Health Transition Review* 3, no. 2 (October 1993): 159–75; King and Hill, *Women's Education in Developing Countries: Barriers, Benefits, and Policies*.

87. Sandra D. Lane, "From Population Control to Reproductive Health: An Emerging Policy Agenda," *Social Science & Medicine* 39, no. 9 (November 1, 1994): 1303–14.

88. "Resolution 1838: Population Growth and Economic Development," United Nations, December 18, 1962, 25, www.un.org/en/ga/search/view_doc.asp?symbol=A/RES/1838(XVII).

89. As M. B. Kuumba summarizes with regard to population control, "Balance is achieved through preventive "checks" (i.e., avoiding childbirth and family rearing) and positive "checks" (i.e., high mortality among certain groups) on population growth." M. Bahati Kuumba, "A Cross-Cultural Race/Class/Gender Critique of Contemporary Population Policy: The Impact of Globalization," *Sociological Forum* 14, no. 3 (1999): 447–63.

90. Mohan Rao and Sarah Sexton, eds., *Markets and Malthus: Population, Gender and Health in Neo-Liberal Times* (New Delhi: SAGE Publications India, 2010), 6.

91. Steven Polgar, "Birth Planning: Between Neglect and Coercion," in *Population and Social Organisations*, ed. Moni Nag (The Hague: Mouton Publisher, 1975), 177–202. Thank you to Kirk Anderson for this insight.

92. As many scholars, such as Angela Davis, M. B. Kuumba, and Dorothy Roberts have shown, these efforts targeted Black, Latina, and Native American women in the United States as well as in countries in the Global South; Dorothy E. Roberts, *Killing the Black Body: Race, Reproduction, and the Meaning of Liberty*, 2nd ed. (New York: Vintage Books, 2017); M. Bahati Kuumba, "A Cross-Cultural Race/Class/Gender Critique of Contemporary Population Policy: The Impact of Globalization."

93. M. Bahati Kuumba, "A Cross-Cultural Race/Class/Gender Critique of Contemporary Population Policy: The Impact of Globalization," 448.

94. For further discussion of the political economy of reproductive control of racialized women's bodies from slavery and the birth of capitalism forward, see: Ibid.; M. Bahati Kuumba, "Reproductive Imperialism: Population and Labor of Underdeveloped World Women" (working paper, Women in International Development, Michigan State University, East Lansing, 1996).

95. For an excellent and extensive discussion of Pearl's biological experiments and his theories of demographic transition in French colonial Algeria, see: Michelle Murphy, "Economization of Life: Calculative Infrastructures of Population and Economy," in *Relational Architectural Ecologies: Architecture, Nature and Subjectivity*, ed. Peg Rawes (London: Routledge, 2013), 140; Murphy, *Seizing the Means of Reproduction: Entanglements of Feminism, Health, and Technoscience.*

96. Murphy, *Seizing the Means of Reproduction: Entanglements of Feminism, Health, and Technoscience*, 145.

97. Murphy, *Seizing the Means of Reproduction: Entanglements of Feminism, Health, and Technoscience.*

98. Ibid., 144.

99. Murphy, "Economization of Life: Calculative Infrastructures of Population and Economy," 145.

100. Lane, "From Population Control to Reproductive Health: An Emerging Policy Agenda" Rao and Sexton, *Markets and Malthus: Population, Gender and Health in Neo-Liberal Times*; Murphy, *Seizing the Means of Reproduction: Entanglements of Feminism, Health, and Technoscience.*

101. "Family Planning Timeline," USAID, n.d., accessed August 17, 2017, www.usaid.gov/sites/default/files/documents/1864/timeline_b.pdf.

102. Ibid.

103. Ibid.

104. The original name of UNFPA was changed to the United Nations Population Fund in 1987. UNFPA remained its official abbreviation. "About Us," United Nations Population Fund, n.d., accessed August 17, 2017, www.unfpa.org/about-us.

105. Ibid.

106. Ibid.

107. Mohan Rao and Sarah Sexton, eds., *Markets and Malthus: Population, Gender and Health in Neo-Liberal Times* (New Delhi: SAGE Publications India, 2010). For a discussion of Puerto Rico, see: Laura Briggs, *Reproducing Empire: Race, Sex, Science, and US Imperialism in Puerto Rico* (Berkeley: University of California Press, 2003).

108. World Health Organization, "Eliminating Forced, Coercive and Otherwise Involuntary Sterilization: An Interagency Statement OHCHR, UN Women, UNAIDS, UNDP, UNFPA, UNICEF and WHO" (joint statement, World Health Organization, Geneva, Switzerland, 2014), 2, http://apps.who.int/iris/bitstream/10665/112848/1/9789241507325_eng.pdf.

109. Murphy, *Seizing the Means of Reproduction: Entanglements of Feminism, Health, and Technoscience.*

110. Murphy, "Economization of Life: Calculative Infrastructures of Population and Economy," 148.

111. Murphy, *Seizing the Means of Reproduction: Entanglements of Feminism, Health, and Technoscience*, 149.

112. "United Nations Conferences on Population," *UN Department of Economic and Social Affairs*, accessed April 3, 2016, www.un.org/en/development/desa/population/events/conference/index.shtml.

113. Geoffrey Gilbert, *World Population: A Reference Handbook* (Santa Barbara: ABC-CLIO, 2005), 68.

114. Robert Cassen, *Population and Development: Old Debates, New Conclusions* (New Brunswick, N.J.: Transaction Publishers, 1994), ix.

115. Sonia Corrêa and Rebecca Lynn Reichmann, *Population and Reproductive Rights: Feminist Perspectives from the South* (Londony: Zed Books, 1994).

116. United Nations Population Division, "United Nations Conferences on Population."

117. Corrêa and Reichmann, *Population and Reproductive Rights*, 1.

118. "Population Dynamics and Educational Development: A Selection of Papers Presented at the Seminar," UNESCO Regional Office for Education in Asia, 1974, 24, http://unesdoc.unesco.org/images/0001/000122/012293eo.pdf.

119. Lisa Ann Richey, "Reproductive Health, Family Planning, and HIV/AIDS: Dangers of (Dis)integration in Tanzania and Uganda," in *Markets and Malthus: Population, Gender and Health in Neo-Liberal Times*, ed. Mohan Rao and Sarah Sexton (New Delhi: SAGE Publications India, 2010), 265–98.

120. "Family Planning Timeline" (Population Assistance policy paper, USAID, Washington, D.C., September 1982), www.usaid.gov/sites/default/files/documents/1864/populat.pdf; Kamran Asdar Ali, "Structural Adjustment, Impotence, and Family Planning: Men's Voices in Egypt," in *Markets and Malthus: Population, Gender and Health in Neo-Liberal Times*, ed. Mohan Rao and Sarah Sexton (New Delhi: SAGE Publications India, 2010), 219.

121. United Nations International Conference on Population, "Text of Declaration by International Population Conference in Mexico City," *New York Times*, August 16, 1984, www.nytimes.com/1984/08/16/world/text-of-declaration-by-international-population-conference-in-mexico-city.html.

122. Corrêa and Reichmann, *Population and Reproductive Rights*.

123. World Health Organization, "Eliminating Forced, Coercive and Otherwise Involuntary Sterilization: An Interagency Statement OHCHR, UN Women, UNAIDS, UNDP, UNFPA, UNICEF and WHO," 3.

124. Ibid.

125. "Part IV: An Action Framework for Population Education on the Eve of the Twenty-First Century," United Nations, April 1983, www.un.org/popin/confcon/poped/part4wp.htm.

126. Federico Mayor, "94-09-06: Statement of UNESCO, Mr. Federico Mayor," United Nations International Conference on Population and Development, 1994, www.un.org/popin/icpd/conference/una/940906194128.html.

127. Ibid.

128. Jan Visser, "Learning without Frontiers—Distance Education for the Nine High-Population Countries," UNESCO, February 1994, www.unesco.org/education/lwf/doc/de9.html.

129. Mayor, "94-09-06: Statement of UNESCO, Mr. Federico Mayor."

130. Ibid.

131. World Health Organization, "Eliminating Forced, Coercive and Otherwise Involuntary Sterilization: An Interagency Statement OHCHR, UN Women, UNAIDS, UNDP, UNFPA, UNICEF and WHO," 10.

132. As recently as November 2014, questions of coerced sterilization of poor women in the Indian state of Chhattisgarh continued, see: Babatunde Osotimehin and Melesse Tewodros, "Joint Statement in Response to the Tragic Deaths and Injuries Sustained by Women Undergoing Sterilization in the Indian

State of Chhattisgarh," United Nations Population Fund and International Planned Parenthood Federation, November 13, 2014, www.ippf.org/news/Joint-statement-response-tragic-deaths-and-injuries-sustained-women-undergoing-sterilization-In; For a critical discussion on the economic and human rights case for population control policies, see: Gita Sen, Adrienne Germain, and Linda Chen, eds., *Population Policies Reconsidered: Health, Empowerment, and Rights*, Harvard Series on Population and International Health (Cambridge, Mass.: Harvard University Press, 1994), https://iwhc.org/resources/population-policies-reconsidered-health-empowerment-rights/.

133. Ester Boserup, *Woman's Role in Economic Development* (London: George Allen & Unwin, 1970); Naila Kabeer, *Reversed Realities: Gender Hierarchies in Development Thought* (London: Verso, 1994); Christine Heward, "Introduction: The New Discourses of Gender, Education, and Development," in *Gender, Education and Development: Beyond Access to Empowerment*, ed. Christine Heward and Sheila Bunwaree (London : Zed Books, 1998), 1–14.

134. Boserup, *Woman's Role in Economic Development*, 208.

135. Kabeer, *Reversed Realities: Gender Hierarchies in Development Thought*, 35.

136. Vavrus, *Desire and Decline: Schooling amid Crisis in Tanzania*, 27.

137. Kabeer, *Reversed Realities: Gender Hierarchies in Development Thought*.

138. For the history of the four UN conferences on women, see United Nations Department of Public Information, "The Four Global Women's Conferences 1975–1995: Historical Perspective," UN Women, June 2000, www.un.org/womenwatch/daw/followup/session/presskit/hist.htm.

139. Ibid.

140. Ibid.

141. "Convention on the Elimination of All Forms of Discrimination against Women," UN Women, June 30, 2014, www.un.org/womenwatch/daw/cedaw/.

142. United Nations Department of Public Information, "The Four Global Women's Conferences 1975–1995: Historical Perspective."

143. Ibid.

144. Vavrus, *Desire and Decline: Schooling amid Crisis in Tanzania*.

145. Ibid.

146. Ibid., 28.

147. Marianne H. Marchand and Jane L. Parpart, eds., *Feminism/Postmodernism/Development* (London: Routledge, 1995).

148. Eva M. Rathgeber, "WID, WAD, GAD: Trends in Research and Practice," *Journal of Developing Areas* 24, no. 4 (1990): 489–502.

149. Parpart, "Deconstructing the Development 'Expert': Gender, Development and the 'Vulnerable Groups.'"

150. Marchand and Parpart, *Feminism/Postmodernism/Development*, 14.

151. Vavrus, *Desire and Decline: Schooling amid Crisis in Tanzania.*

152. Parpart, "Deconstructing the Development 'Expert': Gender, Development and the 'Vulnerable Groups."

153. Jackson, "Rescuing Gender from the Poverty Trap."

154. Vavrus, *Desire and Decline: Schooling amid Crisis in Tanzania*, 34.

155. "EFA Global Monitoring Report 2003/4: Gender and Education for All—The Leap to Equality." United Nations Educational, Scientific and Cultural Organization, 2003, http://unesdoc.unesco.org/images/0013/001325/132513e.pdf.

156. Ibid.

157. Vavrus, *Desire and Decline: Schooling amid Crisis in Tanzania.*

158. The World Bank, "World Bank Group Historical Chronology."

159. Cortina, "Global Priorities and Local Predicaments in Education."

160. Elizabeth Boner Helene, "The Making of the 'Entrepreneur' in Tanzania: Experimenting with Neo-Liberal Power through Discourses of Partnership, Entrepreneueship, and Participatory Education" (doctoral dissertation, University of California, Berkeley, 2011), http://escholarship.org/uc/item/6cj0p3dh#page-5.

161. Agamben, *The Signature of All Things: On Method*; Foucault, *Power/Knowledge: Selected Interviews and Other Writings, 1972–1977*; Ferguson, *The Anti-Politics Machine: Development, Depoliticization, and Bureaucratic Power in Lesotho.*

162. All interviews were conducted in confidentiality, and the names of interviewees are withheld by mutual agreement. Interview with Nike Foundation official, 2007.

163. Interview with official in one of the Nike Foundation partner organizations, 2009.

164. I was invited to participate in the World Bank's Global Symposium on Gender, Education, and Development, a small, closed event at its headquarters in Washington, D.C., in fall 2007, as a graduate student researcher.

165. "President Robert B. Zoellick Announces 6 New World Bank Group Commitments on Gender Equality," World Bank, April 11, 2008, http://go.worldbank.org/S1YV8VKGL0.

166. "The World Bank Launches Private-Public Initiative to Empower Adolescent Girls," World Bank: News & Broadcast, October 10, 2008, http://web.worldbank.org/WBSITE/EXTERNAL/NEWS/0,,contentMDK:21935449~pagePK:34370~piPK:34424~theSitePK:4607,00.html.

167. Ibid.

168. "CGI Annual Meeting 2008: Multimedia: Global Health—Healthy Transitions for Adolescent Girls," Clinton Global Initiative (CGI), 2008, accessed August 17, 2017, www.clintonglobalinitiative.org/ourmeetings/2008/meeting_annual_multimedia.asp?Section=OurMeetings.

169. Amanda Ellis, "Bringing the Private Sector on Board," accessed August 17, 2017, www.slideshare.net/AlexandraBrunais/world-bank-gender-action-plan-newsletter-spring-2009.

170. The members of the Private Sector Leaders Forum included: Boeing International, Carlson, CISCO Systems Inc., Ernst & Young, Goldman Sachs, Grupo Inter-Quimica S.A., Hendrick & Struggles, Husnu Foundation, INSEAD, Nike Foundation, Norfund, McKinsey & Company, Monte Rio Power Corp., PriceWaterhouseCoopers, Shalaknay Law Office, Standard Chartered PLC, SunMedia, Sungjoo International, Unilever, Women Private Equity Fund.

171. *Family Planning = The Girl Effect Dividend*, DFID - UK Department for International Development, July 13, 2013, www.flickr.com/photos/dfid/7561275206/in/album-72157630556042220/.

172. Jad Chaaban and Wendy Cunningham, "Measuring the Economic Gain of Investing in Girls: the Girl Effect Dividend," (*World Bank Policy Research Working Paper No. 5753*, 2011).

173. Hall, *The Hard Road to Renewal*, 8.

CHAPTER 3

1. "The Other Billanthropy: Doing Good the Clinton Way," *Economist*, September 21, 2006, www.economist.com/node/7946259.

2. Goldman Sachs, *10,000 Women*.

3. Rex Tillerson was sworn in as US secretary of state on February 1, 2017. "Rex Tillerson Is Confirmed as Secretary of State amid Record Opposition," *New York Times*, February 1, 2017, www.nytimes.com/2017/02/01/us/politics/rex-tillerson-secretary-of-state-confirmed.html?mcubz=0&_r=0.

4. Chant, "Re-thinking the 'Feminization of Poverty' in Relation to Aggregate Gender Indices."

5. The business of Exxon and Mobil merged in 1999 to form ExxonMobil, the largest corporation in the world. "Exxon-Mobil $82B Deal Done after FTC Approval," CNN Money, November 30, 1999, http://money.cnn.com/1999/11/30/deals/exxonmobil/.

6. As of May 2015, PetroChina surpassed ExxonMobil as the world's largest energy company. John Manfreda, "Exxon Mobil Is No Longer the World's Largest Oil Company," Business Insider, May 14, 2015, www.businessinsider.com/exxon-mobil-is-no-longer-the-worlds-largest-oil-company-2015-5?r=UK.

7. "Learn about the History of ExxonMobil," ExxonMobil, n.d., accessed October 25, 2017, http://corporate.exxonmobil.com/en/company/about-us/history/overview.

8. Michael Watts, "Petro-Violence: Community, Extraction, and Political Ecology of a Mythic Commodity," in *Violent Environments*, ed. Nancy L Peluso and Michael Watts (Ithaca, N.Y.: Cornell University Press, 2001), 189.

9. Ibid.

10. "ExxonMobil," Fortune, accessed October 23, 2017, http://fortune.com/fortune500/exxon-mobil/.

11. Alan Taylor, "The Exxon *Valdez* Oil Spill: 25 Years Ago Today," *Atlantic*, March 24, 2014, www.theatlantic.com/infocus/2014/03/the-exxon-valdez-oil-spill-25-years-ago-today/100703/.

12. Bassey Udo, "Nigeria: Protesters Shut Down ExxonMobil Operations in Eket Over N26.5b Oil Spill Compensation," Premium Times, October 25, 2013, www.premiumtimesng.com/news/147277-protesters-shut-exxonmobil-operations-eket-n26-5b-oil-spill-compensation.html.

13. Lesley Curwen, "Science Climate Conflict Warms Up," BBC News, April 26, 2007, http://news.bbc.co.uk/2/hi/business/6595369.stm.

14. Neela Banerjee, Lisa Song, and David Hasemyer, "Exxon's Own Research Confirmed Fossil Fuels' Role in Global Warming Decades Ago," Inside Climate News, September 16, 2015, http://insideclimatenews.org/news/15092015/Exxons-own-research-confirmed-fossil-fuels-role-in-global-warming.

15. Justin Gillis and Clifford Krauss, "ExxonMobil Investigated for Possible Climate Change Lies by New York Attorney General," *New York Times*, November 5, 2015, www.nytimes.com/2015/11/06/science/exxon-mobil-under-investigation-in-new-york-over-climate-statements.html.

16. Kolawole Olaniyan, "Nigeria Oil Judgment a Small Step in the Journey from Travesty to Justice," Business and Human Rights, Amnesty International, December 29, 2012, www.amnesty.org/en/latest/campaigns/2012/12/nigeria-oil-judgment-a-small-step-in-the-journey-from-travesty-to-justice/.

17. For another example, see "ExxonMobil Lawsuit (re Aceh)," Business and Human Rights Resource Centre, accessed August 25, 2015, http://business-humanrights.org/en/exxonmobil-lawsuit-re-aceh.

18. "Women Leaders," ExxonMobil, accessed March 7, 2008, www.exxonmobil.com/Corporate/news_features_20080306_womenleaders.asp.

19. "ExxonMobil Announces New Community Investment Initiative; Programs in Africa, Asia, Middle East, Caspian," ExxonMobil, July 7, 2005, http://ir.exxonmobil.com/phoenix.zhtml?c=115024&p=irol-newsArticle_pf&ID=727331&highlight=.

20. "ExxonMobil—2005 Grants," ExxonMobil, accessed December 9, 2005, http://exxonmobil.com/Corporate/Citizenship/gcr_women_girls_2005grants.asp; ExxonMobil Foundation Awards $5 Million to Educate Women, Girls in Developing Countries," Philanthropy News Digest, accessed September 6, 2017, http://philanthropynewsdigest.org/news/exxonmobil-foundation-awards-5-million-to-educate-women-girls-in-developing-countries.

21. ExxonMobil, "ExxonMobil Announces New Community Investment Initiative; Programs in Africa, Asia, Middle East, Caspian."

22. Andrea Newell, "Investing in Women's Economic Opportunities at ExxonMobil: Lorie Jackson," Triple Pundit: People, Planet, Profit, April 4, 2011, www.triplepundit.com/2011/04/exxonmobil-women-interview-lorie-jackson/.

23. "ExxonMobil Launches Technology Program to Support Women's Economic Advancement at Clinton Global Initiative," Business Wire, September 23, 2009, www.businesswire.com/news/home/20090923005135/en/ExxonMobil-Launches-Technology-Program-Support-Women%E2%80%99s-Economic.

24. Ibid.

25. See the following reports on Goldman Sachs: "Goldman Sachs 2009 Annual Report," Goldman Sachs, April 2009, www.goldmansachs.com/investor-relations/financials/archived/annual-reports/2009-complete-annual.pdf; "Financial Highlights," Goldman Sachs, accessed March 4, 2015, www.goldmansachs.com/our_firm/investor_relations/financial_reports/annual_reports/2005/pdf/Page_IFC_Financ_High.pdf; "Goldman Sachs 2013 Annual Report," April 2014, www.goldmansachs.com/s/2013annualreport/assets/downloads/GS_AR13_Complete_Fin.pdf; "Goldman Sachs 2011 Annual Report," Goldman Sachs, accessed October 25, 2017, www.goldmansachs.com/investor-relations/financials/fulfillment/reports/GS_AR11_AllPages.pdf.

26. Louise Story and Gretchen Morgenson, "S.E.C. Accuses Goldman of Fraud in Housing Deal," *New York Times*, April 16, 2010, www.nytimes.com/2010/04/17/business/17goldman.html.

27. "Senate Subcommittee Investigating Financial Crisis Releases Documents on Role of Investment Banks," Homeland Security and Governmental Affairs: Permanent Subcommittee on Investigations, April 24, 2010, www.hsgac.senate.gov/subcommittees/investigations/media/senate-subcommittee-investigating-financial-crisis-releases-documents-on-role-of-investment-banks.

28. Ibid.

29. Ibid.

30. Matt Taibbi, "The Great American Bubble Machine," *Rolling Stone*, April 5, 2010, www.rollingstone.com/politics/news/the-great-american-bubble-machine-20100405.

31. Greg Smith, "Why I Am Leaving Goldman Sachs," *New York Times*, March 14, 2012, www.nytimes.com/2012/03/14/opinion/why-i-am-leaving-goldman-sachs.html.

32. Owen Davis, "Goldman Sachs Improves to 'Poor' in Reputation Poll, Still Ranks Dead Last," International Business Times, February 7, 2015, www.ibtimes.com/goldman-sachs-improves-poor-reputation-poll-still-ranks-dead-last-1808420.

33. "Regional Grocer Wegmans Unseats Amazon to Claim Top Corporate Reputation Ranking," Harris Poll, February 4, 2015, www.theharrispoll.com/business/Regional-Grocer-Wegmans-Unseats-Amazon.html.

34. Stephanie Strom, "Gift to Teach Business to Third-World Women," *New York Times*, March 6, 2008, www.nytimes.com/2008/03/06/us/06gift.html.

35. Candida G. Brush et al., "Investing in the Power of Women: Progress Report on the Goldman Sachs 10,000 Women Initiative," Babson College, September 11, 2014, www.goldmansachs.com/citizenship/10000women/news-and-events/10kw-progress-report/progress-report-full.pdf.

36. Sandra Lawson, "Global Economics Paper No. 164: Women Hold Up Half the Sky," Goldman Sachs, March 4, 2008, 1, www.goldmansachs.com/our-thinking/investing-in-women/bios-pdfs/women-half-sky-pdf.pdf.

37. Ibid.

38. Ibid.

39. "Goldman Sachs' Reputation Tarnished," *Financial Times*, accessed October 23, 2017, www.ft.com/content/ae3d459a-7f8e-11de-85dc-00144feabdc0?mhq5j=e6.

40. Lisa Chiu, "Goldman Sachs Sets New Standard for Strategic Philanthropy," Deveximpact, June 10, 2013, www.devex.com/news/goldman-sachs-sets-new-standard-for-strategic-philanthropy-81187.

41. Welker, *Enacting the Corporation: An American Mining Firm in Post-Authoritarian Indonesia*; Kirsch, *Mining Capitalism: The Relationships between Corporations and Their Critics*; Rajak, *In Good Company*.

42. Benson and Kirsch, "Capitalism and the Politics of Resignation."

43. Duarte, "What Does a Culture of Corporate Social Responsibility 'Look' Like? A Glimpse into a Brazilian Mining Company"; Rajak, *In Good Company*; Smith and Helfgott, "Flexibility or Exploitation? Corporate Social Responsibility and the Perils of Universalization."

44. Kirsch, *Mining Capitalism: The Relationships between Corporations and Their Critics*, 3.

45. Ibid.

46. Ibid., 1.

47. Kirsch, *Mining Capitalism: The Relationships between Corporations and Their Critics*; Goldman, *Imperial Nature: The World Bank and Struggles for Social Justice in the Age of Globalization*.

48. Antonio Gramsci, *The Gramsci Reader: Selected Writings 1916–1935*, ed. David Forgacs (New York: New York University Press, 2000), 323.

49. Goldman, *Imperial Nature: The World Bank and Struggles for Social Justice in the Age of Globalization*, 7.

50. Kirsch, *Mining Capitalism: The Relationships between Corporations and Their Critics*.

51. Bob Jessop, "Spatial Fixes, Temporal Fixes, and Spatio-Temporal Fixes," in *David Harvey: A Critical Reader*, ed. Noel Castree and Derek Gregory (Oxford:

Blackwell Publishing, 2006), 142–66, http://bobjessop.org/2014/01/16/spatia-fixes-temporal-fixes-and-spatio-temporal-fixes/.

52. Ibid., 147.

53. David Harvey, *The Condition of Postmodernity: An Enquiry into the Origins of Cultural Change* (Oxford: Wiley-Blackwell, 1992), 182–83.

54. Goldman, *Imperial Nature: The World Bank and Struggles for Social Justice in the Age of Globalization.*

55. Wal-Mart Stores, Inc. v. Betty Dukes et al., Supreme Court Reporter (Supreme Court of the United States 2011) No. 10-277.

56. "Wal-mart Settles Sex Bias Claims, but Class Action Refiled," Bloomberg BNA, accessed October 23, 2017, www.bna.com/walmart-settles-sex-n73014444958/.

57. Kirsch, *Mining Capitalism: The Relationships between Corporations and Their Critics*, 4.

58. Penny Abeywardena, "How Walmart Is Reimagining Its Investments to Empower Girls and Women," Clinton Foundation, April 29, 2014, www.clintonfoundation.org/blog/2014/04/29/how-walmart-reimagining-its-investments-empower-girls-and-women.

59. "Walmart Launches Global Women's Economic Empowerment Initiative," Walmart, September 14, 2011, http://corporate.walmart.com/_news_/news-archive/2011/09/14/walmart-launches-global-womens-economic-empowerment-initiative.

60. "Wal-Mart Class Website," CohenMilstein, accessed April 4, 2016, www.walmartclass.com/public_home.html.

61. Abeywardena, "How Walmart Is Reimagining Its Investments to Empower Girls and Women."

62. Ibid.

63. Jamie Peck, "Global Policy Models, Globalizing Poverty Management: International Convergence or Fast-Policy Integration?," *Geography Compass* 5, no. 4 (April 3, 2011): 165–81, doi:10.1111/j.1749-8198.2011.00417.x.

64. Stephen J. Ball, *Global Education Inc.: New Policy Networks and the Neoliberal Imaginary* (New York: Routledge, 2012), preface.

65. Peck, "Global Policy Models, Globalizing Poverty Management: International Convergence or Fast-Policy Integration?" Ferguson, *The Anti-Politics Machine: Development, Depoliticization, and Bureaucratic Power in Lesotho.*

66. Stuart Hall, ed., *Representation: Cultural Representations and Signifying Practices* (London: Sage Publications, 1997).

67. For a more complete articulation of poverty as spectacle, see: Kathryn Moeller, "Poverty as Spectacle," (forthcoming manuscript), consulted October 25, 2017.

68. Guy Debord, *Society of the Spectacle*, trans. Donald Nicholson-Smith (St. Petersburg, Fla.: Red & Black, 1970), 4.

69. Debord, *Society of the Spectacle.*

70. Ibid.; Hall, *Representation: Cultural Representations and Signifying Practices*; Edward W. Said, *Orientalism* (New York: Pantheon Books, 1978).

71. Hall, *Representation: Cultural Representations and Signifying Practices*, 260.

72. For a discussion of the ways in which the Carnegie Corporation mobilized a regime of "global whiteness" through the Poor White Study in South Africa, see Tiffany Willoughby-Herard, *Waste of a White Skin: The Carnegie Corporation and the Racial Logic of White Vulnerability* (Berkeley: University of California Press, 2015) 3.

73. Hall, *Representation: Cultural Representations and Signifying Practices*, 260.

74. Debord, *Society of the Spectacle*, 10.

75. Hall, *Representation: Cultural Representations and Signifying Practices*, 197.

76. Hall, *Representation: Cultural Representations and Signifying Practices*; Anne McClintock, *Imperial Leather: Race, Gender, and Sexuality in the Colonial Contest* (New York: Routledge, 1995); Mohanty, "Under Western Eyes: Feminist Scholarship and Colonial Discourses."

CHAPTER 4

1. "The Girl Effect Media Kit," Nike Foundation, 2008, accessed November 2, 2009, www.nikefoundation.com/files/ [C05.97] The_Girl_Effect_Media_Kit.pdf.

2. All translations are my own.

3. The funding by the Inter-American Development Bank did not continue through the duration of the NGO program in Rio de Janeiro.

4. Nike Foundation, "The Girl Effect Media Kit."

5. Nike Foundation, "Request for Proposals: 'She's an Economic Powerhouse: Economic Empowerment Models for Girls,'" October 2007.

6. Ibid.; Moeller, "Searching for Adolescent Girls in Brazil: The Transnational Politics of Poverty in 'The Girl Effect,'" 579.

7. The Nike Foundation uses very different numbers to conceptualize this population ranging from 250 million to 5 or 6 hundred million in different documents. For example, see: Girleffect.org, "The Girl Effect: Your Move," NoVo Foundation, 2012, http://novofoundation.org/wp-content/uploads/2012/07/Girl_Effect_Your_Move.pdf.

8. Moeller, "Searching for Adolescent Girls in Brazil: The Transnational Politics of Poverty in 'The Girl Effect,'" 579; Nike Foundation, "Request for

Proposals: 'She's an Economic Powerhouse: Economic Empowerment Models for Girls.'"

9. Nike Foundation, "The Girl Effect Media Kit."

10. In accordance with the protection of human subjects, all individuals in my study are given pseudonyms.

11. Carnaval is an annual holiday in Brazil that occurs before the beginning of the Christian liturgical season of Lent.

12. Rani of Sirmur was a widow of the Raja, the prince of the region of Sirmur, who was deposed and banished by the British in the nineteenth century.

13. Spivak, *A Critique of Postcolonial Reason: Toward a History of the Vanishing Present.*

14. David Valentine, *Imagining Transgender: An Ethnography of a Category* (Durham, N.C.: Duke University Press, 2007).

15. Personal e-mail communication with the Nike Foundation, August 11, 2017.

16. Michael Omi and Howard Winant, *Racial Formation in the United States: From the 1960s to the 1990s*, 2nd ed. (New York: Routledge, 1994).

17. In Brazil, there are the official racial categories for the census created by the Instituto Brasileiro de Geografia e Estatística, including *branco* (white), *pardo* (Brown), *preto* (Black), *amarelo* (yellow), and *indígena* (indigenous). Then there are the racial categories through which people identify themselves and their communities, particularly politically and/or based on ancestry, or are identified by others, including *Negro* (Black), *Afro-Brasileiro* (Afro-Brazilian), and *Moreno* (Brown or mixed).

18. Francine Twine Winddance, *Racism in a Racial Democracy: The Maintenance of White Supremacy in Brazil* (New Brunswick, N.J.: Rutgers University Press, 1998).

19. Ruth Levine et al., "Girls Count: A Global Investment & Action Agenda," Center for Global Development, January 14, 2008, http://www.cgdev.org/publication/girls-count-global-investment-action-agenda.

20. Personal communication with Nike Foundation, August 11, 2017.

21. The Girl Effect, an exhibit of photos and videos, Mercy Corps Action Center Gallery, Portland, Oregon, November 2010–January 2011.

22. Michael Wyness, *Childhood and Society: An Introduction to the Sociology of Childhood* (New York: Palgrave Macmillan, 2006), 117.

23. Ibid., 118.

24. Alan Prout, *The Future of Childhood: Towards the Interdisciplinary Study of Children* (London: RoutledgeFalmer, 2005); Philippe Ariès, *Centuries of Childhood: A Social History of Family Life* (New York: Knopf Doubleday Publishing Group, 1960).

25. Barrie Thorne, *Gender Play: Girls and Boys in School* (New Brunswick, N.J.: Rutgers University Press, 2004).

26. Ibid.

27. Leigh Gilmore and Elizabeth Marshall, "Girls in Crisis: Rescue and Transnational Feminist Autobiographical Resistance," *Feminist Studies* 36, no. 3 (October 1, 2010): 667–90.

28. Catherine Driscoll, *Girls: Feminine Adolescence in Popular Culture and Cultural Theory* (New York: Columbia University Press, 2002), 6.

29. Levine et al., "Girls Count: A Global Investment & Action Agenda."

30. Driscoll, *Girls: Feminine Adolescence in Popular Culture and Cultural Theory*, 6.

31. Ibid.

32. Ibid., 7.

33. Stan Emert, "Maria Eitel, Nike Foundation (CGI 2010)," Rainmakers.TV, October 1, 2010, http://rainmakers.tv/maria-eitel-nike-foundation-cgi-2010/.

34. "Nike Foundation," Nike Foundation, n.d., accessed October 15, 2006, www.nikefoundation.com.

35. "Adolescent Girls: The Most Powerful Force of Change on the Planet" (internal document, Nike Foundation, Beaverton, Oregon, September 2009).

36. Ibid.

37. Kanani, "The Nike Foundation on Unleashing the 'Girl Effect.'"

38. Ibid.

39. In his critique of the "culture of poverty," Eduardo Bonilla-Silva explains that the theory is based on the idea that "the poor develop a culture based on adaptations to their poverty status, which is then transmitted from generation to generation and becomes an obstacle for moving out of poverty." Eduardo Bonilla-Silva, *Racism without Racists: Color-Blind Racism and the Persistence of Racial Inequality in the United States* (Lanham, Md.: Rowman & Littlefield, 2006), 275.

40. In his book, *The End of Poverty*, economist Jeffery Sachs argues that "one sixth of humanity" is "caught in the poverty trap;" yet, as he posits, the "end of poverty is possible in our time." Jeffrey Sachs, *The End of Poverty: Economic Possibilities for Our Time* (New York: Penguin Books, 2006).

41. Molyneux, "Mothers at the Service of the New Poverty Agenda."

42. "Adolescent Girls in Focus at the World Economic Forum," World Bank: Gender and Development, February 26, 2009, http://web.worldbank.org/WBSITE/EXTERNAL/TOPICS/EXTGENDER/0,,contentMDK:22059153~menuPK:336906~pagePK:64020865~piPK:149114~theSitePK:336868,00.html.

43. "Gender Action Plan: Gender Equality as Smart Economics," World Bank, n.d., accessed August 22, 2017, http://web.worldbank.org/WBSITE/EXTERNAL/TOPICS/EXTGENDER/0,,contentMDK:21983335~pagePK:210058~piPK:210062~theSitePK:336868,00.html.

44. World Bank, "Adolescent Girls in Focus at the World Economic Forum."

45. "World Bank Development Report 2012: Gender Equality and Development," World Bank, 2011, https://siteresources.worldbank.org/INTWDR2012

/Resources/7778105-1299699968583/7786210-1315936222006/Complete-Report .pdf.

46. Nike Foundation, "Nike Foundation."

47. Bachetta, "Openings: Reflections on Transnational Feminist Alliances."

48. Martin Carnoy et al., "How Schools and Students Respond to School Improvement Programs: The Case of Brazil's PDE," *Economics of Education Review* 27, no. 1 (2008): 22–38; David Plank, *The Means of Our Salvation: Public Education in Brazil, 1930–1995* (Boulder, Colo.: Westview Press, 1996); David N. Plank, "The Politics of Basic Education in Brazil," *Comparative Education Review* 34, no. 4 (1990): 538–59.

49. "Brazilian Universities Take Affirmative Action," BBC News, accessed March 5, 2016, www.bbc.com/news/business-23862676.

50. Lisa Delpit, *Other People's Children: Cultural Conflict in the Classroom*, 1st ed. (New York: New Press, 2006).

CHAPTER 5

1. "The Revolution," Nike Foundation, accessed March 11, 2012, www.girleffect .org/learn/the-revolution.

2. Anna Lowenhaupt Tsing, *Friction: An Ethnography of Global Connection* (Princeton: Princeton University Press, 2005).

3. Ibid., 7.

4. "Request for Proposals. She's an Economic Powerhouse: Economic Empowerment Models for Girls," Nike Foundation, October 2007, 2.

5. Personal communication with Nike Foundation, August 11, 2017, and September 7, 2017.

6. NGO questionnaire documents received in 2009 and 2010.

7. Based on personal communication with Nike Foundation, August 11, 2017.

8. Paul Rabinow, *French Modern: Norms and Forms of the Social Environment* (Cambridge, Mass.: MIT Press, 1989).

9. Thomas S. Popkewitz, ed., *Educational Knowledge: Changing Relationships between the State, Civil Society, and the Educational Community* (Albany: State University of New York Press, 2000).

10. Ibid.

11. Graham Burchell, Colin Gordon, and Peter Miller, eds., *The Foucault Effect: Studies in Governmentality* (Chicago: University of Chicago Press, 1991).

12. Ibid., 100.

13. Michel Foucault, *The History of Sexuality, Vol. 1: An Introduction*, trans. Robert Hurley (New York: Vintage Books, 1978).

14. Popkewitz, *Educational Knowledge: Changing Relationships between the State, Civil Society, and the Educational Community*, 12.

15. Ibid.

16. Valentine, *Imagining Transgender: An Ethnography of a Category.*

17. Susan Brin Hyatt, "From Citizen to Volunteer: Neoliberal Governance and the Erasure of Poverty," in *The New Poverty Studies: The Ethnography of Power, Politics, and Impoverished People in the United States*, ed. Judith G. Goode and Jeff Maskovsky (New York: New York University Press, 2001), 205.

18. Barbara Cruikshank, *The Will to Empower: Democratic Citizens and Other Subjects* (Ithaca: Cornell University Press, 1999).

19. Li, *The Will to Improve: Governmentality, and the Practice of Politics.*

20. Ibid., 4.

21. Ibid.

22. Mercy Tembom and Lucia Fort, eds., *Girls' Education in the 21st Century: Gender Equality, Empowerment, and Economic Growth* (Washington, D.C.: World Bank, 2008), http://siteresources.worldbank.org/EDUCATION/Resources/278200-1099079877269/547664-1099080014368/DID_Girls_edu.pdf; Herz and Sperling, *What Works in Girls' Education*; Psacharopoulos and Patrinos, "Returns to Investment in Education"; King and Hill, *Women's Education in Developing Countries: Barriers, Benefits, and Policies*; Summers, "The Most Influential Investment."

23. Vavrus, *Desire and Decline: Schooling amid Crisis in Tanzania*; John Knodel and Gavin W. Jones, "Post-Cairo Population Policy: Does Promoting Girls' Schooling Miss the Mark?," *Population and Development Review* 22, no. 4 (1996): 683–702.

24. Jennifer Johnson-Hanks, *Uncertain Honor: Modern Motherhood in an African Crisis* (Chicago: University Of Chicago Press, 2005); Davis, *Women, Race, & Class.*

25. *Davos Annual Meeting 2009—The Girl Effect on Development*, World Economic Forum, 2009, www.youtube.com/watch?v=CQc7NZPjqBA.

26. Larry Elliot, "Girls' Education Goes Prada Courtesy of Anne Hathaway and Christy Turlington," Guardian, October 7, 2010, www.theguardian.com/global-development/poverty-matters/2010/oct/07/girls-education-hathaway-turlington-agi.

27. When I left Brazil in August 2010, the program managers or other Nike Foundation employees had not visited the NGO. The exception was a prior visit by an individual contracted by the Nike Foundation. In October 2010, foundation staff visited Brazil to meet with the grantees in its portfolio.

28. Personal communication with Nike Foundation, 2013.

29. An example of this is Saartjie Baartman, a Black, Khoekhoe young woman from southern Africa, referred to as "The Hottentot Venus," who was placed on live exhibition in London and Paris for a period of nine years beginning in 1810. Ellen Samuels, "Examining Millie and Christine McKoy: Where Enslavement and Enfreakment Meet," *Signs* 37, no. 1 (2011): 53–81; John Willinsky, *Learning*

to Divide the World: Education at Empire's End (Minneapolis: University of Minnesota Press, 1998); Hall, *Representation: Cultural Representations and Signifying Practices*; McClintock, *Imperial Leather: Race, Gender, and Sexuality in the Colonial Contest.*

30. Donna M. Goldstein, *Laughter Out of Place: Race, Class, Violence, and Sexuality in a Rio Shantytown* (Berkeley: University of California Press, 2013).

31. I am grateful to Roshank Kheshti for this idea.

32. Chant, "Re- thinking the 'Feminization of Poverty' in Relation to Aggregate Gender Indices," 206.

33. Foucault, *Discipline and Punish: The Birth of the Prison*, 170.

34. Personal communication with Nike Foundation, August 15, 2013.

CHAPTER 6

1. For further reading look at: Rachel R. Chapman, *Family Secrets: Risking Reproduction in Central Mozambique* (Nashville: Vanderbilt University Press, 2011); Wanda S. Pillow, *Unfit Subjects: Educational Policy and the Teen Mother* (New York: RoutledgeFalmer, 2004).

2. Victoria Bernal and Inderpal Grewal, "The NGO Form: Feminist Struggles, States, and Neoliberalism," in *Theorizing NGOs: States, Feminisms, and Neoliberalism* (Durham, N.C.: Duke University Press, 2014), 1–18; Tiffany King Lethabo and Ewuare Osayande, "The Filth on Philanthropy: Progressive Philanthropy's Agenda to Misdirect Social Justice Movements," in *The Revolution Will Not Be Funded: Beyond the Non-Profit Industrial Complex*, ed. INCITE! Women of Color against Violence (Durham, N.C.: Duke University Press, 2007).

3. Lauren Leve, "Failed Development and Rural Revolution in Nepal: Rethinking Subaltern Consciousness and Women's Empowerment," in *Theorising NGOs: States, Feminisms, and Neoliberalism*, ed. Victoria Bernal and Inderpal Grewal (Durham, N.C.: Duke University Press, 2014), 50–92.

4. Bernal and Grewal, "The NGO Form: Feminist Struggles, States, and Neoliberalism," 7.

5. Timoth Mitchell, "Society, Economy, and the State Effect," in *State/Culture: State-Formation after the Cultural Turn.*, ed. George Steinmetz (Ithaca and London: Cornell University Press, 1999), 76–97.

6. Bernal and Grewal, "The NGO Form: Feminist Struggles, States, and Neoliberalism," 7.

7. David Adams, *Urban Planning and the Development Process* (London: Routledge, 1994), 142.

8. Mani, *Contentious Traditions: The Debate on Sati in Colonial India.*

9. Luzia Maria Heilborn et al., eds., *O aprendizado da sexualidade: Reproducao e trajectorias sociais de jovens Brasileiros* (Rio de Janeiro: Fiocruz Garamond, 2006).

10. Edna Roland, "*Direitos reprodutivos e racismo no Brasil,*" *Estudos Feministas* 3, no. 2 (1995): 506–14.

11. Ibid.; And for a discussion on reproductive control of the Black body in particular, in the United States as well as other countries, see: Roberts, *Killing the Black Body: Race, Reproduction, and the Meaning of Liberty.*

12. Nigel Brooke and Mary Witoshynsky, eds., *Os 40 anos da Fundação Ford no Brasil. The Ford Foundation's 40 Years in Brazil* (São Paulo: Ford Foundation, 2002), 353, http://docplayer.com.br/32508-Os-40-anos-da-fundacao-ford-no-brasil-the-ford-foundation-s-40-years-in-brazil.html.

13. Ibid.

14. Personal communication with Nike Foundation, August 11, 2017 and August 31, 2017.

15. Aluizio Freire, "*Cabral defende aborto contra violência no Rio de Janeiro,*" G1, October 24, 2007, http://g1.globo.com/Noticias/Politica/0,,MUL155710-5601,00-CABRAL+DEFENDE+ABORTO+CONTRA+VIOLENCIA+NO+RIO+DE+JANEIRO.html.

16. "*Solução simplista,*" Centro Latino-Americano em Sexualidade e Direitos Humanos, October 30, 2007, www.clam.org.br/publique/cgi/cgilua.exe/sys/start.htm?infoid=3395&sid=7.

17. Ibid.

18. Ibid.

19. Roberts, *Killing the Black Body: Race, Reproduction, and the Meaning of Liberty*, xvi; Davis, *Women, Race, & Class.*

20. "Current Partners," Nike Foundation, accessed September 11, 2017, https://web.archive.org/web/20061117044230/www.nike.com/nikebiz/nikefoundation/approach.jhtml?pg=currentpartners.

21. When I use the term "developmental death" I am thinking about development through an international development lens.

22. Thomas Princen and Matthias Finger, *Environmental NGOs in World Politics: Linking the Local and the Global* (London: Routledge, 1994).

23. Interview with GJO staff member.

24. This information was based on a conversation I had with GJO staff members, April 2010.

25. Kothari, "Critiquing 'Race' and Racism in Development Discourse and Practice"; White, "Thinking Race, Thinking Development."

26. Welker, *Enacting the Corporation: An American Mining Firm in Post-Authoritarian Indonesia.*

27. Bernal and Grewal, "The NGO Form: Feminist Struggles, States, and Neoliberalism," 7.

28. Ibid.

CONCLUSION

1. With a few exceptions, the Nike Foundation phased out NGO partnerships as their grant agreements ended, often after three years, and they did not issue additional rounds of RFPs. The Grassroots Girls Initiative, comprised of a group of organizations committed to working with girls on the ground, including Global Fund for Children, Global Fund for Women, Mama Cash, American Jewish World Service, Firelight Foundation, and EMpower, is a notable exception that has received funding during the duration of the Nike Foundation's portfolio on adolescent girls.

2. The Girl Effect, "The Girl Effect Accelerator," accessed September 15, 2017, http://girleffectaccelerator.com/.

3. Nike Foundation, "Girl Effect Accelerator Culminating Event," Eventbrite, November 11, 2014, www.eventbrite.com/e/girl-effect-culminating-event-tickets-13367128441?aff=efbneb.

4. "The Girl Effect Accelerator provided information on what investment meant in this context: The term *patient capital* has become synonymous with investing across early stage ventures in emerging markets. Although important, we also believe it is critical to make 'impatient capital' available to these same companies. To this end we have launched a 500k working capital fund designed to provide capital in the form of a short-term debt to the ten ventures who participate in the Girl Effect Accelerator. It will play a crucial role in providing the participating ventures with fast acting, low-interest rate, non-collateral tied, and immediately available debt financing. Unreasonable Capital will also be committing to invest into each venture and we are hosting a private investor gathering designed to align our select companies with some of the world's top performing investment funds and foundations," Girl Effect Accelerator, accessed September 15, 2017, http://girleffectaccelerator.com/.

5. Personal communication with Nike Foundation, August 11, 2017.

6. "Girl Effect," Girl Effect, accessed August 30, 2017, www.girleffect.org/.

7. I received this e-mail from a grantee of the Nike Foundation on January 29, 2016.

8. Personal communication with Nike Foundation, August 11, 2017.

9. "IRS Form 990PF for Nike Foundation," Citizenaudit.org, accessed August 30, 2017, http://pdfs.citizenaudit.org/2017_03_PF/93-1159948_990PF_201605.pdf.

10. Barry, "Ethical Capitalism."

11. In 2005/2006, Nike, Inc. first disclosed its contract factories. Nike, Inc., "Nike Publishes List of Global Contract Factories in Push for Greater Transparency and Collaboration to Improve Footwear and Apparel Industry Labor Conditions – Press Releases," CSR Newswire, April 13, 2005, www.csrwire.com/press_releases/24956-Nike-Publishes-List-of-Global-Contract-Factories-in-Push-for-Greater-Transparency-and-Collaboration-to-Improve-Footwear-and-Apparel-Industry-Labor-Conditions.

12. For example, see the following articles for issues regarding controversies with Nike, Inc.'s labor monitoring practices and accusations of labor abuses in contract factories: "What Did Nike Just Do?," USAS: Organizing for Student and Worker Power, November 19, 2015, http://usas.org/2015/11/19/what-did-nike-just-do/; Dave Jamieson, "Watchdog Group Kept Out of Nike Supplier's Factory after Worker Strike, Huffington Post, March 3, 2016, www.huffingtonpost.com/entry/nike-labor-rights-vietnam_us_56d893f2e4b0000de403b7d0.

13. Suzanne Bergeron and Stephen Healy, "Beyond the Business Case: A Community Economics Approach to Gender, Development and Social Economy" (draft paper prepared for the UNRISD Conference on Potential and Limits of Social and Solidarity Economy, Geneva, 2013, 6–80.

Bibliography

Abeywardena, Penny. "How Walmart Is Reimagining Its Investments to Empower Girls and Women." *Clinton Foundation*, April 29, 2014, www.clintonfoundation.org/blog/2014/04/29/how-walmart-reimagining-its-investments-empower-girls-and-women.

Adams, David. *Urban Planning and the Development Process* (New York: Routledge, 2012).

Agamben, Giorgio. *The Signature of All Things: On Method*, trans. Luca D'Isanto and Kevin Attell (Cambridge: MIT Press, 2009).

Aguirre, DeAnne, and Karim Sabbagh. "The Third Billion," Strategy+Business, May 10, 2010, www.strategy-business.com/article/10211?gko=98895.

Ali, Kamran Asdar. "Structural Adjustment, Impotence, and Family Planning: Men's Voices in Egypt," in *Markets and Malthus: Population, Gender and Health in Neo-Liberal Times*, ed. Mohan Rao and Sarah Sexton (New Delhi: Sage Publications India, 2010), 215–44.

Apple, Michael W. *Educating the "Right" Way: Markets, Standards, God, and Inequality* (Abindgon, UK: Taylor & Francis, 2006).

Ariès, Philippe. *Centuries of Childhood: A Social History of Family Life* (New York: Knopf Doubleday, 1960).

Arutyunova, Angelika. "'Investing' in Women's Rights: Challenges and New Trends," *Development* 55, no. 3 (September 2012): 305–10.

Arutyunova, Angelika, and Cindy Clark. "Watering the Leaves, Starving the Roots: The Status of Financing for Women's Rights Organizing and Gender

Equality," Association of Women in Development, October 6, 2013, www.awid.org/sites/default/files/atoms/files/WTL_Starving_Roots .pdf.

Association of Women in Development. "Resourcing Women's Rights," *AWID*, December 17, 2014, www.awid.org/priority-areas/resourcing-womens-rights.

Avon. "Experience Avon's History," *Avon: The Company for Women*, n.d., accessed August 25, 2017, www.avoncompany.com/aboutavon/history/index.html.

AwakenKibera. "The Girl Effect," AwakenKibera, n.d., accessed September 21, 2010, http://awakenkibera.org/the-girl-effect.html.

Bachetta, Paola. "Openings: Reflections on Transnational Feminist Alliances" (paper presented at the *Conference genre et mondealisation, Ministère de la Recherche*, Paris, March 23, 2007).

Baden, Sally. "The Impact of Recession and Structural Adjustment on Women's Work in Selected Developing Countries," Interdepartmental Project on Equality for Women in Employment, International Labour Office, December 1993, www.bridge.ids.ac.uk/sites/bridge.ids.ac.uk/files/reports/re15c.pdf.

Bair, Jennifer. "On Difference and Capital: Gender and the Globalization of Production," *Journal of Women in Culture and Society* 36, no. 1 (2010): 203–26.

Ball, Stephen J. *Global Education Inc.: New Policy Networks and the Neoliberal Imaginary* (New York: Routledge, 2012).

Ballard, Chris, and Glenn Banks. "Resource Wars: The Anthropology of Mining," *Annual Review of Anthropology* 20, no. 15 (May 15, 2003): 287–313.

Banerjee, Neela, Lisa Song, and David Hasemyer. "Exxon's Own Research Confirmed Fossil Fuels' Role in Global Warming Decades Ago," Inside Climate News, September 16, 2015, http://insideclimatenews.org/news/15092015 /Exxons-own-research-confirmed-fossil-fuels-role-in-global-warming.

Barker, Drucilla K., and Edith Kuiper, eds. *Toward a Feminist Philosophy of Economics* (London: Routledge, 2003).

Barry, Andrew. "Ethical Capitalism," in *Global Governmentality: Governing International Spaces*, ed. Wendy Larner and William Walters (London: Routledge, 2004) 195–221.

Becker, Gary S. "Altruism in the Family and Selfishness in the Market Place," *Economica* 48, no. 189 (February 1981): 1–15.

Benson, Peter, and Stuart Kirsch. "Capitalism and the Politics of Resignation," *Current Anthropology* 51, no. 4 (2010): 459–86.

Bent, Emily. "A Different Girl Effect: Producing Political Girlhoods in the 'Invest in Girls' Climate," in *Youth Engagement: The Civic-Political Lives of Children and Youth*, ed. Sandi Nenga K. and Jessica K. Taft (Bingley, UK: Emerald Group, 2013) 3–20.

Bergeron, Suzanne, and Stephen Healy. "Beyond the Business Case: A Community Economics Approach to Gender, Development and Social Economy." In (draft paper prepared for the UNRISD Conference on Potential and Limits of Social and Solidarity Economy, Geneva, 2013, 6-8).

Bernal, Victoria, and Inderpal Grewal. "The NGO Form: Feminist Struggles, States, and Neoliberalism," in *Theorizing NGOs: States, Feminisms, and Neoliberalism*, ed. Victoria Bernal and Inderpal Grewal (Durham, N.C.: Duke University Press, 2014), 1–18.

Bishop, Matthew, and Michael Green. *Philanthrocapitalism: How Giving Can Save the World* (New York: Bloomsbury Press, 2009).

Boner, Elizabeth Helene. "The Making of the 'Entrepreneur' in Tanzania: Experimenting with Neo-Liberal Power through Discourses of Partnership, Entrepreneurship, and Participatory Education," (doctoral dissertation, University of California, Berkeley, 2011, http://escholarship.org/uc/item/6cj0p3dh#page-5.

Bonilla-Silva, Eduardo. *Racism without Racists: Color-Blind Racism and the Persistence of Racial Inequality in the United States* (Lanham, Md.: Rowman & Littlefield, 2006).

Boserup, Ester. *Woman's Role in Economic Development* (London: Allen & Unwin, 1970).

Bou Akar, Hiba. "Contesting Beirut's Frontiers," *City & Society* 24, no. 2 (August 23, 2012): 150–72.

Briggs, Laura. *Reproducing Empire: Race, Sex, Science, and US Imperialism in Puerto Rico* (Berkeley: University of California Press, 2003).

Brooke, Nigel, and Mary Witoshynsky, eds. "*Os 40 anos da Fundação Ford no Brasil*. The Ford Foundation's 40 Years in Brazil," Ford Foundation, 2002. http://docplayer.com.br/32508-Os-40-anos-da-fundacao-ford-no-brasil-the-ford-foundation-s-40-years-in-brazil.html.

Brush, Candida G., Lakshmi Balachandra, Amy Davis, and Patricia G. Greene. "Investing in the Power of Women: Progress Report on the Goldman Sachs 10,000 Women Initiative," Babson College, September 11, 2014, www.goldmansachs.com/citizenship/10000women/news-and-events/10kw-progress-report/progress-report-full.pdf.

Burchell, Graham, Colin Gordon, and Peter Miller, eds. *The Foucault Effect: Studies in Governmentality* (Chicago: University of Chicago Press, 1991).

Business and Human Rights Resource Centre. "ExxonMobil Lawsuit (re Aceh)," Business and Human Rights Resource Centre, accessed August 25, 2015, http://business-humanrights.org/en/exxonmobil-lawsuit-re-aceh.

Calkin, Sydney. "Feminism, Interrupted? Gender and Development in the Era of 'Smart Economics,'" *Progress in Development Studies* 15, no. 4 (2015), http://journals.sagepub.com/doi/pdf/10.1177/1464993415592737.

Calkin, Sydney. "Post-Feminist Spectatorship and the Girl Effect: 'Go Ahead, Really Imagine Her,'" *Third World Quarterly* 36, no. 4 (May 18, 2015): 654–69.

Carnoy, Martin, Amber K. Gove, Susanna Loeb, Jeffrey H. Marshall, and Miguel Socias. "How Schools and Students Respond to School Improvement Programs: The Case of Brazil's PDE," *Economic of Education Review* 27, no. 1 (2008): 22–38.

Casey, Nicholas, and Raphael Pura. "Nike Addresses Abuse Complaints at Malaysia Plant," *Wall Street Journal*, August 4, 2008, www.wsj.com/articles/SB121779204898108093.

Cassen, Robert. *Population and Development: Old Debates, New Conclusions* (New Brunswick, N.J.: Transaction, 1994).

Centro Latino-Americano em Sexualidade e Direitos Humanos. "*Solução simplista*," clam+10, October 30, 2007, www.clam.org.br/publique/cgi/cgilua.exe/sys/start.htm?infoid=3395&sid=7.

Chabaud, Jacqueline. *The Education and the Advancement of Women* (Paris: UNESCO, 1970).

Chant, Sylvia. "Re- thinking the 'Feminization of Poverty' in Relation to Aggregate Gender Indices," *Journal of Human Development* 7, no. 2 (July 2006): 201–20.

Chapman, Rachel R. *Family Secrets: Risking Reproduction in Central Mozambique*. Nashville: Vanderbilt University Press, 2011).

Chevron. "Empowering Women in Brazil," Chevron.com, July 2011, www.chevron.com/Stories/Empowering-Women-in-Brazil.

Chiu, Lisa. "Goldman Sachs Sets New Standard for Strategic Philanthropy," Deveximpact, June 10, 2013, www.devex.com/news/goldman-sachs-sets-new-standard-for-strategic-philanthropy-81187.

Chowdhry, Geeta. "Engendering Development: Women in Development (WID) in International Development Regimes," in *Feminism/Postmodernism/Development*, ed. Marianne H. Marchand and Jane L. Parpart (London: Routledge, 1995), 26–41.

Clean Clothes Campaign. "Gap and Walmart in Bangladesh: A History of Irresponsibility and Empty Promises," Clean Clothes Campaign, n.d., accessed September 22, 2017, https://cleanclothes.org/resources/background/history-gap-and-walmart-bangladesh/.

Clean Clothes Campaign. "Just Pay It: Wage Compensation for Indonesian Nike Workers," Clean Clothes Campaign, January 12, 2012, https://cleanclothes.org/news/2012/01/12/just-pay-it-wage-compensation-for-indonesian-nike-workers.

Clean Clothes Campaign. "Nike," Clean Clothes Campaign, March 31, 2014, https://cleanclothes.org/livingwage/tailoredwages/company-submissions/nike-submission.pdf/view.

Clinton Foundation. "Clinton Global Initiative," n.d., accessed October 30, 2017, www.clintonfoundation.org/clinton-global-initiative.

Clinton Global Initiative (CGI). "CGI Annual Meeting 2008: Multimedia: Global Health—Healthy Transitions for Adolescent Girls," Clinton Global Initiative, 2008, www.clintonglobalinitiative.org/ourmeetings/2008/meeting_annual_multimedia.asp?Section=OurMeetings.

Clinton Global Initiative (CGI). "Plenary Session: Investing in Girls and Women," Clinton Global Initiative, 2009, http://original.livestream.com/cgi_plenary/video/flv_4a4a944a-7a8d-494b-8359-747320d8cd99.

CNN Money. "Exxon-Mobil $82B Deal Done after FTC Approval," CNN Money, November 30, 1999, http://money.cnn.com/1999/11/30/deals/exxonmobil/.

CohenMilstein. "Wal-Mart Class Website," CohenMilstein, accessed April 4, 2016, www.walmartclass.com/public_home.html.

Coleman, Isobel. "Women Are the New Global Growth Engine," *Forbes*, September 15, 2010, www.forbes.com/2010/09/15/women-growth-globalization-leadership-citizenship-strategy.html.

Collins, Jane L. "Mapping a Global Labor Market: Gender and Skill in the Globalizing Garment Industry," *Gender & Society* 16, no. 6 (December 2002): 921–40.

Collins, Jane L. *Threads: Gender, Labor, and Power in the Global Apparel Industry* (Chicago: University of Chicago Press, 2003).

Corrêa, Sonia, and Rebecca Lynn Reichmann. *Population and Reproductive Rights: Feminist Perspectives from the South* (London: Zed Books, 1994).

Cortina, Regina. "Global Priorities and Local Predicaments in Education," in *Distant Alliances: Promoting Education for Girls and Women in Latin America*, ed. Regina Cortina and Nelly P. Stromquist (New York: Routledge-Falmer, 2000), 179–200.

Cortina, Regina, and Nelly P. Stromquist, eds. *Distant Alliances: Promoting Education for Girls and Women in Latin America* (New York: Routledge-Falmer, 2000).

Cruikshank, Barbara. *The Will to Empower: Democratic Citizens and Other Subjects* (Ithaca, N.Y.: Cornell University Press, 1999).

Curwen, Lesley. "Science Climate Conflict Warms Up," BBC News, April 26, 2007, http://news.bbc.co.uk/2/hi/business/6595369.stm.

Cushman, John H. "International Business: Nike Pledges to End Child Labor and Apply U.S. Rules Abroad," *New York Times*, May 13, 1998, www.nytimes.com/1998/05/13/business/international-business-nike-pledges-to-end-child-labor-and-apply-us-rules-abroad.html.

Davis, Angela Y. *Women, Race, & Class* (New York: Vintage Books, 1983).

Davis, Owen. "Goldman Sachs Improves to 'Poor' in Reputation Poll, Still Ranks Dead Last," International Business Times, February 7, 2015, www.ibtimes.com/goldman-sachs-improves-poor-reputation-poll-still-ranks-dead-last-1808420.

Debord, Guy. *Society of the Spectacle*, trans. Donald Nicholson-Smith (St. Petersburg, Fla.: Red & Black, 1970).

Delpit, Lisa. *Other People's Children: Cultural Conflict in the Classroom* (New York: New Press, 2006).

Department for International Development. "Family Planning = The Girl Effect Dividend," UK Department for International Development, July 13, 2013, www.flickr.com/photos/dfid/7561275206/in/album-72157630556042220/.

Desai, Manisha. "Transnational Solidarity: Women's Agency, Structural Adjustment, and Globalization," in *Women's Activism and Globalization: Linking Local Struggles and Transnational Politics*, ed. Nancy A. Naples and Manisha Desai (New York: Routledge, 2002), 15–33.

Driscoll, Catherine. *Girls: Feminine Adolescence in Popular Culture and Cultural Theory* (New York: Columbia University Press, 2002).

Duarte, Fernanda. "What Does a Culture of Corporate Social Responsibility 'Look' Like? A Glimpse into a Brazilian Mining Company," *International Journal of Business Anthropology* 2, no. 1 (April 2011): 106–22.

Economist. "The Good Company: Is Corporate Philanthropy Worthwhile?," *Economist*, February 23, 2006, www.economist.com/node/5517678.

Economist. "The Other Billanthropy: Doing Good the Clinton Way," *Economist*, September 21, 2006, www.economist.com/node/7946259.

Eisenstein, Hester. "A Dangerous Liaison? Feminism and Corporate Globalization," *Science & Society* 69, no. 3 (July 2005): 487–518.

Eisenstein, Hester. *Feminism Seduced: How Global Elites Use Women's Labor and Ideas to Exploit the World* (Boulder, Colo.: Paradigm, 2009).

Eitel, Maria. "Day 1 at Davos: Girls, Economies and Green Innovation," Huffington Post, March 30, 2010, www.huffingtonpost.com/maria-eitel/day-1-at-davos-girls-econ_b_440715.html.

Elias, Juanita. "Davos Woman to the Rescue of Global Capitalism: Postfeminist Politics and Competitiveness Promotion at the World Economic Forum," *International Political Sociology* 7, no. 2 (June 1, 2013): 152–69.

Elliot, Larry. "Girls' Education Goes Prada Courtesy of Anne Hathaway and Christy Turlington," *Guardian*, October 7, 2010, www.theguardian.com/global-development/poverty-matters/2010/oct/07/girls-education-hathaway-turlington-agi.

Elson, Diane. "Male Bias in Macro-Economics: The Case of Structural Adjustment," in *Male Bias in the Development Process*, ed. Diane Elson, 2nd ed. (Manchester, UK: Manchester University Press, 1995), 164–90.

Emert, Stan. "Maria Eitel, Nike Foundation (CGI 2010)," Rainmakers.TV, October 1, 2010, http://rainmakers.tv/maria-eitel-nike-foundation-cgi-2010/.

Escobar, Auturo. *Encountering Development: The Making and Unmaking of the Third World* (Princeton, N.J.: Princeton University Press, 1995).

ExxonMobil. "ExxonMobil Announces New Community Investment Initiative; Programs in Africa, Asia, Middle East, Caspian," ExxonMobil, July 7, 2005, http://ir.exxonmobil.com/phoenix.zhtml?c=115024&p=irol-news Article_pf&ID=727331&highlight=.

ExxonMobil. "ExxonMobil Launches Technology Program to Support Women's Economic Advancement at Clinton Global Initiative," Business Wire, September 23, 2009, www.businesswire.com/news/home/20090923005135/en/ExxonMobil-Launches-Technology-Program-Support-Women%E2%80%99s-Economic.

ExxonMobil. "Groundbreaking Training Program in Cameroon Will Enable Women to Push Economies Forward," Business Wire, October 27, 2009, www.businesswire.com/news/home/20091027006668/en/Groundbreaking-Training-Program-Cameroon-Enable-Women-Push.

ExxonMobil. "Learn about the History of ExxonMobil," ExxonMobil, n.d., accessed August 25, 2017, http://corporate.exxonmobil.com/en/company/about-us/history/overview.

ExxonMobil. "Women Leaders," ExxonMobil, accessed March 7, 2008, www.exxonmobil.com/Corporate/news_features_20080306_womenleaders.asp.

ExxonMobil. "ExxonMobil—2005 Grants," ExxonMobile, accessed December 9, 2005, http://exxonmobil.com/Corporate/Citizenship/gcr_women_girls_2005grants.asp.

Federici, Silvia. *Caliban and the Witch: Women, the Body and Primitive Accumulation* (Brooklyn: Autonomedia, 2004).

Ferguson, James. *The Anti-Politics Machine: Development, Depoliticization, and Bureaucratic Power in Lesotho* (Minneapolis: University of Minnesota Press, 1994).

Ferguson, Lucy, and Daniela Alarcon Moreno. "Gender Expertise and the Private Sector: Navigating the Privatization of Gender Equality Funding," in *The Politics of Feminist Knowledge Transfer: Gender Training and Gender Expertise*, ed. Maria Bustelo, Lucy Ferguson, and Maxime Forest (London: Palgrave Macmillan, 2016).

Ferreira da Silva, Denise. *Toward a Global Idea of Race*. (Minneapolis: University of Minnesota Press, 2007).

Fortune500. "Exxon Mobil (XOM) Stock Price, Financials, and News," *Fortune*, accessed October 30, 2017, http://fortune.com/fortune500/exxon-mobil/.

Foucault, Michel. *Discipline and Punish: The Birth of the Prison*, trans. Alan Sheridan (New York: Vintage Books, 1977).

Foucault, Michel. *Power/Knowledge: Selected Interviews and Other Writings, 1972–1977*, ed. Colin Gordon (New York: Harvester Press, 1980).

Foucault, Michel. *The History of Sexuality, Vol. 1: An Introduction*, trans. Robert Hurley (New York: Vintage Books, 1978).

Fraser, Nancy. "Feminism, Capitalism, and the Cunning of History," *New Left Review*, no. 56 (April 2009): 97–117.

Freire, Aluizio. "*Cabral defende aborto contra violência no Rio de Janeiro.*" G1, Globo.com, October 24, 2007, http://g1.globo.com/Noticias/Politica/0,,MUL155710-5601,00-CABRAL+DEFENDE+ABORTO+CONTRA+VIOLENCIA+NO+RIO+DE+JANEIRO.html.

Fundo Social Elas. Fundo Social Elas, accessed April 4, 2016, www.fundosocialelas.org/.

Galbraith, John Kenneth. *The Great Crash 1929* (New York: Houghton Mifflin Harcourt, 1954).

Gap Inc. "P.A.C.E: Advancing Women to Advance the World," Gap, n.d., accessed May 12, 2010, www.gap.com/products/pace-program.jsp.

Gilbert, Geoffrey. *World Population: A Reference Handbook* (Santa Barbara: ABC-CLIO, 2005).

Gillis, Justin, and Clifford Krauss. "Exxon Mobil Investigated for Possible Climate Change Lies by New York Attorney General," *New York Times*, November 5, 2015, www.nytimes.com/2015/11/06/science/exxon-mobil-under-investigation-in-new-york-over-climate-statements.html.

Gilmore, Leigh, and Elizabeth Marshall. "Girls in Crisis: Rescue and Transnational Feminist Autobiographical Resistance," *Feminist Studies* 36, no. 3 (October 1, 2010): 667–90.

Girl Effect. *The Girl Effect: The Clock Is Ticking*, Girl Effect, 2008, www.girleffect.org/media?id=3453.

Girleffect.org. "The Girl Effect: Your Move," NoVo Foundation, 2012, http://novofoundation.org/wp-content/uploads/2012/07/Girl_Effect_Your_Move.pdf.

Global Exchange. "Nike Campaign," Global Exchange, n.d., accessed June 15, 2012, www.globalexchange.org/fairtrade/sweatfree/nike.

Goldman, Michael. *Imperial Nature: The World Bank and Struggles for Social Justice in the Age of Globalization*. (New Haven, Conn.: Yale University Press, 2005).

Goldman Sachs. "10,000 Women," Goldman Sachs, accessed December 22, 2011, www.goldmansachs.com/citizenship/10000women/.

Goldman Sachs. "Financial Highlights," Goldman Sachs, accessed March 4, 2015, www.goldmansachs.com/our_firm/investor_relations/financial_reports/annual_reports/2005/pdf/Page_IFC_Financ_High.pdf.

Goldman Sachs. "Goldman Sachs 2009 Annual Report," Goldman Sachs, April 2007, www.goldmansachs.com/investor-relations/financials/archived/annual-reports/2009-complete-annual.pdf.

Goldman Sachs. "Goldman Sachs 2013 Annual Report," April 2014, www.goldmansachs.com/s/2013annualreport/assets/downloads/GS_AR13_

Complete_Fin.pdf; http://www.goldmansachs.com/investor-relations/financials/fulfillment/reports/GS_AR11_AllPages.pdf.

Goldstein, Donna M. *Laughter Out of Place: Race, Class, Violence, and Sexuality in a Rio Shantytown* (Berkeley: University of California Press, 2013).

González de la Rocha, Mercedes. "Gender and Ethnicity in the Shaping of Differentiated Outcomes of Mexico's Progresa-Oportunidades Conditional Cash Transfer Programme," in *International Handbook of Gender and Poverty: Concepts, Research, Policy*, ed. Sylvia Chant (Cheltenham, UK: Edward Elgar Publishing, 2010), 248–53.

Gramsci, Antonio. *Selections from the Prison Notebooks of Antonio Gramsci*, ed. and trans. Quintin Hoare and Geoffrey Nowell Smith (New York: International Publishers, 1971).

Gramsci, Antonio. *Selections from the Prison Notebooks of Antonio Gramsci*, trans. Quentin Hoare and Geoffrey Nowell Smith (London: Electric Book Company, 1999), http://abahlali.org/files/gramsci.pdf.

Gramsci, Antonio. *The Gramsci Reader: Selected Writings 1916–1935*, ed. David Forgacs (New York: New York University Press, 2000).

Gregory, Derek. *The Colonial Present: Afghanistan. Palestine. Iraq* (Malden, Mass.: Blackwell, 2004), https://middleeastgeographies.files.wordpress.com/2014/12/gregory-the-colonial-present.pdf.

Grosfoguel, Ramon. *Colonial Subjects: Puerto Ricans in a Global Perspective* (Berkeley: University of California Press, 2003).

Grosfoguel, Ramon, and Margarita Cervantes-Rodriguez, eds. *The Modern/Colonial/Capitalist World-System in the Twentieth Century: Global Processes, Antisystemic Movements, and the Geopolitics of Knowledge* (Westport, Conn.: Praeger, 2002).

Guillaumin, Colette. *Racism, Sexism, Power and Ideology* (London: Routledge, 2002).

Gupta, Akhil, and James Ferguson. *Anthropological Locations: Boundaries and Grounds of a Field Science* (Berkeley: University of California Press, 1997).

Hall, Stuart. "Europe's Other Self," *Marxism Today*, no. 25 (August 1991): 18–19.

Hall, Stuart, ed. *Representation: Cultural Representations and Signifying Practices* (London: Sage Publications, 1997).

Hall, Stuart. *The Hard Road to Renewal: Thatcherism and the Crisis of the Left* (Brooklyn: Verso, 1988).

Hall, Stuart. "The Problem of Ideology: Marxism without Guarantees," *Sage Publications*, Fall 1986, 28–44.

Haraway, Donna. "Situated Knowledges: The Science Question in Feminism and the Privilege of Partial Perspective," *Feminist Studies* 14, no. 3 (1988): 575–99.

The Harris Poll. "Regional Grocer Wegmans Unseats Amazon to Claim Top Corporate Reputation Ranking," *Harris Poll*, February 4, 2015, www.theharrispoll.com/business/Regional-Grocer-Wegmans-Unseats-Amazon.html.

Hart, Gillian. *Disabling Globalization: Places of Power in Post-Apartheid South Africa* (Berkeley: University of California Press, 2003).

Hart, Gillian. "From 'Rotten Wives' to 'Good Mothers': Household Models and the Limits of Economism," *IDS Bulletin* 28, no. 3 (July 1997): 14–25, doi:10.1111/j.1759-5436. 1997.mp28003002.x.

Hart, Gillian. "Gender and Household Dynamics: Recent Theories and Their Implications," in *Critical Issues in Asian Development: Theories, Experiences and Policies*, ed. M. G. Quibria (New York: Oxford University Press, 1995), 39–74.

Harvey, David. *Spaces of Hope* (Berkeley: University of California Press, 2000).

Harvey, David. *Spaces on Neoliberalization: Towards a Theory of Uneven Geographical Development* (Birkenwaldstr, Germany: Franz Steiner Verlag (1656), 2005).

Harvey, David. *The Condition of Postmodernity: An Enquiry into the Origins of Cultural Change* (Oxford: Wiley-Blackwell, 1992).

Hayhurst, Lyndsay. "Corporatising Sport, Gender and Development: Postcolonial IR Feminisms, Transnational Private Governance and Global Corporate Social Engagement," *Third World Quarterly* 32, no. 3 (May 20, 2011): 531–49.

Heilborn, Luzia Maria, L. M. Estela Aquino, Michel Bozon, and Riva Daniel Knauth, eds. *O aprendizado da sexualidade: Reproducao e trajectorias sociais de Jovens Brasileiros* (Rio de Janeiro: Fiocruz Garamond, 2006).

Herz, Barbara Knapp, and Gene B. Sperling. *What Works in Girls' Education: Evidence and Policies from the Developing World* (Washington, D.C.: Council on Foreign Relations Press, 2004).

Heward, Christine. "Introduction: The New Discourses of Gender, Education, and Development," in *Gender, Education and Development: Beyond Access to Empowerment*, ed. Christine Heward and Sheila Bunwaree (London: Zed Books, 1998), 1–14.

Heward, Christine, and Sheila Bunwaree, eds. *Gender, Education and Development: Beyond Access to Empowerment* (London: Zed Books, 1998).

Hickel, Jason. "The 'Girl Effect': Liberalism, Empowerment and the Contradictions of Development," *Third World Quarterly* 35, no. 8 (October 3, 2014): 1355–73.

Hobcraft, John. "Women's Education, Child Welfare and Child Survival: A Review of the Evidence," *Health Transition Review* 3, no. 2 (October 1993): 159–75.

Homeland Security and Governmental Affairs: Permanent Subcommittee on Investigations. "Senate Subcommittee Investigating Financial Crisis Releases Documents on Role of Investment Banks," Homeland Security and Governmental Affairs, April 24, 2010, www.hsgac.senate.gov/subcommittees/investigations/media/senate-subcommittee-investigating-financial-crisis-releases-documents-on-role-of-investment-banks.

Hookway, James, and Anh Thu Nguyen. "Vietnam Workers Strike: Factory Employees Seek Higher Wages as Inflation Soars," *Wall Street Journal*, April 2, 2008, www.wsj.com/articles/SB120704094273579965.

Hyatt, Susan Brin. "From Citizen to Volunteer: Neoliberal Governance and the Erasure of Poverty," in *The New Poverty Studies: The Ethnography of Power, Politics, and Impoverished People in the United States*, ed. Judith G. Goode and Jeff Maskovsky (New York: New York University Press, 2001), 201–35.

International Center for Research on Women. "The Girl Effect: What Do Boys Have to Do with It?," ICRW, 2010, www.icrw.org/wp-content/uploads/2016/10/The-Girl-Effect-What-Do-Boys-Have-to-do-with-it.pdf.

International Center for Research on Women, Oak Foundation, and Dalberg and Witter Ventures. "The Business Case for Women's Economic Empowerment: An Integrated Approach," ICRW, 2014, www.icrw.org/publications/business-case-womens-economic-empowerment-integrated-approach.

Jackson, Cecile. "Rescuing Gender from the Poverty Trap," *World Development* 24, no. 3 (March 1996): 489–504.

Jamieson, Dave. "Watchdog Group Kept out of Nike Supplier's Factory after Worker Strike," Huffington Post, March 3, 2016, www.huffingtonpost.com/entry/nike-labor-rights-vietnam_us_56d893f2e4b0000de403b7d0.

Jessop, Bob. "Spatial Fixes, Temporal Fixes, and Spatio-Temporal Fixes," in *David Harvey: A Critical Reader*, ed. Noel Castree and Derek Gregory (Oxford: Blackwell, 2006) 142–66, http://bobjessop.org/2014/01/16/spatial-fixes-temporal-fixes-and-spatio-temporal-fixes/.

Johnson-Hanks, Jennifer. *Uncertain Honor: Modern Motherhood in an African Crisis* (Chicago: University of Chicago Press, 2005).

Joo, Thomas Wuil. "Corporate Governance: Law, Theory and Policy," Social Science Research Network, October 10, 2004, http://papers.ssrn.com/abstract=602704.

Kabeer, Naila. *Gender Mainstreaming in Poverty Eradication and the Millennium Development Goals: A Handbook for Policy-Makers and Other Stakeholders* (London: Commonwealth Secretariat, 2003).

Kabeer, Naila. *Reversed Realities: Gender Hierarchies in Development Thought* (London: Verso, 1994).

Kanani, Rahim. "The Nike Foundation on Unleashing the 'Girl Effect,'" Huffington Post, April 20, 2011, www.huffingtonpost.com/rahim-kanani/nike-foundation-girl-effect_b_850551.html.

Kapur, Devesh, John P. Lewis, and Richard Webb. "Perspectives," Brookings Institution Press, 1997, http://documents.worldbank.org/curated/en/1997/01/13074578/world-bank-first-half-century-vol-2-2-perspectives.

Karabel, Jerome, and A. H. Halsey, eds. *Power and Ideology in Education* (Oxford: Oxford University Press, 1977).

Karim, Lamia. *Microfinance and Its Discontents: Women in Debt in Bangladesh* (Minneapolis: University of Minnesota Press, 2011).

Keady, Jim. "Are Nike's Factory Workers Paid a Living Wage? (video blog)," Huffington Post, accessed April 24, 2012, www.huffingtonpost.com/jim-keady/nike-sweatshops-wages_b_1021155.html.

Kendall, Nancy O'Gara. "Global Policy in Practice: The 'Successful Failure' of Free Primary Education in Malawi," (doctoral dissertation, Stanford University, Palo Alto, Calif., 2004).

King, Elizabeth M. "Does Education Pay in the Labor Market? The Labor Force Participation, Occupation, and Earnings of Peruvian Women. Living Standards Measurement Study Working Paper Number 67," World Bank, 1990, http://documents.worldbank.org/curated/en/174511468776408219/pdf/multi-page.pdf.

King, Elizabeth M., and Anne Hill, eds. *Women's Education in Developing Countries: Barriers, Benefits, and Policies* (Baltimore: John Hopkins University Press, 1993), http://documents.worldbank.org/curated/en/1993/06/440603/womens-education-developing-countries-barriers-benefits-policies.

King, Tiffany Lethabo, and Ewuare Osayande. "The Filth on Philanthropy: Progressive Philanthropy's Agenda to Misdirect Social Justice Movements," in *The Revolution Will Not Be Funded: Beyond the Non-Profit Industrial Complex*, ed. INCITE! Women of Color against Violence (Durham, N.C.: Duke University Press, 2007).

Kirk, Jackie. "Impossible Fictions: The Lived Experiences of Women Teachers in Karachi," *Comparative Education Review* 48, no. 4 (2004): 374–95.

Kirsch, Stuart. *Mining Capitalism: The Relationships between Corporations and Their Critics* (Berkeley: University of California Press, 2014).

Klein, Naomi. *No Logo: Taking Aim at the Brand Bullies* (New York: Picador, 2000).

Knodel, John, and Gavin W. Jones. "Post-Cairo Population Policy: Does Promoting Girls' Schooling Miss the Mark?," *Population and Development Review* 22, no. 4 (1996): 683–702.

Koffman, Ofra, and Rosalind Gill. "'The Revolution Will Be Led by a 12-Year-Old Girl': Girl Power and Global Biopolitics," *Feminist Review* 105, no. 1 (November 2013): 83–102.

Kohl-Arenas, Erica. *The Self-Help Myth: How Philanthropy Fails to Alleviate Poverty*, vol. 1. (Oakland: University of California Press, 2015).

Kothari, Uma, ed. *A Radical History of Development Studies: Individual, Institutions, and Ideologies* (London: Zed Books, 2006).

Kothari, Uma. "Critiquing 'Race' and Racism in Development Discourse and Practice," *Progress in Development Studies* 6, no. 1 (2006): 1–7.

Koyama, Jill P. *Making Failure Pay: For-profit Tutoring, High-stakes Testing, and Public Schools* (Chicago: University of Chicago Press, 2010).

Kristof, Nicholas. "Where Sweatshops Are a Dream," *New York Times*, January 14, 2009, www.nytimes.com/2009/01/15/opinion/15kristof.html.

Kuumba, M. Bahati. "A Cross-Cultural Race/Class/Gender Critique of Contemporary Population Policy: The Impact of Globalization," *Sociological Forum* 14, no. 3 (1999): 447–63.

Kuumba, M. Bahati. *Reproductive Imperialism: Population and Labor of Underdeveloped World Women,* (working paper, Women in International Development, Michigan State University, East Lansing, Mich., 1996.

Lane, Sandra D. "From Population Control to Reproductive Health: An Emerging Policy Agenda," *Social Science & Medicine* 39, no. 9 (November 1, 1994): 1303–14.

Lave, Jean, and Etienne Wegner. *Situated Learning: Legitimate Peripheral Participation* (London: Cambridge University Press, 1991).

Lawson, Sandra. "Global Economics Paper No: 164: Women Hold up Half the Sky." Goldman Sachs, March 4, 2008, www.goldmansachs.com/our-thinking/investing-in-women/bios-pdfs/women-half-sky-pdf.pdf.

Leve, Lauren. "Failed Development and Rural Revolution in Nepal: Rethinking Subaltern Consciousness and Women's Empowerment," in *Theorising NGOs: States, Feminisms, and Neoliberalism*, ed. Victoria Bernal and Inderpal Grewal (Durham, N.C.: Duke University Press, 2014), 50–92.

Levine, Ruth, Cynthia Lloyd, Margaret Greene, and Caren Grown. "Girls Count: A Global Investment & Action Agenda," Center for Global Development, January 14, 2008, www.cgdev.org/publication/girls-count-global-investment-action-agenda.

Lewis, Kristin. "The Gender Dividend: A Business Case for Gender Equality," UN Women, 2011, www2.unwomen.org/~/media/headquarters/media/publications/en/unwomenthegenderdividend.pdf?v=1&d=20140917T100949.

Li, Murray Tania. *The Will to Improve: Governmentality, and the Practice of Politics* (Durham, N.C.: Duke University Press, 2007).

Locke, Richard. "The Promise and Perils of Globalization: The Case of Nike," Industrial Performance Center, Massachusetts Institute of Technology, July 2002, https://ipc.mit.edu/sites/default/files/documents/02-007.pdf.

Lugones, Maria. "Heterosexualism and the Colonia Modern Gender System," *Hypatia* 22, no. 1 (2007): 186–209.

Manfreda, John. "Exxon Mobil Is No Longer the World's Largest Oil Company," Business Insider, May 14, 2015, www.businessinsider.com/exxon-mobil-is-no-longer-the-worlds-largest-oil-company-2015-5?r=UK.

Mani, Lata. *Contentious Traditions: The Debate on Sati in Colonial India* (Berkeley: University of California Press, 1998).

Mani, Lata. "Production of an Official Discourse on Sati in Early Nineteenth-Century Bengal," in *Women and Social Reform in Modern India: A Reader*, ed. Sumit Sarkar and Tanika Sarkar (Bloomington: Indiana University Press, 2008), 38–57.

Marchand, Marianne H., and Jane L. Parpart, eds. *Feminism/Postmodernism /Development* (London: Routledge, 1995).

Marcus, George E. "Ethnography in/of the World System: The Emergence of Multi-Sited Ethnography," *Annual Review of Anthropology* 24 (1995): 95–117.

Marx, Karl. *Grundrisse* (London: Penguin Books, 1973).

Massey, Doreen. *Space, Place and Gender* (Cambridge: Polity Press, 1994).

Mayor, Federico. "94-09-06: Statement of UNESCO, Mr. Federico Mayor," United Nations Population Information Network, 1994, www.un.org /popin/icpd/conference/una/940906194128.html.

McClintock, Anne. *Imperial Leather: Race, Gender, and Sexuality in the Colonial Contest* (New York: Routledge, 1995).

McGirt, Ellen. "Meet the League of Extraordinary Women: 60 Influencers Who Are Changing the World," Fast Company, June 2012, www.fastcompany .com/1839862/meet-league-extraordinary-women-60-influencers-who -are-changing-world.

McGoey, Linsey. "Philanthrocapitalism and Its Critics," *Poetics* 40, no. 2 (April 2012): 185–99.

McKinsey & Company. "The Business of Empowering Women: Where, Why, and How," McKinsey&Company, January 2010, http://mckinseyonsociety .com/the-business-of-empowering-women/.

McLaren, Peter. "The Ethnographer as Postmodern Flaneur: Critical Reflexivity and Posthybridity as Narrative Engagement," in *Representation and the Text: Re-Framing the Narrative Voice*, ed. William G. Tierney and Yvonna S. Lincoln (Albany: State University of New York Press, 1997), 143–78.

Melamed, Jodi. "Racial Capitalism," *Critical Ethnic Studies* 1, no. 1 (2015): 76–85.

Mies, Maria. *Patriarchy and Accumulation on a World Scale: Women in the International Division of Labour* (London: Zed Books, 1986).

Mills, Mary Beth. "Gender and Inequality in the Global Labor Force," *Annual Review of Anthropology* 32, no. 2003 (2003): 41–62, doi:10.1146/annurev .anthro.32.061002.093107.

Minh-Ha, Trinh T. *Woman, Native, Other: Writing Postcoloniality and Feminism* (Bloomington: Indiana University Press, 2009).

Mitchell, Timothy. "Society, Economy, and the State Effect," in *State/Culture: State-Formation after the Cultural Turn*, ed. George Steinmetz (Ithaca, N.Y.: Cornell University Press, 1999), 76–97.

Moeller, Kathryn. "A Critical Feminist and Race Critique of Thomas Piketty's Capital in the Twenty-First Century," *British Journal of Sociology of Education* 37, no. 6 (2016): 810–22.

Moeller, Kathryn. "Investing in the Girl Effect in Brazil: Corporatized Development, Girls' Education, and the Transnational Politics of Poverty," (PhD thesis, University of California, Berkeley, 2012).

Moeller, Kathryn. "Searching for Adolescent Girls in Brazil: The Transnational Politics of Poverty in 'The Girl Effect,'" *Feminist Studies* 40, no. 3 (2014): 575–601.

Mohanty, Chandra Talpade. "Under Western Eyes: Feminist Scholarship and Colonial Discourses," in *Third World Women and the Politics of Feminism*, ed. Talpade Chandra Mohanty, Ann Russo, and Lourdes Torres (Bloomington: Indiana University Press, 1991).

Molyneux, Maxine. "Mothers at the Service of the New Poverty Agenda: Progresa/Oportunidades, Mexico's Conditional Transfer Programme," *Social Policy & Administration* 40, no. 4 (July 19, 2006): 425–49.

Muirhead, Sophia. "Corporate Contributions: The View from Fifty Years," Conference Board, June 1999, www.conference-board.org/publications/publicationdetail.cfm?publicationid=429.

Mulher360. "Corporate Movement for Women's Economic Development," Walmart Brasil, 2015, www.walmartbrasil.com.br/wm/wp-content/uploads/2015/08/Movimento-Mulher-360-En.pdf.

Mundy, Karen. "Educational Multilateralism in a Changing World Order: UNESCO and the Limits of the Possible," *International Journal of Educational Development* 19, no. 1 (1999): 27–52.

Mundy, Karen. "Retrospect and Prospect: Education in a Reforming World Bank," *International Journal of Educational Development* 22, no. 5 (September 2002): 483–508.

Murphy, Michelle. "Economization of Life: Calculative Infrastructures of Population and Economy," in *Relational Architectural Ecologies: Architecture, Nature and Subjectivity*, ed. Peg Rawes (London: Routledge, 2013), 139–55.

Murphy, Michelle. *Seizing the Means of Reproduction: Entanglements of Feminism, Health, and Technoscience* (Durham, N.C.: Duke University Press, 2012).

Nader, Laura. "Up the Anthropologist: Perspectives Gained from Studying Up," in *Reinventing Anthropology*, ed. Dell Hymes (New York: Pantheon, 1972), 284–311.

Nash, June C., and Maria P. Fernandez-Kelly, eds. *Women, Men, and the International Division of Labor* (Albany: State University of New York Press, 1984).

Newell, Andrea. "Investing in Women's Economic Opportunities at ExxonMobil: Lorie Jackson." TriplePundit, April 4, 2011, www.triplepundit.com/2011/04/exxonmobil-women-interview-lorie-jackson/.

Ngai, Pun. *Made in China: Women Factory Workers in a Global Workplace* (Durham, N.C.: Duke University Press, 2005).

Nike Foundation. "Adolescent Girls: The Most Powerful Force of Change on the Planet (Internal Document)," September 2009.

Nike Foundation. *The Girl Effect: I Dare You to See I Am the Answer*, Nike Foundation, 2010, www.youtube.com/watch?v=C44BOxKhwsQ.

Nike Foundation. "Girl Effect Accelerator Culminating Event," Eventbrite, November 11, 2014, www.eventbrite.com/e/girl-effect-culminating-event-tickets-13367128441?aff=efbneb.

Nike Foundation. "Investor News Details: Nike Foundation Steps on to New Field," Nike News, March 8, 2005, http://investors.nike.com/investors/news-events-and-reports/investor-news/investor-news-details/2005/Nike-Foundation-Steps-on-to-New-Field/default.aspx.

Nike Foundation. "Nike Foundation," Nike Foundation, n.d., accessed April 10, 2008, www.nikefoundation.com.

Nike Foundation. "Request for Proposals: 'She's an Economic Powerhouse: Economic Empowerment Models for Girls,'" Nike Foundation, October 2007, www.nikefoundation.com.

Nike Foundation. "The Girl Effect Media Kit," Nike Foundation, 2008, www.nikefoundation.com/files/ [C05.97] The_Girl_Effect_Media_Kit.pdf.

Nike Foundation. "The Revolution," Nike Foundation, accessed March 11, 2012, www.girleffect.org/learn/the-revolution.

Nike, Inc. "Nike Publishes List of Global Contract Factories in Push for Greater Transparency and Collaboration to Improve Footwear and Apparel Industry Labor Conditions—Press Releases," CSR Newswire, April 13, 2005, www.csrwire.com/press_releases/24956-Nike-Publishes-List-of-Global-Contract-Factories -in-Push-for-Greater-Transparency-and-Collaboration-to-Improve-Footwear-and-Apparel-Industry-Labor-Conditions.

Nike, Inc. "Our Work," Nike, Inc., n.d., accessed June 21, 2012, http://nikeinc.com/pages/our-work.

O Movimento. "O Movimento," *Movimento Mulher 360*, n.d., accessed October 30, 2107, http://movimentomulher360.com.br/institucional/o-movimento/.

Olaniyan, Kolawole. "Nigeria Oil Judgment a Small Step in the Journey from Travesty to Justice," Amnesty International, December 29, 2012, www.amnesty.org/en/latest/campaigns/2012/12/nigeria-oil-judgment-a-small-step-in-the-journey-from-travesty-to-justice/.

Omi, Michael, and Howard Winant. *Racial Formation in the United States: From the 1960s to the 1990s*, 2nd ed. (New York: Routledge, 1994).

Ong, Aihwa. "The Gender and Labor Politics of Postmodernity," *Annual Review of Anthropology* 20, no. 1991 (1991): 279–309.

Organisation for Economic Co-operation and Development. "The Global Economy: Strengthening Growth and Job Creation - Statement at G20 Leader's Summit," *OECD*, 2014, www.oecd.org/g20/summits/brisbane/the-global-economy-strengthening-growth-and-job-creation.htm.

Osotimehin, Babatunde, and Melesse Tewodros. "Joint Statement in Response to the Tragic Deaths and Injuries Sustained by Women Undergoing Sterilization in the Indian State of Chhattisgarh," United Nations Population Fund and International Planned Parenthood Federation, November 13, 2014, www.ippf.org/news/Joint-statement-response-tragic-deaths-and-injuries-sustained-women-undergoing-sterilization-In.

Oxfam Australia. "Nike Watch," Oxfam, n.d., accessed October 30, 2017, www.oxfam.org.au/what-we-do/ethical-trading-and-business/workers-rights-2/nike/.

Parpart, Jane. "Deconstructing the Development 'Expert': Gender, Development and the 'Vulnerable Groups,'" in *Feminism/Postmodernism/Development*, ed. Marianne H. Marchand (London: Routledge, 2003), 221–43).

Peck, Jamie. "Geographies of Policy from Transfer-Diffusion to Mobility-Mutation," *Progress in Human Geography* 35, no. 6 (February 21, 2011): 773–97.

Peck, Jamie. "Global Policy Models, Globalizing Poverty Management: International Convergence or Fast-Policy Integration?," *Geography Compass* 5, no. 4 (April 3, 2011): 165–81.

Peck, Jamie, and Nik Theodore. "Mobilizing Policy: Models, Methods, and Mutations," *Geoforum* 41, no. 2 (March 2010): 169–74.

Peet, Richard. *Unholy Trinity: The IMF, World Bank and WTO* (London: Zed Books, 2003).

Philanthropy News Digest. "NIKE, NoVo Foundation Commit $100 Million to the Girl Effect," Philanthropy News Digest, May 28, 2008, http://philanthropynewsdigest.org/news/nike-novo-foundation-commit-100-million-to-the-girl-effect.

Piketty, Thomas. *Capital in the Twenty-First Century*, trans. Arthur Goldhammer (Cambridge, Mass.: Belknap Press of Harvard University Press, 2014).

Pillow, Wanda S. *Unfit Subjects: Educational Policy and the Teen Mother* (New York: RoutledgeFalmer, 2004).

Plank, David. *The Means of Our Salvation: Public Education in Brazil, 1930–1995* (Boulder, Colo.: Westview Press, 1996).

Plank, David N. "The Politics of Basic Education in Brazil," *Comparative Education Review* 34, no. 4 (1990): 538–59.

Polanyi, Karl. *The Great Transformation: The Political and Economic Origins of Our Time* (Boston: Beacon Press, 1944).

Polgar, Steven. "Birth Planning: Between Neglect and Coercion," in *Population and Social Organisations*, ed. Moni Nag (The Hague: Mouton Publishers, 1975), 177–202.

Popkewitz, Thomas S., ed. *Educational Knowledge: Changing Relationships between the State, Civil Society, and the Educational Community* (Albany: State University of New York Press, 2000).

Prahalad, C. K. *The Fortune at the Bottom of the Pyramid: Eradicating Poverty through Profits* (Upper Saddle River, N.J.: Pearson FT Press, 2009).

Prahalad, C. K., and Stuart L. Hart. "The Fortune at the Bottom of the Pyramid," Strategy+Business, January 10, 2002, www.strategy-business.com/article/11518?gko=9a4ba.

Princen, Thomas, and Matthias Finger. *Environmental NGOs in World Politics: Linking the Local and the Global* (London: Routledge, 1994).

Propera - International Network of Women's Funds. "International Network of Women's Funds," INWF, accessed October 30, 2017, www.prospera-inwf.org/.

Prout, Alan. *The Future of Childhood: Towards the Interdisciplinary Study of Children*, Future of Childhood Series (London: RoutledgeFalmer, 2005).

Prügl, Elisabeth. "Corporate Social Responsibility and the Neoliberalization of Feminism," in *Gender Equality and Responsible Business: Expanding CSR Horizons*, ed. Kate Grosser, Lauren McCarthy, and Maureen Kilgour (Sheffield, UK: Greenleaf Publishing, 2016), 46–54.

Prügl, Elisabeth, and Jacqui True. "Equality Means Business? Governing Gender through Transnational Public-Private Partnerships," *Review of International Political Economy* 21, no. 6 (2014): 1137–69, doi:10.1080/09692290.2013.849277.

Psacharopoulos, George, and Harry Anthony Patrinos. "Returns to Investment in Education: A Further Update," Social Science Research Network, September 30, 2002.

Psacharopoulos, George, and Maureen Woodhall. *Education for Development: An Analysis of Investment Choices* (Oxford: Oxford University Press, 1986).

Quijano, Anibal. "Coloniality of Power, Eurocentrism, and Latin America," *Nepantla: Views from the South* 1, no. 3 (2000): 533–80.

Rabinow, Paul. *French Modern: Norms and Forms of the Social Environment* (Cambridge, Mass.: MIT Press, 1989).

Rajak, Dinah. "'HIV/AIDS Is Our Business': The Moral Economy of Treatment in a Transnational Mining Company," *Journal of the Royal Anthropological Institute* 16, no. 3 (August 5, 2010): 551–71, doi:10.1111/j.1467-9655.2010.01639.x.

Rajak, Dinah. *In Good Company: An Anatomy of Corporate Social Responsibility* (Palo Alto, Calif.: Stanford University Press, 2011).

Rankin, Katharine N. "Governing Development: Neoliberalism, Microcredit, and Rational Economic Woman," *Economy and Society* 30, no. 1 (2001): 18–37.

Rao, Mohan, and Sarah Sexton, eds. *Markets and Malthus: Population, Gender and Health in Neo-Liberal Times* (New Delhi: SAGE Publications India, 2010).

Rathgeber, Eva M. "WID, WAD, GAD: Trends in Research and Practice," *Journal of Developing Areas* 24, no. 4 (1990): 489–502.

Razavi, Shahra. "Fitting Gender into Development Institutions," *World Development* 25, no. 7 (July 1977): 1111–1125.

Richey, Lisa Ann. "Reproductive Health, Family Planning, and HIV/AIDS: Dangers of (Dis)integration in Tanzania and Uganda," in *Markets and Malthus: Population, Gender and Health in Neo-Liberal Times*, ed. Mohan Rao and Sarah Sexton (New Delhi: SAGE Publications India, 2010), 265–98.

Roberts, Adrienne. "The Political Economy of 'Transnational Business Feminism,'" *International Feminist Journal of Politics* 17, no. 2 (January 28, 2014): 209–31.

Roberts, Dorothy E. *Killing the Black Body: Race, Reproduction, and the Meaning of Liberty*, 2nd ed. (New York: Vintage Books, 2017).

Robertson, Susan, Karen Mundy, and Antoni Verger, eds. *Public Private Partnerships in Education: New Actors and Modes of Governance in a Globalizing World* (Cheltenham, UK: Edward Elgar Publishing, 2012).

Robinson, Cedric J. *Black Marxism: The Making of the Black Radical Tradition* (Chapel Hill: University of North Carolina Press, 1983).

Rofel, Lisa. *Other Modernities: Gendered Yearnings in China after Socialism* (Berkeley: University of California Press, 1999).

Roland, Edna. *"Direitos reprodutivos e racismo no Brasil," Estudos Feministas* 3, no. 2 (1995): 506–14.

Rostow, W. W. *The Stages of Economic Growth. A Non-Communist Manifesto* (Cambridge, UK: Cambridge University Press, 1960).

Roy, Ananya. *City Requiem, Calcutta: Gender and the Politics of Poverty* (Minneapolis: University of Minnesota Press, 2003).

Roy, Ananya. "'Ethical Subjects: Market Rule in an Age of Poverty,'" *Public Culture* 24, no. 1 (2012): 105–8.

Roy, Ananya. *Poverty Capital: Microfinance and the Making of Development* (New York: Routledge, 2010).

Sachs, Jeffrey. *The End of Poverty: Economic Possibilities for Our Time* (New York: Penguin Books, 2006).
Said, Edward W. *Orientalism* (New York: Pantheon Books, 1978).
Salzinger, Leslie. *Gender in Production: Making Workers in Mexico's Global Factories* (Berkeley: University of California Press, 2003).
Samuels, Ellen. "Examining Millie and Christine McKoy: Where Enslavement and Enfreakment Meet," *Signs* 37, no. 1 (2011): 53–81.
Sawyer, Suzana. "Disabling Corporate Sovereignty in a Transnational Lawsuit," *PoLAR: Political and Legal Anthropology Review* 29, no. 1 (May 2006): 23–43.
Schultz, T. Paul. "Women and Development: Objectives, Frameworks, and Policy Interventions," World Bank, April 30, 1989, http://documents.worldbank.org/curated/en/1989/04/437022/women-development-objectives-frameworks-policy-interventions.
Schultz, Theodore W. "Investment in Human Capital," *American Economic Review* 51, no. 1 (May 1961): 1–17.
Schwittay, Anke Fleur. "Digital Citizens, Inc.: Producing Corporate Ethics, Flexible Networks and Mobile Entrepreneurs in the Global Marketplace," (PhD thesis, University of California, Berkeley, Calif., 2006).
Scott, Linda, Catherine Dolan, Mary Johnstone-Louis, et al. "Enterprise and Inequality: A Study of Avon in South Africa," *Entrepreneurship Theory and Practice* 36, no. 3 (2012): 543–68.
Scott, Joan W. "Gender: A Useful Category of Historical Analysis," *American Historical Review* 91, no. 5 (1986): 1053–75.
Sen, Gita, Adrienne Germain, and Linda Chen, eds. *Population Policies Reconsidered: Health, Empowerment, and Rights*. Harvard University Press, 1994, https://iwhc.org/resources/population-policies-reconsidered-health-empowerment-rights/.
Shain, Farzana. "'The Girl Effect': Exploring Narratives of Gendered Impacts and Opportunities in Neoliberal Development," *Sociological Research Online* 18, no. 2 (2012): 9.
Siddiqi, Dina M. "Do Bangladeshi Factory Workers Need Saving? Sisterhood in the Post-Sweatshop Era," *Feminist Review* 91, no. 1 (2009): 154–74.
Smith, Greg. "Why I Am Leaving Goldman Sachs," *New York Times*, March 14, 2012, www.nytimes.com/2012/03/14/opinion/why-i-am-leaving-goldman-sachs.html.
Smith, Jessica, and Frederico Helfgott. "Flexibility or Exploitation? Corporate Social Responsibility and the Perils of Universalization," *Anthropology Today* 26, no. 3 (June 2010): 20–23.
Spivak, Gayatri Chakravorty. *A Critique of Postcolonial Reason: Toward a History of the Vanishing Present* (Cambridge, Mass.: Harvard University Press, 1999).

Spivak, Gayatri Chakravorty, and Sneja Gunew. "Questions of Multiculturalism," in *The Cultural Studies Reader*, ed. Simon During (London: Routledge, 1993), 193–202.

Stiglitz, Joseph E. *Globalization and Its Discontents* (New York: W.W. Norton & Company, 2003).

Story, Louise, and Gretchen Morgenson. "S.E.C. Accuses Goldman of Fraud in Housing Deal," *New York Times*, April 16, 2010, www.nytimes.com/2010/04/17/business/17goldman.html.

Streeten, Paul, Frances Stewart, Shahid Javid Burki, et al. "Poverty and Basic Needs," World Bank, September 1, 1980, http://documents.worldbank.org/curated/en/1980/09/6454349/poverty-basic-needs.

Strom, Stephanie. "Gift to Teach Business to Third-World Women," *New York Times*, March 6, 2008, www.nytimes.com/2008/03/06/us/06gift.html.

Stromquist, Nelly P. "The Impact of Structural Adjustment Programmes in Africa and Latin America," in *Gender, Education and Development: Beyond Access to Empowerment*, ed. Christine Heward and Sheila Bunwaree (London: Zed Books, 1998), 17–32.

Summers, Lawrence. "Investing in All the People," World Bank, 1992, www-wds.worldbank.org/servlet/WDSContentServer/WDSP/IB/1992/05/01/000009265_3961003011714/Rendered/PDF/multi_page.pdf.

Summers, Lawrence. "The Most Influential Investment," *Scientific American*, August 1992, www.scientificamerican.com/article/the-most-influential-investment/.

Switzer, Heather. "(Post)Feminist Development Fables: The Girl Effect and the Production of Sexual Subjects," *Feminist Theory* 14, no. 3 (December 1, 2013): 345–60, doi:10.1177/1464700113499855.

Taibbi, Matt. "The Great American Bubble Machine," *Rolling Stone*, April 5, 2010, www.rollingstone.com/politics/news/the-great-american-bubble-machine-20100405.

Taylor, Alan. "The Exxon Valdez Oil Spill: 25 Years Ago Today," *Atlantic*, March 24, 2014, www.theatlantic.com/infocus/2014/03/the-exxon-valdez-oil-spill-25-years-ago-today/100703/.

Tembom, Mercy, and Lucia Fort, eds. *Girls' Education in the 21st Century: Gender Equality, Empowerment, and Economic Growth*. (Washington, D.C.: World Bank, 2008), http://siteresources.worldbank.org/EDUCATION/Resources/278200-1099079877269/547664-1099080014368/DID_Girls_edu.pdf.

Teodor, Shanin. "The Idea of Progress," in *The Post-Development Reader*, ed. Majid Rahnema and Victoria Bawtree (Chicago: University of Chicago Press, 1997), 65–71, http://pages.uoregon.edu/aweiss/intl422_522/The%20Idea%20of%20Progress.pdf.

The Third Billion. "The Third Billion," The Third Billion, accessed July 17, 2013, https://web.archive.org/web/20130625122005/http://thethirdbillion.org/.

Thorne, Barrie. *Gender Play: Girls and Boys in School* (New Brunswick, N.J.: Rutgers University Press, 2004).

Tsing, Anna Lowenhaupt. *Friction: An Ethnography of Global Connection* (Princeton: Princeton University Press, 2005).

Udo, Bassey. "Nigeria: Protesters Shut Down ExxonMobil Operations in Eket Over N26.5b Oil Spill Compensation," Premium Times, October 25, 2013, www.premiumtimesng.com/news/147277-protesters-shut-exxonmobil-operations-eket-n26-5b-oil-spill-compensation.html.

UN Global Compact. "The Ten Principles," *United Nations Global Compact*, n.d., accessed October 30, 2017, www.unglobalcompact.org/what-is-gc/mission/principles.

UNESCO. "Access of Girls and Women to Education in Rural Areas: A Comparative Study," UNESCO, 1964, http://unesdoc.unesco.org/images/0000/000013/001322eo.pdf.

UNESCO. "Access of Women to Out-of-School Education," UNESCO, accessed April 1, 2016, http://unesdoc.unesco.org/images/0012/001262/126287EB.pdf.

UNESCO. "Access of Women to the Teaching Profession," UNESCO, 1961, http://unesdoc.unesco.org/images/0012/001262/126291EB.pdf.

UNESCO. "General Conference, 15th Session: International Education Year," UNESCO, September 12, 1968, http://unesdoc.unesco.org/images/0016/001601/160197eb.pdf.

UNESCO. "Introducing UNESCO," UNESCO, accessed June 24, 2014, http://en.unesco.org/about-us/introducing-unesco.

UNESCO. "United Nations Educational, Scientific and Cultural Organization (UNESCO)," United Nations in Ethiopia, n.d., accessed October 30, 2017, http://et.one.un.org/content/unct/ethiopia/en/home/resources/un-agencies-profiles/united-nations-educational—scientific-and-cultural-organization.html.

UNESCO Regional Office for Education in Asia. "Population Dynamics and Educational Development: A Selection of Papers Presented at the Seminar," UNESCO Regional Office for Education in Asia, 1974, http://unesdoc.unesco.org/images/0001/000122/012293eo.pdf.

UNICEF. *The Invisible Adjustment: Poor Women and the Economic Crisis* (Santiago, Chile: UNICEF, 1989).

United Nations. "Part IV: An Action Framework for Population Education on the Eve of the Twenty-First Century," United Nations, April 1983, www.un.org/popin/confcon/poped/part4wp.htm.

United Nations. "Resolution 1838: Population Growth and Economic Development," United Nations, December 18, 1962, www.un.org/en/ga/search/view_doc.asp?symbol=A/RES/1838(XVII).

United Nations. "Short History of the Commission on the Status of Women," UNCSW, n.d., October 30, 2017, www.un.org/womenwatch/daw/CSW60YRS /CSWbriefhistory.pdf.

United Nations. "The Universal Declaration of Human Rights," United Nations, December 10, 1948, www.un.org/en/universal-declaration-human-rights /index.html.

United Nations. "United Nations Millennium Development Goals," United Nations, n.d., accessed October 30, 2017, www.un.org/millenniumgoals/.

United Nations Department of Public Information. "The Four Global Women's Conferences 1975–1995: Historical Perspective," UN Women, June 2000, www.un.org/womenwatch/daw/followup/session/presskit /hist.htm.

United Nations Educational, Scientific and Cultural Organization [UNESCO]. "EFA Global Monitoring Report 2003/4: Gender and Education for All—The Leap to Equality," United Nations Educational, Scientific and Cultural Organization, 2003, http://unesdoc.unesco.org/images/0013/001325 /132513e.pdf.

United Nations International Conference on Population. "Text of Declaration by International Population Conference in Mexico City," *New York Times*, August 16, 1984, www.nytimes.com/1984/08/16/world/text-of-declaration-by-international-population-conference-in-mexico-city.html.

United Nations Population Division. "United Nations Conferences on Population," UN Department of Economic and Social Affairs, accessed April 3, 2016, www.un.org/en/development/desa/population/events/conference /index.shtml.

United Nations Population Fund. "About Us," UNFPA, n.d., accessed October 30, 2017, www.unfpa.org/about-us.

United Nations Women, "Convention on the Elimination of All Forms of Discrimination against Women," UN Women, June 30, 2014, www.un.org /womenwatch/daw/cedaw/.

United Nations Women. "International Women's Day: History of the Day," n.d., accessed October 30, 2017, www.un.org/en/events/womensday/history .shtml.

United States Agency for International Development [USAID]. "Family Planning Timeline," n.d. https://www.usaid.gov/sites/default/files /documents/1864/timeline_b.pdf.

United States Agency for International Development [USAID]. "Population Assistance," United States Agency for International Development, September 1982, www.usaid.gov/sites/default/files/documents/1864/populat.pdf.

United Students Against Sweatshops. "What Did Nike Just Do?" *USAS: Organizing for Student and Worker Power*, November 19, 2015. http://usas .org/2015/11/19/what-did-nike-just-do/.

Unterhalter, Elaine. *Gender, Schooling and Global Social Justice: Foundations and Futures of Education*. London & New York: Routledge, 2007.

Valentine, David. *Imagining Transgender: An Ethnography of a Category* (Durham, N.C.: Duke University Press, 2007).

Vavrus, Frances Katherine. *Desire and Decline: Schooling amid Crisis in Tanzania* (Bern, Switzerland: Peter Lang Publishing, 2003).

Verisk Maplecroft. "Mapping the Vulnerability of Adolescent Girls in the Developing World," Verisk Maplecroft, accessed April 24, 2012, http://maplecroft.com/about/news/girls_discovered_nov_09.html.

Visser, Jan. "Learning without Frontiers—Distance Education for the Nine High-Population Countries," UNESCO, February 1994, www.unesco.org/education/lwf/doc/de9.html.

Walmart. "Walmart Launches Global Women's Economic Empowerment Initiative," Walmart, September 14, 2011, http://corporate.walmart.com/_news_/news-archive/2011/09/14/walmart-launches-global-womens-economic-empowerment-initiative.

Wal-Mart Stores, Inc. v. Betty Dukes et al., Supreme Court Report No. 10-277, 2011.

Watts, Michael. "Petro-Violence: Community, Extraction, and Political Ecology of a Mythic Commodity," in *Violent Environments*, ed. Nancy L Peluso and Michael Watts (Ithaca, N.Y.: Cornell University Press, 2001), 189–212.

Welker, Marina. *Enacting the Corporation: An American Mining Firm in Post-Authoritarian Indonesia* (Berkeley: University of California Press, 2014).

White, Sarah. "Thinking Race, Thinking Development" *Third World Quarterly* 23, no. 3 (2002): 407–19.

Willinsky, John. *Learning to Divide the World: Education at Empire's End* (Minneapolis: University of Minnesota Press, 1998).

Willoughby-Herard, Tiffany. *Waste of a White Skin: The Carnegie Corporation and the Racial Logic of White Vulnerability* (Berkeley: University of California Press, 2015).

Winddance, Francine Twine. *Racism in a Racial Democracy: The Maintenance of White Supremacy in Brazil* (New Brunswick, N.J.: Rutgers University Press, 1998).

World Bank. "Adolescent Girls in Focus at the World Economic Forum," World Bank, February 26, 2009, http://web.worldbank.org/WBSITE/EXTERNAL/TOPICS/EXTGENDER/0,,contentMDK:22059153~menuPK:336906~pagePK:64020865~piPK:149114~theSitePK:336868,00.html.

World Bank. "Documents & Reports," World Bank, accessed October 23, 2011, www-wds.worldbank.org/WBSITE/EXTERNAL/EXTWDS/0,,detailPagemenuPK:64187510~menuPK:64187513~pagePK:64187848~

piPK:64187934~searchPagemenuPK:64187283~siteName:WDS~theSitePK:523679,00.html.

World Bank. "Gender Action Plan: Gender Equality as Smart Economics," World Bank, n.d., accessed October 30, 2017, http://web.worldbank.org/WBSITE/EXTERNAL/TOPICS/EXTGENDER/0,,contentMDK:21983335~pagePK:210058~piPK:210062~theSitePK:336868,00.html.

World Bank. "President Robert B. Zoellick Announces 6 New World Bank Group Commitments on Gender Equality," World Bank, April 11, 2008, http://go.worldbank.org/S1YV8VKGL0.

World Bank. *Priorities and Strategies for Education: A World Bank Review* (Washington, D.C.: International Bank for Reconstruction and Development/World Bank, 1995).

World Bank. "The World Bank Launches Private-Public Initiative to Empower Adolescent Girls," World Bank: News & Broadcast, October 10, 2008, http://web.worldbank.org/WBSITE/EXTERNAL/NEWS/0,,contentMDK:21935449~pagePK:34370~piPK:34424~theSitePK:4607,00.html.

World Bank. *World Bank Development Report 2012: Gender Equality and Development* (Washington, D.C.: World Bank, 2011), https://siteresources.worldbank.org/INTWDR2012/Resources/7778105-1299699968583/7786210-1315936222006/Complete-Report.pdf.

World Bank. "World Bank Education Sector Working Paper 1971," World Bank, 1971, http://documents.worldbank.org/curated/en/149071468338353096/Education-sector-working-paper.

World Bank. "World Bank Education Sector Working Paper 1974," World Bank, December 31, 1974, http://documents.worldbank.org/curated/en/868961468741007167/Education.

World Bank. "World Bank Group Historical Chronology," World Bank, n.d., accessed October 30, 2017, www.worldbank.org/en/about/archives/history/chronology.

World Business Council for Sustainable Development. "WBCSD—World Business Council for Sustainable Development," n.d., accessed October 30, 2017, www.wbcsd.org/home.aspx.

World Economic Forum. *Davos Annual Meeting 2009—The Girl Effect on Development*, World Economic Forum, 2009, www.youtube.com/watch?v=CQc7NZPjqBA.

World Health Organization. "Eliminating Forced, Coercive and Otherwise Involuntary Sterilization: An Interagency Statement: OHCHR, UN Women, UNAIDS, UNDP, UNFPA, UNICEF and WHO," World Health Organization, 2014, http://apps.who.int/iris/bitstream/10665/112848/1/9789241507325_eng.pdf.

Wright, Melissa W. *Disposable Women and Other Myths of Global Capitalism* (New York: Routledge, 2006).

Wright, Stephen. "Nike Faces New Worker Abuse Claims in Indonesia," Huffington Post, July 2011, www.huffingtonpost.com/2011/07/13/nike-faces-new-worker-abuse-indonesia_n_896816.html.

Wyness, Michael. *Childhood and Society: An Introduction to the Sociology of Childhood* (London, UK: Palgrave Macmillan, 2006).

Index

Figures and tables are indicated by page numbers followed by *fig.* and *tab.* respectively.